CATALAN
PRACTICAL
DICTIONARY

CATALAN
PRACTICAL
DICTIONARY

Catalan-English/ English-Catalan

A. Scott Britton

Hippocrene Books, Inc.
New York

for Jonas
✳ ✳ ✳

For information, address:
HIPPOCRENE BOOKS, INC.
171 Madison Avenue
New York, NY 10016
www.hippocrenebooks.com

*Cataloging-in-Publication Data available from
the Library of Congress*

ISBN 13: 978-0-7818-1368-6

Printed in the United States of America

CONTENTS

INTRODUCTION

Catalan, or, *català*, as it is known to its speakers, is a Romance language spoken by well over nine million people worldwide. Some Catalan speakers can be found in North and South America. The majority of speakers, however, reside in the Mediterranean area, with the highest concentration occurring in Spain's Catalonia and Valencia regions.

Catalan enjoys a co-official status in many of the areas where it is spoken, and it is *the* official language in the small mountain nation of Andorra, nestled between France and Spain. Notions of a Catalonia that is entirely independent from Spain (the region is already classified as an autonomous state with a considerable degree of freedom) are ever-looming, and continue to fuel fierce pride in the culture and language of the region.

* * *

While readers who possess some knowledge of other Romance languages, particularly Spanish, Portuguese, and French, will no doubt feel a significant sense of familiarity with the Catalan language, this dictionary is meant to serve anyone with a desire to speak, write, or read Catalan, regardless of experience.

An exhaustive pronunciation guide with example English sounds is provided below, as well as a discussion of the basics of Catalan grammar. These resources, taken with the more than 16,000 entries in this dictionary, are designed to help users communicate in Catalan with few, if any, additional materials.

PRONUNCIATION

Vowels

a Stressed: *t_a_ll*
Unstressed: *banan_a_*

e Stressed: 1. *m_e_t*   2. *m_a_ke*
Unstressed: *tel_e_phone*

i Stressed and unstressed: *chlor_i_ne*
Unstressed and connecting two other vowels: *_y_ellow*
Silent when followed by *x*

o Stressed: 1. *sl_o_t*   2. *c_o_ne*
Unstressed: *m_oo_n*

u Stressed and unstressed: *r_u_by*
Unstressed and connecting two other vowels: *_w_in*
Silent when following *g* or *q* and then followed by an
 e or *i*. This rule is negated and *u* is pronounced like
 w when it is marked with a dieresis (ü).
 U following *g* or *q* and then itself followed by *a* or *o*
 is also pronounced like *w*. Examples: *g_u_ava*, *q_u_ick*.

Consonants

b   *best*

c   1. *cat*
    2. When followed by *e* or *i*: *center*

ç   *simple*

d   1. In the initial position or following *n*, *m*, or *l*: *dinner*
    2. At the end of words: *hut*
    3. In the interior of words and followed by a vowel: *them*

f   *family*

g   1. *gift*
    2. When followed by *e* or *i*: *pleasure*
    3. At the end of a word: *kick*, except when the ending is
       -aig, *-eig*, *-oig*, *-uig*, or stressed *-ig* directly after a
       consonant, then pronounced like *-tch* in *pitch*

h   Silent, except in some loanwords, when it is aspirated.

j   *treasure*

k   *kilometer*

l   1. *lamp*
    2. double *l* (*ll*): similar to the *y* in *yes*
    3. two *l*s separated by a dot (*l·l*) are pronounced
       separately in succession, as in *intelligent*

m   *march*

n   _n_ever, except before _f_ or _v_, then pronounced roughly
        like English _m_

p   _p_ath

q   _q_uote

r   1. Trilled in the initial position and when doubled
        2. Usually silent when appearing at the end of a word
        3. Like English _r_ in all other instances

s   _s_tick, except when appearing between two vowels,
        when it is pronounced like English _z_, except
        double _s_, when it reverts to the sound of English _s_

t   _t_art

v   tri_b_ute

w   sounds like English _b_ (found only in loanwords)

x   1. te_x_t
        2. At the beginning of a word and within a word and
        preceded by _i_: _sh_out

y   _y_ard

z   _z_ap

Cluster

ix   _sh_are

GRAMMAR

Nouns

Gender

Nouns in Catalan are either feminine or masculine.

> For example:
> Feminine: **la metàfora** *metaphor*
> Masculine: **el llibre** *book*

Some nouns don't inherently reflect gender. These are words that correspond to occupation, where the actor can be either feminine or masculine.

> For example, the word **cantant** *singer*:
>
> **la cantant** *(female) singer* is as viable as
> **el cantant** *(male) singer*

Plurals

Nouns in Catalan reflect number, as well. Plurals are often formed with the simple addition of *-s* at the end of the word:

> **premi** *award*
> **premis** *awards*

In cases where the singular word ends in an unstressed *-a*, replace the *-a* with *-es*:

> **pàgina** *page*
> **pàgines** *pages*

To form the plural of words ending in a stressed vowel, replace the vowel with its unstressed form and add -*ns*:

pistó *piston*
pistons *pistons*

Words ending in -*ç*, -*s*, -*x*, and other 's' sounds (-*sc*, -*st*, -*xt*)
usually end with -*os* in their plural forms:

procés *process*
processos *processes*

Articles

Articles in Catalan appear before the noun, and reflect its
gender and number. The definite article (*the*) is:

el (masculine singular)   **els** (masculine plural)
la (feminine singular)   **les** (feminine plural)
l' *el*, *els*, *la*, and *les* become *l'* when the noun begins
      with a vowel or the letter *h*

The indefinite articles (*a* or *an*) are:

un (masculine singular)   **uns** (masculine plural)
una (feminine singular)   **unes** (feminine plural)

Adjectives

Most adjectives in Catalan appear after the noun they modify
(although, there are exceptions):

ou <u>fregit</u> *fried egg*

In this dictionary adjectives are presented in their masculine
form. Forming the feminine is often as simple as adding an

-a to the end of the word:

> **gos <u>dolent</u>** *bad dog*
> **sang <u>dolenta</u>** *bad blood*

The list below demonstrates some common gender form changes:

-e	becomes *-a*	*-it*	becomes *-ida*
-at	becomes *-ada*	*-oc*	becomes *-oga*
-ec	becomes *-ega*	*-ós*	becomes *-osa*
-eig	becomes *-etja*	*-os*	becomes *-ossa*
-ic	becomes *-iga*	*-ou*	becomes *-ova*
-ig	becomes *-itja*	*-ut*	becomes *-uda*

Example: **compte <u>tancat</u>** *closed account*
          porta <u>tancada</u> *closed door*

Adjectives in Catalan also reflect number. The rules of pluralization for adjectives are the same as those for nouns:

> **casa <u>buida</u>** *empty house*
> **cases <u>buides</u>** *empty houses*

Adverbs

Many adverbs in Catalan end in *-ment*, effectively equating them with the English adverbial ending *-ly*. As a result, forming adverbs in Catalan is often as easy as adding the *-ment* ending to Catalan adjectives:

> **intel·ligent** *intelligent*
> **intel·ligent<u>ment</u>** *intelligent<u>ly</u>*

Pronouns

Subject Pronouns

Subject pronouns appear before the verb in Catalan. While they are often omitted (the conjugated verb itself conveys the necessary information), their inclusion can act as a form of emphasis.

	Singular	*Plural*
1st per.	**jo** *I*	**nosaltres** *we*
2nd per.	**tu** *you (fam.)*	**vosaltres** *you (fam.)*
3rd per.	**ell** *he*	**ells** *they (m.)*
	ella *she*	**elles** *they (f.)*
	vostè *you (form.)*	**vostès** *you (form.)*

Examples: **jo** tinc *I have*

          nosaltres parlem *we talk*

Object Pronouns

Like subject pronouns, object pronouns usually occur before the verb. But there are some important exceptions to this rule. For instance, object pronouns will occur *after* the verb (post position) when the verb is in command or infinitive form.

	Before Verb		*After Verb*	
Singular				
1st per. *me*:	em	m'	-me	'm
2nd per. *you*:	et	t'	-te	't
3rd per. *him*:	el[1], li[2]	l'[1], li[2]	-lo[1], -li[2]	'l[1], -li[2]
her:	la[1], li[2]	l'[1], li[2]	-la[1], -li[2]	-la[1], -li[2]
it:	ho	ho	-ho	-ho

	Before Verb		After Verb	
Plural				
1st per. us:	ens	ens	-nos	'ns
2nd per. you:	us	us	-vos	-us
3rd per. them (m.):	els	els	-los	'ls
them (f.):	les[1], els[2]	les[1], els[2]	-les[1], -los[2]	-les[1], 'ls[2]

[1] Direct object pronoun
[2] Indirect object pronoun

Examples: **L'estima.** *He loves her.*
          Li comprarè un cafè. *I will buy her a coffee.*

Post Position

Examples:
          command form: **Ajudi'm!** *Help me!*
          with infinitives: **dir-ho** *to say it*

Verbs

Verbs are catalogued and sorted in their infinitive form (to ~).
The infinitive is conjugated to indicate who is using the verb,
and how they're using it. Catalan verbs are generally grouped
into three categories: *-ar* verbs, *-er/-re* verbs, and *-ir* verbs.
Basic conjugation tables for examples of each verb type are
provided below.

Key to the conjugation tables

I	we
you (*sing.*, *fam.*)	you (*pl.*, *fam.*)
he, she, you (*sing.*, *form.*)	they (*m.*), they (*f.*), you (*pl.*, *form.*)

-ar verbs: Example using **caminar** 'to walk'

Present	camino	caminem
	camines	camineu
	camina	caminen

Imperfect	caminava	caminàvem
	caminaves	caminàveu
	caminava	caminaven

Preterit	caminí/vaig caminar	caminàrem/vam caminar
	caminares/vas caminar	caminàreu/vau caminar
	caminà/va caminar	caminaren/van caminar

Future	caminaré	caminarem
	caminaràs	caminareu
	caminarà	caminaran

Imperative	—	caminem
	camina	camineu
	camini	caminin

Gerund	caminant

-er/-re verbs: Example using **voler** 'to want'

Present	vull	volem
	vols	voleu
	vol	volen

Imperfect	volia	volíem
	volies	volíeu
	volia	volien

Preterit	volguí/vaig voler	volguérem/vam voler
	volgueres/vas voler	volguéreu/vau voler
	volgué/va voler	volgueren/van voler

Future	voldré	voldrem
	voldràs	voldreu
	voldrà	voldran

Imperative	—	vulguem
	vulgues	vulgueu
	vulgui	vulguin

Gerund	volent	

-ir verbs: Example using **tenir** 'to have'

Present	tinc	tenim
	tens	teniu
	té	tenen

Imperfect	tenia	teníem
	tenies	teníeu
	tenia	tenien

Preterit	tinguí/vaig tenir	tinguérem/vam tenir
	tingueres/vas tenir	tinguéreu/vau tenir
	tingué/va tenir	tingueren/van tenir

Future	tindré	tindrem
	tindràs	tindreu
	tindrà	tindran

Imperative   —   tinguem
                  té/tingues   teniu/tingueu
                  tingui   tinguin

Gerund   tenint

ABBREVIATIONS

abbr.	abbreviation
adj.	adjective
adv.	adverb
art.	article
conj.	conjunction
def.	definite
dem.	demonstrative
f.	feminine
fam.	familiar
form.	formal
gram.	grammatical
indef.	indefinite
interj.	interjection
lit.	literally
m.	masculine
mech.	mechanical
med.	medical
n.	noun
num.	number
per.	person
phr.	phrase
phys.	physical
pl.	plural
pos.	possessive
prep..	preposition
pron.	pronoun
psych.	psychological
rel.	relative
sing.	singular
v.	verb
zool.	zoological

CATALAN-ENGLISH
DICTIONARY

A

a *prep.* at; in; on, upon; into, to
a baix *adv.* downstairs
a bord *adv.* aboard | *phr.* on board
a casa *adv.* indoors
a contracor *adv.* unwillingly
a dalt *adv.* upstairs
a l'aire lliure *adj.* outdoor(s)
a l'estranger *adv.* abroad
a la graella *adj.* charcoal-grilled, grilled
a la tarda *adv.* p.m. *(early)*
a més *adv.* furthermore, moreover
a part *adv.* apart, aside
a part de *prep.* apart from
a penes *adv.* hardly
a peu *phr.* on foot
a prop de *prep.* close to
a qualsevol lloc *adv.* anywhere, wherever
a quarts *adj.* quartered
a tot arreu *adv.* everywhere
a través *prep.* across
a través de *prep.* through
a ultramar *adv.* overseas
abadia *n.f.* abbey
abaixar *v.* lower
abandonar *v.* abandon, forsake, desert
abandonat *adj.* abandoned, deserted
abans *adv.* beforehand
abans de *prep.* before
abast *n.m.* scope
abdomen *n.m.* abdomen
abella *n.f.* bee

abellar *n.m.* apiary
abocar *v.* dump
abonat *n.* subscriber
aborigen *adj.* aboriginal
abraçada *n.f.* hug
abraçar *v.* embrace, hug
abreviatura *n.f.* abbreviation
abric *n.m.* coat, overcoat; shelter
abric de pell *n.m.* fur coat
abril *n.m.* April
abrogar *v.* repeal
abruptament *adv.* steeply
abrupte *adj.* abrupt
abscés *n.m.* abscess
absència *n.f.* absence
absent *adj.* absent
absenta *n.f.* absinthe
absis *n.f.* apse
absoldre *v.* acquit
absolució *n.f.* acquittal
absolut *adj.* absolute
absolutament *adv.* absolutely
absorbir *v.* absorb, engross
absort *adj.* absorbed
abstenir-se *v.* refrain
abstracte *adj.* abstract
absurd *adj.* absurd
abús *n.m.* abuse
acabament *n.m.* completion
acabar *v.* finish
acabat *adj.* finished
acadèmia *n.f.* academy
acadèmic *adj.* academic
acampador *n.* camper
acariciar *v.* pet

accelerador *n.m.* accelerator
accent *n.m.* accent
acceptable *adj.* acceptable
acceptar *v.* accept
accés *n.m.* access
accident *n.m.* accident
accident vascular cerebral
 (AVC) *n.m.* stroke
accidental *adj.* accidental
accidentalment *adv.* accidentally
acció *n.f.* action
accionista *n.* shareholder
acer *n.m.* steel
acer inoxidable *n.m.* stainless
 steel
àcid *n.m.* acid
acidificar *v.* acidify
aclarir *v.* clarify
acne *n.f.* acne
acolliment *n.m.* welcome
acollir *v.* welcome
acomiadament *n.m.* dismissal;
 farewell
acomiadar *v.* dismiss; say goodbye
acompanyar *v.* accompany
acomplir *v.* accomplish
aconseguir *v.* achieve
aconsellar *v.* advise
acord *n.m.* accordance, agreement;
 chord
acre *adj.* tart | *n.m.* acre
acrílic *adj.* acrylic
acte *n.m.* act
actitud *n.f.* attitude
actiu *adj.* active
activament *adv.* actively
activar *v.* activate
activista *n.f.* activist
activitat *n.f.* activity

actor *n.m.* actor
actriu *n.f.* actress
actuació *n.f.* performance, gig
actual *adj.* current
actualitats *n.f.* current affairs
actualitzar *v.* refresh
actualitzat *adj.* updated
actualment *adv.* currently
acumulació *n.f.* accumulation
acumular *v.* accumulate
acupuntura *n.f.* acupuncture
acusació *n.f.* prosecution
acusar *v.* accuse
acusat *n.* defendant
adaptador *n.m.* adapter
adaptar *v.* adapt
addicció *n.f.* addiction
addició *n.f.* addition
addicional *adj.* additional
addicte *adj.* addicted
additiu alimentari *n.m.* food
 additive
adepte *adj.* adept
adequadament *adv.* adequately
adequat *adj.* adequate, suited
adeu *phr.* goodbye, bye
adherir *v.* adhere
adhesió *n.f.* adherence; adhesion
adhesiu *adj.* adhesive
adjacent *adj.* adjacent
adjectiu *n.m.* adjective
adjunt *adj.* attached
adjuntar *v.* attach
admetre *v.* admit
administració *n.f.* administration,
 management
administrador de correu *n.*
 postmaster
administratiu *adj.* administrative
admiració *n.f.* admiration

admirar *v.* admire
admissió *n.f.* admission, admittance
ADN *n.m.* DNA
adolorit *adj.* sore
adoptar *v.* adopt
adorable *adj.* adorable
adoració *n.f.* worship
adorar *v.* adore, worship
adormit *adj.* asleep
adornar *v.* garnish
adquirir *v.* acquire
adquisició *n.f.* acquisition
adreça *n.f.* address
adulació *n.f.* adulation, flattery
adult *n.* adult
adverbi *n.m.* adverb
adversari *n.* adversary
adversitat *n.f.* adversity
advertiment *n.m.* warning
advertir *v.* warn
advocat *n.* attorney, lawyer
aeri *adj.* aerial
aeròbic *n.m.* aerobic
aerolínia *n.f.* airline
aeroport *n.m.* airport
afaitar-se *v.* shave
afalagar *v.* flatter
afamat *adj.* hungry
afecció cardíaca *n.f.* heart condition
afectació *n.f.* affectation
afectar *v.* affect
afecte *n.m.* affection
afegir *v.* add
aficionat *n.* fan; amateur | *adj.* keen on
afilat *adj.* sharp
afiliació *n.f.* membership, affiliation

afinar *v.* tune
afinitat *n.f.* affinity
afirmació *n.f.* affirmation
afirmar *v.* affirm
aflicció *n.f.* affliction
afligir *v.* afflict
afluència *n.f.* affluence
afluixar *v.* unscrew
afores *n.m.* outskirts
afortunadament *adv.* fortunately
afortunat *adj.* lucky
africà *adj.* African
Àfrica *n.f.* Africa
agafar *v.* clutch, grab, hold; catch
agència *n.f.* agency
agent *n.* agent
àgil *adj.* agile, nimble, limber
agitació *n.f.* agitation
agitar *v.* agitate
agost *n.m.* August
agradable *adj.* enjoyable, nice, pleasant, pleasing
agradablement *adv.* nicely, pleasantly
agradar *v.* fancy, like
agraïment *n.m.* thanks
agrair *v.* thank
agraït *adj.* thankful, grateful
agrari *adj.* agrarian
agre *adj.* sour
agrella *n.f.* sorrel
agressió *n.f.* aggression
agressiu *adj.* aggressive
agreujament *n.* aggravation
agreujar *v.* aggravate
agrícola *adj.* agricultural
agricultura *n.f.* agriculture, farming
agronomia *n.f.* agronomy

agulla *n.f.* needle, pin; spire
agulla hipodèrmica *n.f.*
  hypodermic needle
agut *adj.* acute, sharp, keen
agutzil *n.m.* bailiff
ahir *adv.* yesterday
aigua *n.f.* water
aigua calenta *n.f.* hot water
aigua dolça *n.f.* fresh water
aigua mineral *n.f.* mineral water
aigua potable *n.f.* drinkable water
aigua tònica *n.f.* tonic water
aiguafort *n.m.* etching
aiguamel *n.f.* mead
aigües baixes *n.f.* shallow water
aïllament *n.m.* isolation
aïllar *v.* isolate
aïllat *adj.* isolated
aire *n.m.* air | *adj.* **a l'aire lliure**
  outdoor(s)
aire condicionat *n.m.* air conditioning
aixafar *v.* crush, squash
aixafat *adj.* crushed
aixecar *v.* lift
aixeta *n.f.* faucet
així *adv.* thus
ajornament *n.m.* postponement,
  continuance
ajornar *v.* postpone, procrastinate
ajuda *n.f.* aid
ajudant *n.* assistant
ajudant de cambra *n.m.* valet
ajudar *v.* help
ajuntar-se *v.* rally; get closer
ajust *n.m.* adjustment
ajustar *v.* adjust
al costat de *prep.* alongside,
  beside, next to
al llarg de *prep.* throughout,
  along

al revés *adv.* upside down
al vespre *adv.* p.m. *(later)*
al voltant *adv.* around | *adj.*
  surrounding
ala *n.f.* wing
ala delta *n.f.* hang glider
Alabama *n.* Alabama
alarma *n.f.* alarm
alarma d'incendis *n.f.* fire alarm
alarmant *adj.* alarming
alarmat *adj.* alarmed
Alaska *n.* Alaska
alba *n.f.* dawn
Albània *n.f.* Albania
albercoc *n.* apricot
alberg *n.m.* hostel
albergínia *n.f.* eggplant
àlbum *n.m.* album
alçada *n.f.* height
alcalde *n.m.* mayor
alcohol *n.m.* alcohol | *adj.* **sense**
  ~ non-alcoholic
alcohòlic *adj./n.* alcoholic
aldarull *n.m.* rampage, riot
alè *n.m.* breath
aleatori *adj.* random
alegrar *v.* rejoice
alegre *adj.* cheerful
alegrement *adv.* cheerfully
alegria *n.f.* joy
alemany *adj./n.* German
Alemanya *n.f.* Germany
alfabet *n.m.* alphabet
alfabètic *adj.* alphabetical
alfabèticament *adv.* alphabetically
alfàbrega *n.f.* basil
alga *n.f.* seaweed
àlgebra *n.f.* algebra
algú *pron.* anybody, anyone,
  somebody, someone

algun: en ~ lloc *adv.* somewhere
alguna cosa *pron.* something
alguns *pron.* some
àlies *n.m.* alias
aliat *adj.* allied | *n.* ally
aliment *n.m.* nourishment
aliment modificat genèticament
  n.m. genetically modified food
alimentar *v.* feed
alineació *n.f.* alignment
alinear *v.* align
all *n.m.* garlic
allà *adv.* there
allau *n.f.* avalanche
al·legació *n.f.* allegation
al·legar *v.* plead
al·lergen *n.m.* allergen
al·lèrgia *n.f.* allergy
al·lèrgic *adj.* allergic
alletar *v.* breastfeed
alleujament *n.m.* alleviation,
  relief
alleujar *v.* relieve
allí *adv.* there
alliberar *v.* release
allò *dem pron.* that
allotjament *n.m.* accommodation
al·lusió *n.f.* allusion
almoina *n.f.* alms
àloe *n.m.* aloe
alosa *n.f.* lark
alquímia *n.f.* alchemy
alt *adj.* high, tall
alta qualitat *adj.* high-quality
alta tecnologia *adj.* high-tech
altar *n.m.* altar
altaveu *n.m.* speaker *(audio*
  equipment)
alteració *n.f.* alteration
alterar *v.* alter

alternador *n.m.* alternator
alternatiu *adj.* alternative
alternativa *n.f.* alternative
alternativament *adv.* alternatively
altímetre *n.m.* altimeter
altiplà *n.m.* plateau
altitud *n.f.* altitude
altrament *adv.* otherwise
altre *adj.* other; **un** ~ another |
  adv. **en** ~ **lloc** elsewhere
altura sobre el nivell del mar
  n.f. height above sea level
alumini *n.m.* aluminum
alvocat *n.m.* avocado
amable *adj.* gentle, amiable, kind
amablement *adv.* kindly
amagar *v.* hide
amanida *n.f.* salad
amanida Cèsar *n.f.* Caesar salad
amaniment *n.m.* salad dressing
amant *n.* lover
amarant *n.m.* amaranth
amarg *adj.* bitter
amb *prep.* with
amb aire condicionat *adj.* air-
  conditioned
amb amargura *adv.* bitterly
amb classe *adj.* classy
amb confiança *adv.* confidently
amb cura *adv.* carefully | *adj.*
  caring
amb èxit *adv.* successfully
amb fermesa *adv.* firmly
amb la mirada perduda *adv.*
  blankly
amb mantega *adj.* buttered
amb molt de gust *adv.* gladly
amb plom *adj.* leaded
amb tristesa *adv.* sadly
ambaixada *n.f.* embassy

ambaixador *n.m.* ambassador
ambició *n.f.* ambition
ambient *n.m.* setting
ambiental *adj.* environmental
ambigu *adj.* ambiguous
ambigüitat *n.f.* ambiguity
amblar *v.* amble
ambrosia *n.f.* ambrosia
ambulància *n.f.* ambulance
ambulatori *adj.* out-patient
amenaça *n.f.* threat, menace
amenaçador *adj.* threatening
amenaçar *v.* threaten
americà *adj.* American
Amèrica del Nord *n.f.* North America
Amèrica del Sud *n.f.* South America
ametlla *n.f.* almond
amfitrió *n.* host
amic *n.* friend
amígdala *n.f.* tonsil
amigdalitis *n.f.* tonsilitis
aminoàcid *n.m.* amino acid
amistat *n.f.* friendship, amity
amistós *adj.* friendly, amicable
amnèsia *n.f.* amnesia
amnistia *n.f.* amnesty
amo *n.m.* master
amor *n.m.* love
amotinat *adj.* mutinous
ampere *n.m.* ampere
amplada *n.f.* width
ample *adj.* wide, broad; loose-fitting
ampli *adj.* ample
àmpliament *adv.* widely
amplificació *n.f.* amplification
amplificador *n.m.* amplifier
amplificar *v.* amplify

ampolla *n.f.* ampule, bottle
amulet *n.m.* amulet
amunt *adv.* up
anacard *n.m.* cashew
analfabet *adj.* illiterate
analfabetisme *n.m.* illiteracy
analgèsic *n.m.* painkiller
anàlisi *n.f.* analysis
analista *n.* analyst
analitzar *v.* analyze
analogia *n.f.* analogy
anar *v.* go
anar a cavall *v.* ride a horse
anar amb bicicleta *v.* ride a bicycle
anar amb compte *v.* beware
anar amb cotxe *v.* ride in a car
anar amb pressa *v.* rush
anar de viatge *v.* tour; travel
anarquista *n.* anarchist
anatomia *n.f.* anatomy
ancià *adj.* elderly
àncora *n.f.* anchor
ancoratge *n.m.* anchorage
Andorra *n.f.* Andorra
ànec *n.m.* duck
aneguet *n.m.* duckling
anell *n.m.* ring
anèmia *n.f.* anemia
anèmic *adj.* anemic
anestèsia *n.f.* anesthesia
anestèsic *adj.* anesthetic
anet *n.m.* dill
àngel *n.m.* angel
angina *n.f.* angina
Anglaterra *n.f.* England
angle *n.m.* angle
anglès *adj./n.m.* English
angoixa *n.f.* agony *(mental)*
angoixar *v.* agonize

anguila *n.f.* eel
angular *adj.* angular
anihilació *n.f.* annihilation
anihilar *v.* annihilate
ànima *n.f.* soul
animació *n.f.* animation
animal *n.m.* animal
animat *adj.* animated, lively
animositat *n.f.* animosity
anís *n.m.* anise
anit *n.f.* last night
aniversari *n.m.* anniversary;
  birthday
anomenat *adj.* renowned
anònim *adj.* anonymous
anonimat *n.m.* anonymity
anorac *n.m.* anorak
ansietat *n.f.* anxiety
ansiós *adj.* anxious
ansiosament *adv.* anxiously
ant *n.m.* moose; elk
Antàrtida *n.f.* Antarctica
antena *n.f.* antenna
anterior *adj.* former, previous,
  prior
anteriorment *adv.* formerly,
  previously
anti *prefix* anti-
anti-govern *adj.* anti-government
antiadherent *adj.* non-stick
antibales *adj.* bullet-proof
antibiòtic *n.m.* antibiotic
antic *adj.* ancient
anticipar *v.* anticipate
anticoncepció *n.f.* contraception
anticonceptiu *adj./n.m.*
  contraceptive
anticongelant *n.m.* antifreeze
anticòs *n.m.* antibody
antídot *n.m.* antidote

antiguitat *n.* antique
antihigiènic *adj.* unsanitary
antílop *n.m.* antelope
antinuclear *adj.* antinuclear
antipatia *n.f.* antipathy
antipàtic *adj.* unfriendly
antiquat *adj.* outdated
antisèptic *adj./n.m.* antiseptic
antologia *n.f.* anthology
anual *adj.* annual
anualment *adv.* annually
anunci *n.m.* announcement,
  advertisement
anunciar *v.* announce, advertise
anxova *n.f.* anchovy
any *n.m.* year
any nou *n.m.* New Year; New
  Year's Day
any que ve *adv.* next year
apagar *v.* switch off; quench
apagat *adv.* off *(switch, etc.)*
aparcament *n.m.* parking
aparcament de llarg termini
  n.m. long-term parking
aparcar *v.* park
aparèixer *v.* appear
aparell digestiu *n.m.* digestive
  system
aparença *n.f.* appearance
aparent *adj.* apparent
aparentment *adv.* apparently
apartament *n.m.* apartment
apassionadament *adv.*
  passionately
apassionat *adj.* passionate
àpat *n.m.* meal
apedaçar *v.* patch
apel·lació *n.f.* appeal
apendicitis *n.f.* appendicitis
apèndix *n.m.* *(anat.)* appendix

aperitiu *n.m.* aperitif; appetizer
apetitós *adj.* appetizing
api *n.m.* celery
apilar *v.* pile
apinyat *adj.* crowded
aplaudir *v.* cheer, clap
aplicar *v.* apply
apoderat *n.m.* proxy
apogeu *n.m.* heyday
apologia *n.f.* apology
apostar *v.* bet
apòstrof *n.m.* apostrophe
apreciar *v.* appreciate
aprendre *v.* learn
aprenent *n.* apprentice
apressar *v.* hurry
apropar *v.* approach
apropiat *adj.* appropriate, proper, suitable
aprovació *n.f.* approval
aprovar *v.* approve (of)
aproximadament *adv.* roughly, approximately
aproximat *adj.* approximate
apuntalar *v.* prop
apuntar *v.* aim
apunyalar *v.* slash
aquarel·la *n.f.* watercolor
aquari *n.* Aquarius; aquarium
aquàrium *n.m.* aquarium
aqüeducte *n.m.* aqueduct
aquell(a) *dem. adj.* that *(far)*
aquelles *adj.* those
aquells *adj.* those
aquest(a) *dem. adj.* that *(near)*
aquest(a) *pron.* this
aquesta nit *adv.* tonight
aquestes *pron.* these
aquests *pron.* these
aquí *adv.* here, hither

ara *adv.* now
àrab *adj.* Arab | *n.m.* Arabic
arada *n.f.* plow
arador *n.* plowman
aranja *n.f.* grapefruit
aranya *n.f.* spider
arbitratge *n.m.* arbitration
àrbitre *n.* referee
arbre *n.m.* tree; axle
arbre de fulla perenne *n.m.* evergreen
arbre genealògic *n.m.* family tree
arbre jove *n.m.* sapling
arbust *n.m.* bush
arc *n.m.* arch
arc de Sant Martí *n.m.* rainbow
arca *n.f.* ark
ardit *n.m.* ruse
àrea *n.f.* area
àrea de conservació *n.f.* conservation area
àrea de pícnic *n.f.* picnic area
arenes movedisses *n.f.* quicksand
areng *n.m.* herring
Argentina *n.f.* Argentina
argila *n.f.* clay
argot *n.m.* slang
argument *n.m.* argument; plot
àries *n.* Aries
aristocràcia *n.f.* aristocracy
aristòcrata *n.* aristocrat
Arizona *n.* Arizona
Arkansas *n.* Arkansas
arma *n.f.* weapon
arma de foc *n.f.* gun
arma nuclear *n.f.* nuclear bomb
armadura *n.f.* armor
armari *n.m.* cupboard, locker, wardrobe

armat *adj.* armed
Armènia *n.f.* Armenia
armeria *n.f.* armory
armes *n.f.* arms
armes nuclears *n.f.* nuclear weapons
armilla salvavides *n.f.* life jacket, life preserver
arna *n.f.* moth
arnès *n.m.* harness
aroma *n.f.* aroma
aromatització *n.f.* flavoring
aromatitzat *adj.* flavored
arpa *n.f.* harp
arquebisbe *n.m.* archbishop
arqueologia *n.f.* archeology
arqueològic *adj.* archeological
arquitecte *n.* architect
arquitectònic *adj.* architectural
arquitectura *n.f.* architecture
arracada *n.f.* earring
arranjament *n.m.* arrangement
arranjar *v.* arrange
arrebossament *n.m.* breading
arrebossar *v.* batter *(food)*
arrebossat *adj.* breaded
arreglar *v.* fix
arrel *n.f.* root
arrendament *n.m.* lease
arrestar *v.* arrest
arribada *n.f.* arrival
arribar *v.* arrive, reach
arrissar *v.* curl, crimp, ripple
arrissat *adj.* curly, rippled
arròs *n.m.* rice
arròs llarg *n.m.* long-grain rice
arrossegar *v.* drag
arrossegar-se *v.* creep
arruïnar *v.* ruin
arruïnat *adj.* ruined

arsenal *n.m.* arsenal
arsènic *n.m.* arsenic
art *n.m.* art
art prehistòric *n.m.* prehistoric art
art tradicional *n.* folk art
artell *n.m.* knuckle
artèria *n.f.* artery
artesà *n.* artisan
artesanies *n.f.* crafts
àrtic *n.* Arctic
article *n.m.* article, item
articles de luxe *n.m.* luxury goods
articulista *n.* columnist
artificial *adj.* artificial
artificialment *adv.* artificially
artilleria *n.f.* artillery
artista *n.* artist; entertainer
artístic *adj.* artistic
artritis *n.f.* arthritis
arts gràfiques *n.m.* graphic arts
arts liberals *n.m.* liberal arts
arxiu *n.m.* archive
arxiu *n.m.* file *(records)*
arxivar *v.* file *(records)*
ascendent *adj.* upward
ascendir *v.* rise
ascensor *n.m.* elevator
asceta *n.* ascetic
Àsia *n.f.* Asia
asiàtic *adj.* Asian
asil *n.m.* asylum
asma *n.f.* asthma
asmàtic *adj.* asthmatic
aspartam *n.m.* aspartame
aspecte *n.m.* aspect
àspic *n.m.* aspic
aspirar *v.* aim *(to aspire)*
aspirina *n.f.* aspirin
aspre *adj.* coarse, rough
assaborir *v.* savor

assaig *n.m.* essay; rehearsal
assaigs nuclears *n.m.* nuclear testing, nuclear tests
assajar *v.* rehearse
assalt *n.m.* assault
assaltat *adj.* assaulted
assaonar *v.* season
assassí *n.* assassin, murderer | *adj.* murderous
assassinar *v.* assassinate, murder
assassinat *n.m.* assassination, murder
assecador de cabells *n.m.* hair dryer, blow-dryer
assecadora *n.f.* dryer
assecar amb assecador *v.* blow-dry
assedegat *adj.* thirsty
assegurança *n.f.* insurance, health insurance
assegurar *v.* assure, ensure, secure
assemblar-se *v.* resemble, look like
assentir *v.* agree
assenyalar *v.* point to
assequible *adj.* obtainable
assetjament *n.m.* harassment, molestation
assetjar *v.* harass, molest
assignació *n.f.* allocation
assignar *v.* allocate
assistència *n.f.* assistance
assistir *v.* assist; attend
associació *n.f.* association
associar *v.* associate
assolellat *adj.* sunny
assoliment *n.m.* accomplishment, achievement
assortit *adj.* assorted
assumpte *n.m.* affair; issue

asterisc *n.m.* asterisk
asteroide *n.m.* asteroid
astrologia *n.f.* astrology
astronauta *n.* astronaut
astrònom *n.* astronomer
astronomia *n.f.* astronomy
astut *adj.* cunning
atac *n.m.* attack
atac de cor *n.m.* heart attack
atacar *v.* pounce
atemptat *n.m.* attempt
atenció *n.f.* attention
ateu *n.* atheist
àtic *n.m.* penthouse
atletisme *n.m.* athletics
atmosfera *n.f.* atmosphere
àtom *n.m.* atom
atòmic *adj.* atomic
atordir *v.* stun
atracció *n.f.* attraction
atractiu *adj.* attractive, handsome, sexy
atrapament *n.m.* entrapment
atrapar *v.* overtake; catch, trap
atreure *v.* attract
atribut *n.m.* attribute
aturar *v.* stop
aturat *adj.* unemployed; stopped
atzavara *n.f.* agave
audiència *n.f.* audience
audífon *n.m.* hearing aid
audioguia *n.f.* audio-guide
auditiu *adj.* auditory
auditori *n.m.* auditorium
augmentar *v.* increase
aula *n.f.* classroom
aurora *n.f.* aurora
auspici *n.m.* auspice
auster *adj.* austere
austeritat *n.f.* austerity

Austràlia *n.f.* Australia
australià *adj.* Australian
Àustria *n.f.* Austria
autèntic *adj.* authentic
autenticitat *n.f.* authenticity
autobús *n.m.* bus
autocar *n.m.* coach
autocràcia *n.f.* autocracy
autòcrata *n.* autocrat
autoestop: fer ~ *v.* hitchhike
automàtic *adj.* automatic
automàticament *adv.*
  automatically
automòbil *n.m.* automobile
autopista *n.f.* motorway
autor *n.* author; originator
autoritat *n.f.* authority
autoritzar *v.* authorize, entitle
autoritzat *adj.* authorized
auxiliar *n.* auxiliary
avaluació *n.f.* appraisal,
  assessment, evaluation
avaluar *v.* appraise, assess,
  evaluate
avançar *v.* advance
avançat *adj.* advanced
avantatge *n.m.* advantage
avantbraç *n.m.* forearm

avantguarda *n.f.* avant-garde
avantpassat *n.* ancestor
avaria *n.f.* breakdown
avellana *n.f.* hazelnut
aventura *n.f.* adventure; venture
aventurar *v.* venture
avergonyir *v.* embarrass, shame
avergonyit *adj.* embarrassed,
  ashamed
aversió *n.f.* dislike
avet *n.m.* fir
avi *n.m.* grandfather | *n.* grand-
  parent
àvia *n.f.* grandmother
aviació *n.f.* aviation
aviat *adv.* shortly, soon
avinguda *n.f.* avenue
avió *n.m.* aircraft, airplane, plane
aviram *n.m.* poultry
avorrir *v.* bore
avorrit *adj.* bored, boring, dull
avortament *n.m.* abortion
avortament espontani *n.m.*
  miscarriage
avortar *v.* abort
avui *adv.* today
Azerbaidjan *n.m.* Azerbaijan

B

bacallà *n.m.* cod
bacterià *adj.* bacterial
bacteris *n.m.* bacteria
badall *n.m.* yawn
badallar *v.* yawn
badia *n.f.* bay
bàdminton *n.m.* badminton
baia *n.f.* berry
baia de Boysen *n.m.* boysenberry
baix *adj.* low, down; bass; **més ~**
lower | *adv.* **a ~** downstairs
baix en greixos *adj.* low-fat
baix en calories *adj.* low-calorie
bala *n.f.* bullet
Balança *n.f.* Libra
balbotejar *v.* babble
balcó *n.m.* balcony
balderament *adv.* loosely
balena *n.f.* whale
balisa *n.f.* beacon
ballador *n.* dancer
ballar *v.* dance
ballet *n.m.* ballet
bàlsam *n.m.* balm
bambú *n.m.* bamboo
banc *n.m.* bank; bench
banda ampla *n.f.* broadband
bandera *n.f.* flag
bandit *n.m.* bandit, outlaw
banquer *n.* banker
banqueta *n.f.* bench
bany *n.m.* bath
bany d'or *n.m.* gold plate
banya *n.f.* antler
banyador *n.m.* bathing suit,
swimsuit

banyar *v.* bathe
baptisme *n.m.* baptism
bar *n.m.* bar, tavern
baralla *n.f.* quarrel
baralla de cartes *n.f.* playing
cards, deck of cards
barana *n.f.* railing
barat *adj.* inexpensive, cheap;
més ~ cheaper
barata *adv.* cheaply
barba *n.f.* beard
barber *n.m.* barber
barbeta *n.f.* chin
barnús *n.m.* robe
baròmetre *n.m.* barometer
barra d'eines *n.f.* toolbar
barra d'espai *n.f.* spacebar
barra de pa *n.f.* bread loaf
barra de xocolata *n.f.* chocolate
bar
barra lateral *n.f.* sidebar
barranc *n.m.* ravine
barreja *n.f.* mixture
barrejar *v.* blend, mix
barrejat *adj.* mixed
barrera *n.f.* barrier
barret *n.m.* hat
barri *n.m.* neighborhood
barril *n.m.* barrel
base *n.f.* base, basis
base de dades *n.f.* database
bàsic *adj.* basic
bàsicament *adv.* basically
bàsquet *n.m.* basketball
bassal *n.m.* puddle

bastant *adv.* quite
bastida *n.f.* scaffold
bastonets *n.m.* chopsticks
batalla *n.f.* battle
batec *n.m.* heartbeat
bategar *v.* pulsate
batre *v.* pound
batut *n.m.* milkshake
bé *adv.* well
bebè *n.m.* baby
bec *n.m.* beak
beguda *n.f.* beverage, drink
beguda destil·lada *n.f.* hard liquor
begudes espirituoses *n.f.* spirits
  (alcohol)
beina *n.f.* pod
beix *adj.* beige
Bèlgica *n.f.* Belgium
Belize *n.m.* Belize
bellament *adv.* beautifully
bellesa *n.f.* beauty
bena *n.f.* bandage
benefici *n.m.* benefit, behalf
beneficis *n.m.* proceeds
beneir *v.* bless
benèvol *adj.* benevolent
benevolència *n.f.* benevolence
benigne *adj.* benign
béns *n.m.* goods
béns immobles *n.m.* real estate
Benvingut! *phr.* Welcome!
bergant *n.* rascal, rogue
berruga *n.f.* wart
besar *v.* kiss
bessó *n.* twin
Bessons *n.m.* Gemini
bestiar boví *n.m.* cattle
besuc *n.m.* sea bream
beure *v.* drink
biberó *n.m.* feeding bottle

Bíblia *n.f.* Bible
biblioteca *n.f.* library
bibliotecari *n.* librarian
bicarbonat de sodi *n.m.* baking
  soda
bicicleta *n.f.* bicycle
bidet *n.m.* bidet
Bielorússia *n.f.* Belarus
bigoti *n.m.* moustache, mustache
bigotis *n.m.* whisker
bilingüe *adj.* bilingual
billar *n.m.* billiards
binari *adj.* binary
binocles *n.m.* binoculars
biodegradable *adj.* biodegradable
biodiversitat *n.f.* biodiversity
biografia *n.f.* biography
biologia *n.f.* biology
biològic *adj.* biological
biòpsia *n.f.* biopsy
biotecnologia *n.f.* biotechnology
biquini *n.m.* bikini
bisbe *n.m.* bishop
bisó *n.m.* bison
bistec *n.m.* steak
bisturí *n.m.* scalpel
bitlles *n.f.* bowling
bitllet *n.m.* ticket; banknote
blanc *adj.* white; **en ~** blank
blat *n.m.* wheat
blat de moro *n.m.* corn, maize
blat integral *n.m.* whole wheat
blau *adj.* blue | *n.m.* bruise | *v.*
  fer un ~ bruise
bleda *n.f.* Swiss chard, chard
blini *n.m.* pancake
bloc *n.m.* block; pad (of paper)
bloq maj *n.f.* caps lock
bo *adj.* good
boca *n.f.* mouth

boicot *n.m.* boycott
boicotejar *v.* boycott
boig *adj.* crazy, mad
boira *n.f.* fog
boirós *adj.* foggy
bol *n.m.* bowl
bola de bitlles *n.f.* bowling ball
bolet *n.m.* mushroom
bolígraf *n.m.* pen
Bolívia *n.f.* Bolivia
bolquer *n.m.* diaper
bomba *n.f.* bomb; pump
bombar *v.* pump
bombardeig *n.m.* bombardment
bombardejar *v.* bombard
bomber *n.* firefighter
bombers *n.m.* fire department
bombeta *n.f.* lightbulb
bombolla *n.f.* bubble
Bon Nadal *phr.* Merry Christmas
Bon profit! *phr.* Bon appetit!,
  Enjoy your meal!
Bon viatge! *phr.* Bon voyage!
bona disposició *n.f.* willingness
Bona sort! *phr.* Good luck!
bondat *n.f.* kindness
bonic *adj.* beautiful, pretty
bony *n.m.* lump
boom *n.m.* boom
borratxo *adj.* drunk
borrós *adj.* blurred
borsa *n.f.* stock exchange
bosc *n.m.* forest, woods
Bòsnia i Hercegovina *n.f.*
  Bosnia and Herzegovina
bossa *n.f.* bag, pouch
bossa d'escombraries *n.f.*
  garbage bag
bossa de mà *n.f.* handbag
bossa de plàstic *n.f.* plastic bag

bot salvavides *n.m.* lifeboat
bota *n.f.* boot
botànic *adj.* botanical
botiga *n.f.* shop, minimart
botiga de comestibles *n.f.*
  grocery store
botiga de conveniència *n.f.*
  convenience store
botiga de discos *n.f.* music store
botiga de licors *n.f.* liquor store
botiga de regals *n.f.* gift shop
botiga de regals *n.f.* gift store
botiguer *n.* shopkeeper; grocer
botó *n.m.* button
botzina *n.f.* horn
boxa *n.f.* boxing
boysenberry *n.m.* boysenberry
braç *n.m.* arm
braçalet *n.m.* bracelet
braille *n.m.* braille
branca *n.f.* branch
Brasil *n.m.* Brazil
bresca *n.f.* honeycomb
bressol *n.m.* crib
bressol portàtil *n.m.* portable crib
bretxa *n.f.* gap
brètzel *n.f.* pretzel
breu *adj.* brief
breument *adv.* briefly
brillant *adj.* bright, brilliant, shiny
brillantment *adv.* brightly
brillar *v.* shine
brisa *n.f.* breeze
britànic *adj.* British
brodat *n.m.* embroidery
broma *n.f.* joke, prank; pleasantry
  | *v.* **fer** ~ joke
bromejar *v.* prank
broncejat *adj./n.m.* tan
bronquitis *n.f.* bronchitis

bronze *n.m.* bronze
bronzejat *n.m.* suntan
broqueta *n.f.* skewer
bròquil *n.m.* broccoli
brot *n.m.* sprout; outbreak
brotar *v.* sprout
brots d'alfals *n.m.* alfalfa sprouts
brotxa d'afaitar *n.f.* shaving
  brush
brou *n.m.* broth
brownie *n.m.* brownie
bruixa *n.f.* witch
bruixeria *n.f.* witchcraft
brúixola *n.f.* compass
brunch *n.m.* brunch
brusa *n.f.* blouse
bruscament *adv.* sharply
brut *adj.* dirty, gross
brutícia *n.f.* dirt; mess
BTT (Bicicleta Tot Terreny) *n.f.*
  mountain bike
bufada *n.f.* puff
bufanda *n.f.* scarf
bufar *v.* blow, puff
bufeta *n.f.* bladder
bugada *n.f.* laundry
bugaderia *n.f.* laundromat,

  laundry facilities, launderette
buit *adj.* empty, hollow | *n.m.*
  void
Bulgària *n.f.* Bulgaria
bullit *adj.* boiled
bullidor *n.m.* kettle
bullir *v.* boil
bullir a foc lent *v.* simmer
bungalou *n.m.* bungalow
bunyol *n.m.* fritter
burgès *adj.* bourgeois
burla *n.f.* mockery
burlar-se de *v.* make fun of
burocràcia *n.f.* bureaucracy
buròcrata *n.* bureaucrat
burrito *n.m.* burrito
burxar *v.* poke
buscar *v.* seek
busseig *n.m.* diving
bústia *n.f.* mailbox, letter box,
  postbox
butà *n.m.* butane gas
butllofa *n.f.* blister
butterscotch *n.m.* butterscotch
butxaca *n.f.* pocket

C

cabana *n.f.* hut
cabanya *n.f.* cottage
cabaret *n.m.* cabaret
cabell *n.m.* hair
cabestrell *n.m.* sling
cabina *n.f.* cabin
cabina telefònica *n.f.* phone booth
cable *n.m.* cable
cabra *n.f.* goat
caça *n.f.* hunting
caçador *n.* hunter
caçar *v.* hunt
cacau *n.m.* cocoa
cacauet *n.m.* peanut
cactus *n.m.* cactus
cada *pron.* each; every
cada vegada més *adv.*
  increasingly
cadell *n.m.* puppy
cadena *n.f.* chain
cadenat *n.m.* padlock
cadira *n.f.* chair
cadira de rodes *n.f.* wheelchair
caducar *v.* expire
cafè *n.m.* coffee
cafè exprés *n.m.* espresso
cafeïna *n.f.* caffeine | *adj.* sense ~
  caffeine-free
cafeteria *n.f.* cafeteria, café
caiguda *n.f.* fall
caixa *n.f.* box
caixa d'eines *n.f.* toolbox
caixa de canvis *n.f.* gearbox
caixa de cartró *n.f.* carton
caixa de la cadena *n.f.* chain guard

caixa enregistradora *n.f.* cash
  register
caixer *n.* cashier
caixer automàtic *n.m.* ATM
calaix *n.m.* drawer
calamar *n.m.* squid
calamitat *n.f.* calamity
calci *n.m.* calcium
calçotets *n.m.* briefs, underpants;
  pants
càlcul *n.m.* calculation
càlcul renal *n.m.* kidney stone
calculador *adj.* calculating
calculadora *n.f.* calculator
calcular *v.* calculate, compute
calcular malament *v.* miscalculate
caldera *n.f.* boiler
caldo *n.m.* bouillon
calefacció *n.f.* heating
calefacció central *n.f.* central
  heating
calendari *n.m.* calendar
calent *adj.* hot, warm; més ~
  warmer
calfreds *n.f.* chills
Califòrnia *n.* California
cal·ligrafia *n.f.* calligraphy
calma *n.f.* composure
calmar *v.* soothe
calor *n.f.* heat, warmth
caloria *n.f.* calorie
cama *n.f.* leg
camamilla *n.f.* camomile
cambra *n.f.* chamber
cambra d'aire *n.f.* inner tube

cambra de bany *n.f.* bathroom
cambrer *n.m.* waiter; bartender
cambrera *n.f.* waitress; maid
càmera *n.f.* camera
càmera rèflex *n.f.* SLR camera
camí *n.m.* lane, trail, path, way
camí de muntanya *n.m.*
  mountain path
caminar *v.* walk, step
camió *n.m.* truck, lorry
camió d'escombraries *n.m.*
  garbage truck
camioneta *n.f.* pickup *(truck)*
camisa *n.f.* shirt
camp *n.m.* countryside; field
camp a través *n.m.* cross-country
camp d'arròs *n.m.* paddy
camp de golf *n.m.* golf course
camp de joc *n.m.* playing field
campament *n.m.* camp
campana *n.f.* bell
campanya *n.f.* campaign
càmping *n.m.* campground
campionat *n.m.* championship
Canadà *n.m.* Canada
canadenc *adj.* Canadian
canal *n.m.* canal, channel
cancel·lar *v.* cancel
cancel·lat *adj.* canceled
canceller *n.* chancellor
càncer *n.m.* cancer
cancerigen *adj.* carcinogenic
cancerós *adj.* cancerous
cançó *n.f.* song
cançó de bressol *n.f.* lullaby
candeler *n.m.* candlestick
candidat *n.m.* candidate, nominee
canell *n.m.* wrist
cangur *n.m.* kangaroo | *n.* baby-
  sitter

canoa *n.f.* canoe
canós *adj.* gray-haired
cansalada *n.f.* bacon
cansar *v.* tire
cansat *adj.* tired
cant *n.m.* singing
cantalup *n.m.* cantaloupe
cantant *n.* singer
cantar *v.* sing
canvi *n.m.* switch, change
canvi de divises *n.m.* currency
  exchange
canviar *v.* change, shift, switch
canya *n.f.* reed
canya de pescar *n.f.* fishing rod
canyella *n.f.* cinnamon
cap *n.m.* chief, boss, head | *pron.*
  none
cap a *prep.* toward(s)
cap a dins *adv.* inwards
cap amunt *adv.* upwards
cap avall *adv.* downward
cap d'any *n.m.* New Year's Eve
cap de setmana *n.m.* weekend
cap de turc *n.m.* scapegoat
capa *n.f.* layer, coating
capa d'ozó *n.f.* ozone layer
capaç *adj.* able, capable; ~ **de**
  capable of
capacitat *n.f.* ability, capability;
  capacity
capbussar-se *v.* dive
capçalera *n.f.* header, heading
capella *n.f.* chapel
capità *n.m.* captain
capital *n.f.* capital
capítol *n.m.* chapter
Capricorn *n.m.* Capricorn
capritxós *adj.* capricious
càpsula *n.f.* capsule

captaire *n.m.* beggar
captiu *n.* captive
captivitat *n.f.* captivity
capturar *v.* capture
caputxa *n.f.* hood
caqui *n.m.* persimmon
car *adj.* expensive
cara *n.f.* face
carbassó *n.m.* zucchini, squash
característic *adj.* characteristic
característica *n.f.* characteristic, feature
caramel *n.m.* caramel, toffee
caramel·litzat *adj.* caramelized
carbassa *n.f.* gourd
carbassa de rabequet *n.f.* pumpkin
carbó *n.m.* coal
carbó vegetal *n.m.* charcoal
carbohidrat *n.m.* carbohydrate
carbonatat *adj.* carbonated
carboni *n.m.* carbon
carburador *n.m.* carburetor
cargol *n.m.* snail; screw
cargolar *v.* screw
caricatura *n.f.* caricature
caritat *n.f.* charity
carmanyola *n.f.* lunch box
carn *n.f.* flesh, meat
carn curada *n.f.* cured meat
carn de be *n.f.* mutton
carn de porc *n.f.* pork
carn de vaca *n.f.* beef
carn del pit *n.f.* brisket
carn freda *n.f.* cold cuts, lunch-meat
carn picada *n.f.* minced meat
carnaval *n.m.* carnival
carnet d'assegurança *n.m.* insurance card

carnet d'identitat *n.m.* identity card, ID card
carnet de conduir *n.m.* driver's license
carnisser *n.* butcher
Carolina del Nord *n.* North Carolina
Carolina del Sud *n.* South Carolina
carpa *n.f.* carp
càrrega *n.f.* burden
càrrega de la prova *n.f.* burden of proof
carregament *n.m.* shipment
carregar *v.* load
carrer *n.m.* street
carrer principal *n.m.* main street
carrera a peu *n.f.* running
carrera *n.f.* career; race
carreró *n.m.* alley
carreró sense sortida *n.m.* dead end
carretera *n.f.* highway, road
carretera principal *n.f.* main road
carretó *n.m.* trolley
carro *n.m.* cart
carta *n.f.* letter *(postal)*; card
cartell *n.m.* pòster, placard
carter *n.m.* postman
cartera *n.f.* portfolio; wallet
cartílag *n.m.* cartilage
cartó *n.m.* cardboard
carxofa *n.f.* artichoke
cas *n.m.* case | *v.* **no fer** ~ ignore
casa *n.f.* house, home, household | *adv.* **a** ~ indoors
  casa gran *n.f.* mansion
casament *n.m.* wedding
casar-se *v.* marry

casat *adj.* married
casc *n.m.* helmet
cascada *n.f.* waterfall
caseller *n.m.* locker for baggage
casino *n.m.* casino
casset *n.f.* cassette
cassola *n.f.* baking pan, pan, saucepan, casserole
castanya *n.f.* chestnut
castell *n.m.* castle
castellà *n.m.* Castillian, Spanish
càstig *n.m.* punishment
castigar *v.* punish
català *adj./n.* Catalan
catàleg *n.m.* catalog
Catalunya *n.f.* Catalonia
catedral *n.f.* cathedral
categoria *n.f.* category
categoria gramatical *n.f.* part of speech
catifa *n.f.* carpet, rug
catòlic *adj./n.* Catholic
catorzè *adj.* fourteenth
catorze *num.* fourteen
catre *n.m.* cot
caure *v.* fall
causa *n.f.* cause
cautela *n.f.* caution
cautelós *adj.* careful
cautxú *n.m.* rubber
cava *n.f.* champagne
cavall *n.m.* horse
cavalleria *n.f.* cavalry
cavar *v.* dig
caviar *n.m.* caviar
cavitat *n.f.* cavity
CD *n.m.* compact disc, CD
ceba *n.f.* onion
cec *adj.* blind
cedir *v.* relent, relinquish

cel *n.m.* sky; heaven
celebració *n.f.* celebration
celebrar *v.* celebrate
cella *n.f.* eyebrow
cèl·lula *n.f.* cell
cel·lulosa *n.f.* cellulose
cementiri *n.m.* cemetery
cendra *n.f.* ash
cendrer *n.m.* ashtray
cens *n.m.* census
censura *n.f.* censorship
cent *num.* hundred
centenari *n.m.* centenary
centèsim *adj.* hundredth
centígrad *n.m.* centigrade
cèntim *n.m.* cent
centímetre *n.m.* centimeter
centpeus *n.m.* centipede
central *adj.* central
central nuclear *n.f.* nuclear power station
centre *n.m.* center
centre comercial *n.m.* mall
centre de la ciutat *n.m.* downtown, center of town
centre de salut *n.m.* health center
cera *n.f.* wax
ceràmic *adj.* ceramic
ceràmica *n.f.* ceramics
cerca *n.f.* search
cercar *v.* search, look for
cercle *n.m.* circle
cereal *n.m.* cereal
cerimònia *n.f.* ceremony
cert *adj.* certain
certament *adv.* certainly
certificat *n.m.* certificate
cervell *n.m.* brain
cervesa *n.f.* beer, ale
cerveseria *n.f.* brewery

cérvol *n.m.* deer, venison
cessar *v.* cease
chutney *n.m.* chutney
cibercafè *n.m.* Internet café
cibulet *n.m.* chives
cicatriu *n.f.* scar
cicle *n.m.* cycle
ciclisme *n.m.* cycling
ciclista *n.* bicyclist
ciclomotor *n.m.* moped
ciència *n.f.* science
ciències naturals *n.f.* natural
  sciences
científic *adj.* scientific | *n.* scientist
cigar *n.m.* cigar
cigarret *n.m.* cigarette
cigonya *n.f.* stork
cigró *n.m.* chickpea
cilíndric *adj.* cylindrical
cim *n.m.* peak
ciment *n.m.* cement
cinc *num.* five
cinema *n.m.* movie theater, cinema
cinema de terror *n.m.* horror
  films
cinetosi *n.f.* motion sickness
cinquanta *num.* fifty
cinquantè *adj.* fiftieth
cinquè *adj.* fifth
cinta *n.f.* ribbon, tape
cintura *n.f.* waist
cinturó *n.m.* belt
cinturó de seguretat *n.m.* seat
  belt
cinturó salvavides *n.m.* life belt
circuit *n.m.* circuit
circulació *n.f.* circulation
circular *adj.* round
circumstància *n.f.* circumstance
circumstancial *adj.* circumstantial

cirera *n.f.* cherry
cirera marrasquino *n.f.*
  maraschino cherry
cirurgia *n.f.* surgery
cirurgià *n.m.* surgeon
cistella *n.f.* basket
cistitis *n.f.* cystitis
cita *n.f.* appointment, rendezvous
citació *n.f.* quotation, quote;
  subpoena, summons
citar *v.* quote
cítric *n.m.* citrus
citronel·la *n.f.* lemongrass
ciutadà *n.m.* citizen
ciutadania *n.f.* citizenship
ciutat *n.f.* city, town
Ciutat del Vaticà *n.f.* Vatican
  City
civades *n.f.* oats; oatmeal
civil *adj.* civil | *n.m.* civilian
claca *n.f.* quack *(of a duck)*
clacar *v.* quack
clamor *n.m.* clamor, outcry
clapejat *adj.* mottle
clar *adj.* light; clear
clarament *adv.* clearly
clarificat *adj.* clarified
clarivident *adj.* clairvoyant
classe *n.f.* class
classe dirigent *n.m.* establishment
clàssic *adj.* classic; classical
classicisme *n.m.* Classicism
clàssics *n.m.* classics
classificació *n.f.* classification
classificar *v.* classify
clau *n.m.* key; nail
clau de contacte *n.f.* ignition key
clauer *n.m.* key chain, key ring
clàusula *n.f.* clause
clavar *v.* nail, pin

clavell *n.m.* clove
clavícula *n.f.* collarbone
clavilla *n.f.* peg
clementina *n.f.* clementine
clicar *v.* click
client *n.* client; customer
clima *n.m.* climate
clímax *n.m.* climax
clínic *adj.* clinical
clínica *n.f.* clinic
cloïssa *n.f.* clam
clon *n.m.* clone
clonació *n.f.* cloning
clonar *v.* clone
clor *n.m.* chlorine
closca *n.f.* husk, shell
closca d'ou *n.f.* egg shell
club *n.m.* club *(social)*
club gai *n.m.* gay club
clúster *n.m.* cluster
coàgul *n.m.* clot
coagulat *adj.* clotted, congealed
coartada *n.f.* alibi
cobert *adj.* covered
coberta *n.f.* casing, cover; deck *(of a ship)*
coberts *n.m.* cutlery
cobrar *v.* charge
cobrar massa *v.* overcharge
cobriment *n.m.* covering
cobrir *v.* cover
cobrir totalment *v.* overrun
cocaïna *n.f.* cocaine
coco *n.m.* coconut
còctel *n.m.* cocktail
codi *n.m.* code
codi del país *n.m.* country code
codi postal *n.m.* zip code, postal code
còdol *n.m.* pebble

coet *n.m.* rocket
cognom de soltera *n.m.* maiden name
cognom *n.m.* surname, last name
cogombre *n.m.* cucumber
cogombret *n.m.* pickle
coincidir *v.* coincide
coix *adj.* lame
coixí *n.m.* pillow
coixinera *n.f.* pillowcase
col *n.m.* cabbage
col de cabdell *n.f.* collard greens
col verda *n.f.* kale
cola *n.f.* glue
coleslaw *n.f.* coleslaw, slaw
coliflor *n.f.* cauliflower
coll *n.m.* neck
collada *n.f.* mountain pass
collaret *n.m.* necklace
col·lecció *n.f.* collection
col·lecció permanent *n.f.* permanent collection
col·leccionista *n.* collector
col·lega *n.* colleague
col·legi *n.m.* college
collir *v.* pick *(flowers, etc.)*
collita *n.f.* crop, harvest
colom *n.m.* pigeon, dove
Colòmbia *n.f.* Colombia
colomí *n.m.* squab
còlon *n.m. (anat.)* colon
color *n.m.* color | *adj.* **de colors** colored
Colorado *n.* Colorado
colorant *n.m.* coloring
colorant alimentari *n.m.* food coloring
coloret *n.m.* blush
colpejar *v.* strike, hit
cols de Brussel·les *n.m.* Brussels sprouts

columna *n.f.* column
columna vertebral *n.f.* spinal column
colze *n.m.* elbow
com *prep./conj./adv.* as, how, like
coma *n.f.* coma; comma
combinació *n.* combination
combinar *v.* combine
combustible *n.m.* fuel
comèdia *n.f.* comedy
començament *n.m.* start
començar *v.* commence, begin, start
comensal *n.* diner
comentari *n.m.* comment, remark, commentary
comerç *n.m.* trade, trading
comercial *adj.* commercial
comerciant *n.* merchant, dealer, trader
comerciar *v.* trade
comestible *adj.* edible
cometre *v.* commit
comí *n.m.* cumin; caraway
còmic *adj.* comic | *n.m.* comics
comissaria *n.f.* police station
comissió *n.f.* commission
comitè *n.m.* committee
commemoració *n.f.* commemoration
commoció *n.f.* concussion
commovedor *adj.* moving, poignant
còmodament *adv.* comfortably
còmode *adj.* comfortable
compacte *adj.* compact
company *n.* companion, mate
company d'habitació *n.* roommate
companyia *n.f.* company

companyia d'assegurances *n.f.* insurance company
comparació *n.f.* comparison
comparar *v.* compare
comparatiu *adj.* comparative
compartir *v.* share
compassió *n.f.* sympathy, pity
compenetració *n.f.* rapport
compensació *n.f.* compensation
compensar *v.* offset; redress
competició *n.f.* competition
competidor *n.* competitor
competir *v.* compete
competitiu *adj.* competitive
complet *adj.* accomplished, complete
completament *adv.* completely
complex turístic *n.m.* resort
complexitat *n.f.* complexity
complicar *v.* complicate
complicat *adj.* complicated, complex, elaborate
complir *v.* comply
complot *n.m.* plot *(plan)*
compondre *v.* compose
component *n.m.* component
comportament *n.m.* behavior
comportar-se *v.* behave
composició *n.f.* composition
compositor *n.* composer
compositor *n.* songwriter
compost *adj.* composed | *n.m.* compost; compound
compota *n.f.* compote
compra *n.f.* purchase; shopping
comprador *n.m.* buyer, purchaser
comprar *v.* buy, purchase, shop
comprendre *v.* comprise; understand
comprensió *n.f.* understanding

comprensiu *adj.* sympathetic
compresa *n.f.* sanitary napkin
compresa freda *n.f.* cold pack
compromís *n.m.* commitment, engagement
comprovar *v.* check
comptable *adj.* countable; accountant
comptador *n.* accountant; meter box
comptaquilòmetres *n.m.* odometer
comptar *v.* count; reckon
comptar amb *v.* rely on
compte *n.m.* account
compte bancari *n.m.* bank account
comptes: en ~ *adv.* instead
comtat *n.m.* county
comú *adj.* common
comunament *adv.* commonly
comunicació *n.f.* communication
comunicar *v.* communicate; convey
comunió *n.f.* communion
comunisme *n.m.* communism
comunista *n.* communist
comunitat *n.f.* community
concebre *v.* conceive
concedir *v.* grant
concentració *n.f.* concentration
concentrar *v.* concentrate
concepció *n.f.* conception
concepte *n.f.* concept
conceptual *adj.* conceptual
concert *n.m.* concert, concerto
concessió *n.f.* concession
concloure *v.* conclude
conclusió *n.f.* conclusion
concret *adj.* concrete
concurs *n.m.* contest, quiz

concurs de TV *n.m.* game show
condensar *v.* condense
condensat *adj.* condensed
condició *n.f.* condition
condicionador *n.m.* conditioner
condicional *adj.* conditional
condiment *n.m.* condiment, relish
condó *n.m.* condom
condol *n.m.* condolence
conducció *n.f.* driving
conductor *n.m.* conductor, driver
conduir *v.* drive, steer
conegut *n.* acquaintance
coneixement *n.m.* consciousness; knowledge
conèixer *v.* know *(relationships)*
conferència *n.f.* conference; lecture
conferenciant *n.* lecturer
confessar *v.* confess
confessió *n.f.* confession
confiança *n.f.* confidence, trust | *adj.* **de ~** reliable
confiat *adj.* confident
confidencial *adj.* confidential
confinar *v.* confine
confinat *adj.* confined
confirmar *v.* confirm, make sure
confiscació *n.f.* seizure
confiscar *v.* seize
confitar *v.* pickle
confitat *adj.* pickled
confitura *n.f.* preserves
conflicte *n.m.* conflict
confondre *v.* confuse, muddle
confort *n.m.* comfort
confós *adj.* confused
confrontar *v.* confront
confús *adj.* confusing

confusió *n.f.* confusion
congelador *n.m.* freezer
congelar *v.* freeze
congelat *adj.* frozen
congolès *adj.* Congolese
congrés *n.m.* congress
conill *n.m.* rabbit
conillet d'Índies *n.m.* guinea pig
conjectura *n.f.* guess
cònjuge *n.* spouse
conjunció *n.f.* conjunction
conjunt: en ~ *adv.* altogether
conjuntament *adv.* jointly
conjur *n.m.* spell *(magic)*
connectar *v.* connect
connectat *adj.* connected
Connecticut *n.* Connecticut
connexió *n.f.* connection
consciència *n.f.* awareness, consciousness
conscient *adj.* aware, conscious
consell *n.m.* counsel, advice, council
conseller *n.* counselor, advisor
consentir *v.* pamper
conseqüència *n.f.* consequence
conseqüentment *adv.* consequently; consistently
conserva: en ~ *adj.* preserved
conservació *n.f.* conservation
conservador *adj.* conservative | *n.* curator
conservant *n.m.* preservative, food preservative
conservar *v.* conserve, preserve
considerable *adj.* considerable
considerablement *adv.* considerably
consideració *n.f.* consideration
considerar *v.* consider, mull

consistent *adj.* consistent
consistir *v.* consist
consolat *n.m.* consulate
consomé *n.m.* consommé
consonant *n.f.* consonant
constant *adj.* constant
constantment *adv.* constantly
constel·lació *n.f.* constellation
constitució *n.f.* constitution
constitucional *adj.* constitutional
constituir *v.* constitute, make up
construcció *n.f.* construction
constructor *n.* builder
construir *v.* construct, build
construït *adj.* built
consulta *n.f.* consultation
consultar *v.* consult
consultor *n.* consultant
consum *n.m.* consumption
consumidor *n.* consumer
contactar *v.* contact
contacte *n.m.* contact
contagiós *adj.* contagious
contaminació *n.f.* pollution
contaminar *v.* pollute
contar *v.* relate
conte *n.m.* tale
contemporani *adj.* contemporary
contenir *v.* contain
content *adj.* glad
context *n.m.* context
contigu *adj.* adjoining
continent *n.m.* continent
continental *adj.* continental
contingut *n.m.* content
continu *adj.* continuous
contínuament *adv.* continuously
continuar *v.* continue
contorn *n.m.* outline *(shape)*
contra *prep.* against

contracte *n.f.* contraction
contracor: a ~ *adv.* unwillingly
contractar *v.* hire, engage
contracte *n.m.* contract
contractista *n.* contractor
contrafort *n.m.* buttress
contrasenya *n.f.* password
contrast *n.m.* contrast | *adj.* **en ~**
  contrasting
contrastar *v.* contrast
contratemps *n.m.* mishap
contribució *n.f.* contribution
contribuent *n.* taxpayer
contribuir *v.* contribute
control *n.m.* control, restraint
controlada *adj.* controlled
controlar *v.* control
contusió *n.f.* contusion
convèncer *v.* convince
convenció *n.f.* convention
convencional *adj.* conventional
convenient *adj.* convenient
convent *n.m.* convent, nunnery
conversa *n.f.* conversation
convertir *v.* convert
convidat *n.* guest
convocar *v.* summon
convulsió *n.f.* seizure
cooperació *n.f.* cooperation
cooperatiu *adj.* cooperative
coordinar *v.* coordinate
cop *n.m.* hit
cop de puny *n.m.* punch *(hit)*
cop i volta: de ~ *adv.* suddenly
copa *n.f.* goblet, wineglass
copejar *v.* tap
copet *n.m.* tap, pat
còpia *n.f.* copy
copiar *v.* copy
cor *n.m.* heart; core; chorus, choir

coratge *n.m.* courage; prowess
corb *adj.* curved; raven
corba *n.f.* curve
corbata *n.f.* tie
corda *n.f.* rope
cordill *n.m.* string
cordó *n.m.* cord, lace, string
coreà *adj./n.* Korean
Corea *n.* Korea
Corea del Nord *n.* North Korea
Corea del Sud *n.* South Korea
coreògraf *n.* choreographer
coreografia *n.f.* choreography
coriandre *n.m.* coriander, cilantro
corona *n.f.* crown
corporació *n.f.* corporation
corporatiu *adj.* corporate
correctament *adv.* correctly,
  properly, rightly
correcte *adj.* correct, right
corredor *n.* broker, runner
correlació *n.f.* correlation
corrent *n.m.* stream, flow
corrent dominant *n.m.* mainstream
córrer *v.* run, race
córrer més ràpid que *v.* outrun
correspondre *v.* correspond
corresponent *adj.* corresponding
corretja del ventilador *n.f.* fan
  belt
correu *n.m.* mail, post
correu aeri *n.m.* airmail
correu de veu *n.m.* voice mail
correu electrònic *n.m.* e-mail
corró *n.m.* rolling pin
corrompre *v.* corrupt
corromput *adj.* corrupted
corrupció *n.f.* corruption
corrupte *adj.* corrupt

cortès *adj.* polite
cortesament *adv.* politely
cortesia *n.f.* courtesy
cortina *n.f.* curtain
cos *n.m.* body
cosa *n.f.* thing
cosí *n.m.* cousin
cosina *n.f.* cousin
cosir *v.* sew, stitch
cosmètic *n.m.* cosmetic
cosmos *n.m.* cosmos
cost *n.m.* cost
costa *n.f.* coast, shore
costa amunt *adj.* uphill
Costa Rica *n.f.* Costa Rica
costar *v.* cost
costat *n.m.* side | *adj.* **de ~** sideways | *prep.* **al ~ de** alongside, beside, next to
costella *n.f.* rib; cutlet
costerut *adj.* steep
costum *n.m.* custom
costura *n.f.* sewing
cotó *n.m.* cotton
cotxe *n.m.* car
cotxinilla *n.f.* multiped
coure *n.m.* copper
coure a foc lent *v.* braise
cova *n.f.* cave
covard *n.m.* coward
CPU *n.f.* CPU
cranc *n.m.* crab
cranc de riu *n.m.* crayfish
crani *n.m.* skull
creació *n.f.* creation
crear *v.* create
creatiu *adj.* creative
creativitat *n.f.* creativity
crèdit *n.m.* credit
creditor *n.* creditor

creença *n.f.* belief
creixement *n.m.* growth
créixens *n.m.* watercress
créixer *v.* grow
crema d'afaitar *n.f.* shaving cream
crema hidratant *n.f.* moisturizing cream
crema solar *n.f.* sunblock, suntan lotion
cremada *n.f.* sunburn
cremallera *n.f.* zipper
cremar *v.* burn
cremat *adj.* burned, burnt
crep *n.m.* crepe, pancake
crespar *v.* ruffle
cresta *n.f.* ridge
creu *n.f.* rood; cross
creuar *v.* cross
creuer *n.m.* cruise
creure *v.* believe
criar *v.* raise *(children/animals)*
criat *n.* servant
criatura *n.f.* creature
cridar *v.* scream, shout, yell
crim *n.m.* crime
criminal *adj./n.* criminal
cripta *n.f.* crypt
crisi *n.f.* crisis
crispetes *n.f.* popcorn
cristall *n.m.* crystal
cristalleria *n.f.* glassware
cristal·litzat *adj.* crystallized
cristià *adj./n.* Christian
crit *n.m.* shout, yell
criteri *n.m.* criteria
crític *adj.* critical | *n.* critic
crítica *n.f.* criticism, critique
criticar *v.* criticize
Croàcia *n.f.* Croatia

cromosoma *n.f.* chromosome
crònic *adj.* chronic
cronòmetre *n.m.* stopwatch
croqueta *n.f.* croquette
crossa *n.f.* crutch
crosta *n.f.* crust; scab
crostat *adj.* crusted
crostó *n.m.* crouton
cru *adj.* raw
crucial *adj.* crucial
cruel *adj.* cruel
crueltat *n.f.* cruelty
cruixent *adj.* crisp
cruixir *v.* crunch
crustaci *n.m.* crustacean
cua *n.f.* tail; queue
cua de bou *n.f.* oxtail
cub *n.m.* cube
Cuba *n.f.* Cuba
cubell *n.m.* bucket
cubicat *adj.* cubed
cuc *n.m.* earthworm, worm
cuidar *v.* look after
cuina *n.f.* cuisine, cooking;
  kitchen; cooker
cuina casolana *n.f.* home-style
  cooking
cuinar *v.* cook
cuiner en cap *n.* chef
cuir *n.m.* leather
cuir cabellut *n.m.* scalp
cuit a foc lent *adj.* simmered
cuixa *n.f.* thigh
culinari *adj.* culinary
cullera *n.f.* spoon

cullerada *n.f.* tablespoon;
  spoonful
cullereta *n.f.* teaspoon
cullerot *n.m.* ladle
culpa *n.f.* guilt, fault *(blame)*
culpable *adj.* guilty
culpar *v.* blame
cultivable *adj.* arable
cultivar *v.* cultivate
cultivat *adj.* cultivated
cultura *n.f.* culture
cultural *adj.* cultural
cupcake *n.m.* cupcake
cupó *n.m.* coupon
cúpula *n.f.* dome
cura *n.f.* care
cura dels nens *n.f.* childcare
curar *v.* cure, heal
curat *adj.* cured
cúrcuma *n.f.* turmeric
curiós *adj.* curious; quaint
curiosament *adv.* curiously
curiositat *n.f.* curiosity
curri *n.m.* curry
curs *n.m.* course
curs d'idioma *n.m.* language
  course
cursa *n.f.* race *(competition)*
cursa de cavalls *n.f.* horse racing
cursor *n.m.* cursor
curt *adj.* short
cuscús *n.m.* couscous
custòdia *n.f.* custody
cutis *n.m.* complexion

D

d'acord *interj.* OK, okay
dades *n.f.* data
Dakota del Nord *n.* North Dakota
Dakota del Sud *n.* South Dakota
d'alguna manera *adv.* somehow
dalt: a ~ *adv.* upstairs
dama d'honor *n.f.* bridesmaid
dames *n.f.* checkers
damunt *adv.* above
dansa *n.f.* dance
dany *n.m.* damage
danyar *v.* harm, damage
darrere *prep.* behind
data *n.f.* date
data de caducitat *n.f.* expiration date
daurat *adj.* gilded, golden; browned
daus *n.m.* dice
d'autoservei *adj.* self-service
davant *adv.* ahead
davantal *n.m.* apron
de *prep.* of | *conj.* than
de bona gana *adv.* willingly
de calvície incipient *adj.* balding
de colors *adj.* colored
de confiança *adj.* reliable
de cop i volta *adv.* suddenly
de costat *adj.* sideways
de fet *adv.* actually
de fusta *adj.* wooden
de la matinada *adv.* a.m. *(early morning)*
de moda *adj.* fashionable
de no fumador *adj.* non-smoking

de nou *adv.* again | *adj.* nutty
de plata *adj.* silver
de por *adj.* scary
de prop *adv.* closely
de qui *adj.* whose
de recanvi *adj.* spare
de segona mà *adj.* secondhand
de servei *phr.* on duty
de sortida *adj.* outgoing *(clerical)*
de totes maneres *adv.* anyway
de vegades *adv.* sometimes
debat *n.m.* debate
debilitat *n.f.* weakness
debut *n.m.* debut
dècada *n.f.* decade
decantador *n.m.* decanter
decantar *v.* decant
decebedor *adj.* disappointing
decebre *v.* disappoint
decebut *adj.* disappointed
decepció *n.f.* disappointment
decidir *v.* decide
decisió *n.f.* decision
declaració *n.f.* statement
declaració duanera *n.f.* customs declaration
declaració jurada *n.f.* affidavit
declarar *v.* declare
declinar *v.* decline
decoració *n.f.* decoration
decorar *v.* decorate
decoratiu *adj.* decorative
decret *n.m.* decree
dedicació *n.f.* dedication
dedicar *v.* dedicate, devote

dedicat *adj.* dedicated, devoted
deduir *v.* deduct
defecte *n.m.* fault *(defect)*
defectuós *adj.* faulty
defensa *n.f.* defense; advocacy
defensa personal *n.f.* self-defense
defensar *v.* defend; advocate
deficiència *n.f.* deficiency
dèficit *n.m.* deficit
definició *n.f.* definition
definir *v.* define
definit *adj.* definite
definitivament *adv.* definitely
degustar *v.* taste
degut *adj.* due
degut procés *n.m.* due process
d'hora *adv.* early
deïtat *n.f.* deity
deixalles *n.f.* refuse; remains
deixar *v.* quit; leave; let
deixar caure *v.* drop
deixar de *v.* give (something) up
deixar perplex *v.* perplex
del matí *adv.* a.m. *(morning)*
del nord *adj.* northern
del sud *adj.* southern
Delaware *n.* Delaware
delegat *n.* delegate
deliberadament *adv.* deliberately
deliberat *adj.* deliberate
delicadesa *n.f.* delicacy
delicat *adj.* delicate
deliciós *adj.* delicious
delicte *n.m.* felony, misdemeanor; offence, offense
delirant *adj.* delirious
delirar *v.* rave
delit *n.m.* delight
demà *adv.* tomorrow
demanar *v.* order

demanda *n.f.* demand
demandant *n.* plaintiff
democràcia *n.f.* democracy
demostració *n.f.* demonstration
demostrar *v.* demonstrate; prove
dempeus *adj.* standing
denim *n.m.* denim
densament *adv.* thickly
densitat *n.f.* density
dent *n.f.* tooth
dent de lleó *n.f.* dandelion
dentadura postissa *n.f.* dentures
dental *adj.* dental
dentista *n.* dentist
departament *n.m.* department
dependència *n.f.* dependence, reliance
dependent *adj.* dependent
dependre *v.* depend
deposició *n.f.* deposition
depreciació *n.f.* depreciation
depredador *n.m.* predator
depressió *n.f.* depression
depriment *adj.* depressing
deprimir *v.* depress
deprimit *adj.* depressed
derivació *n.f.* offshoot
derivar *v.* derive
derivat *adj.* derivative
derrota *n.f.* defeat, rout
derrotar *v.* defeat
des de *prep.* since
desacord *n.m.* disagreement
desactivar *v.* disable
desafiament *n.m.* challenge
desafiar *v.* dare
desafortunadament *adv.* unfortunately
desafortunat *adj.* unfortunate, unlucky

desagradable *adj.* obnoxious, unpleasant
desaparèixer *v.* disappear
desaparició *n.f.* disappearance
desaprovació *adj.* disapproving
desaprovar *v.* disapprove
desastre *n.m.* disaster
desautoritzar *v.* overrule
desavantatge *n.m.* disadvantage
descafeïnat *adj.* decaffeinated
descans *n.m.* rest, recess | *v.* **fer un ~** recess
descansar *v.* rest
descàrrega *n.f.* discharge
descarregable *adj.* downloadable
descarregar *v.* download; unload, discharge
descarregat *adj.* discharged
descendència *n.f.* offspring
descobert *adj.* discovered | *n.m.* overdraft
descobriment *n.m.* discovery, finding
descobrir *v.* discover, detect
descomposició *n.f.* decay
descompte *n.m.* discount
desconcertar *v.* mystify
desconegut *adj.* unfamiliar, unknown | *n.* stranger
descongelar *v.* defrost
desconnectar *v.* unplug
desconnectat *adj.* offline
descortès *adj.* impolite
descripció *n.f.* description
descripció de treball *n.f.* job description
descriure *v.* describe
descuit *n.m.* oversight
desè *adj.* tenth
desembarcador *n.m.* jetty

desembre *n.m.* December
desenfrenat *adj.* rampant
desengreixar *v.* degrease
desenvolupament *n.m.* development
desenvolupar *v.* develop
desert *n.m.* desert
desesperadament *adv.* desperately
desesperat *adj.* desperate
desfer *v.* undo
desfer-se de *v.* get rid of
desfilada *n.f.* parade, pageant
desforestació *n.f.* deforestation
desgana *n.f.* reluctance
deshonest *adj.* dishonest
deshonestament *adv.* dishonestly
desig *n.m.* desire, wish
desigual *adj.* uneven
desigualtat *n.f.* inequality
desinfectar *v.* sanitize, disinfect
desitjar *v.* desire, wish
desmaiar-se *v.* faint
desnatada *adj.* fat-free
desnonament *n.m.* eviction
desnonar *v.* evict
desocupació *n.f.* unemployment
desocupar *v.* vacate
desodorant *n.m.* deodorant
desordenat *adj.* untidy
desordre *n.m.* disorder
despert *adj.* awake
despertar *v.* wake, rouse
despesa *n.f.* expense, expenditure
despietat *adj.* pitiless
despit *n.m.* spite
després *adv.* afterwards, after
després de *prep.* after
despullar *v.* undress, strip
dessuadora *n.f.* sweatshirt
destacar *v.* highlight

destí *n.m.* fate
destil·lar *v.* distill
destil·lat *adj.* distilled
destinació *n.f.* destination
destinatari *n.m.* addressee
destral *n.f.* axe
destret *n.m.* predicament, plight
destrossar *v.* ravage
destrucció *n.f.* destruction
destruir *v.* destroy
destruït *adj.* destroyed
desviació *n.f.* bypass, detour
desviar *v.* sheer
detall *n.m.* detail
detallar *v.* itemize
detallat *adj.* detailed, itemized
detallista *n.* retailer
detectiu *n.* detective
detergent *n.m.* detergent
determinació *n.f.* determination
determinar *v.* determine
determinat *adj.* determined
déu *n.m.* god, God
deu *num.* ten
deure *v.* owe | *n.m.* duty
deures *n.m.* homework
deute *n.m.* debt
deutor *n.* debtor
devorar *v.* devour
dia *n.m.* day; daytime
Dia d'Acció de Gràcies *n.m.* Thanksgiving
Dia de Nadal *n.m.* Christmas Day
dia laborable *n.m.* weekday
diabètic *adj.* diabetic
diabetis *n.f.* diabetes
diable *n.m.* devil
diafragma *n.m.* diaphragm
diagnosi *n.f.* diagnosis
diagnosticar *v.* diagnose

diagrama *n.m.* diagram
dialecte *n.m.* dialect
diàleg *n.m.* dialogue
diamant *n.m.* diamond
diàmetre *n.m.* diameter
diapositiva *n.f.* slide *(visual)*
diari *adj.* daily, everyday | *n.m.* newspaper; diary
diarrea *n.f.* diarrhea
dibuix *n.m.* drawing
dibuixar *v.* draw
dibuixos animats *n.m.* cartoon
diccionari *n.m.* dictionary
dictar *v.* dictate
dictat *n.m.* dictation
dièsel *n.m.* diesel
dieta *n.f.* diet
dietètic *adj.* dietary
difamació *n.f.* libel
difamar *v.* malign
diferència *n.f.* difference
diferent *adj.* different, unlike
diferentment *adv.* differently
diferir *v.* differ
difícil *adj.* difficult
dificultat *n.f.* difficulty
digerir *v.* digest
digital *adj.* digital
digne *adj.* worthy
dijous *n.m.* Thursday
dilema *n.m.* quandary
diligent *adj.* diligent
dilluns *n.m.* Monday
diluir *v.* dilute
dimarts *n.m.* Tuesday
dimecres *n.m.* Wednesday
dimensió *n.f.* dimension
dimissió *n.f.* resignation
dimitir *v.* resign
Dinamarca *n.f.* Denmark

dinàmic *adj.* dynamic
dinamita *n.f.* dynamite
dinar *n.m.* lunch
dinastia *n.f.* dynasty
diners *n.m.* money, cash
dinou *num.* nineteen
dinovè *adj.* nineteenth
dins *prep.* inside, within
diplomàcia *n.f.* diplomacy
diplomàtic *n.* diplomat
dipòsit *n.m.* escrow; tank
dir *v.* say, tell
direcció *n.f.* direction
directament *adv.* directly
directe *adj.* direct
directiu *adj.* managerial
directiva *n.f.* directive
director *n.* director
directori *n.m.* directory
directriu *n.f.* guideline
dirigir *v.* lead, conduct, manage
disbarat *n.m.* nonsense
disc *n.m.* disk, disc; record
discapacitat *n.f.* disability, handicap
disciplina *n.f.* discipline
discoteca *n.f.* discotheque, night club
discrepar *v.* disagree
discriminació *n.f.* discrimination
discriminar *v.* discriminate
disculpar *v.* apologize
Disculpi *phr.* Excuse me *(for pardon)*
discurs *n.m.* discourse, speech, oration
discussió *n.f.* discussion
discutir *v.* discuss; argue
dislocat *adj.* dislocated
disminuir *v.* decrease, lag

disparar *v.* shoot
dispers *adj.* scattered
dispersar *v.* scatter
disponibilitat *n.f.* availability
disponible *adj.* available
disposat *adj.* willing
disposició *n.f.* disposal
dispositiu *n.m.* device
disputa *n.f.* dispute
dissabte *n.m.* Saturday, sabbath
disseny *n.m.* design
dissenyador *n.* designer
dissenyar *v.* design
dissenyat *adj.* designed
disset *num.* seventeen
dissetè *adj.* seventeenth
dissoldre *v.* dissolve
dissolvent *n.m.* solvent
distància *n.f.* distance
distant *adj.* distant
distinció *n.f.* distinction
distingir *v.* distinguish
distint *adj.* distinct
distintiu *adj.* distinctive
distribució *n.f.* distribution
distribuïdor *n.* distributor
distribuir *v.* distribute
districte *n.m.* district
dit *n.m.* finger
dit del peu *n.m.* toe
dit índex *n.m.* forefinger
dita *n.f.* saying
diumenge *n.m.* Sunday
diumenge de rams *n.m.* Palm Sunday
diürètic *n.m.* diuretic
divendres *n.m.* Friday
diversió *n.f.* fun, amusement
diversos *adj.* various, several
divertir *v.* amuse

divertit *adj.* entertaining, amusing, amused, funny, hilarious
dividend *n.m.* dividend
dividir *v.* divide, split
divisió *n.f.* division, split
divorci *n.m.* divorce
divorciat *adj.* divorced
divuit *num.* eighteen
divuitè *adj.* eighteenth
doblar *v.* dub
doblat *adj.* dubbed
doblatge *n.m.* dubbing
doble *adj.* double
doblegar *v.* bend
doblegat *adj.* bent
dòcil *adj.* amenable
document *n.m.* document
document d'identitat *n.m.* identity document
documental *n.m.* documentary
dol *n.m.* mourning
dòlar *n.m.* dollar
dolç *adj.* sweet
dolços *n.m.* candy
dolor *n.m.* pain, ache; grief
dolor agut *n.m.* agony *(physical)*
dolorós *adj.* painful
dolorosament *adv.* painfully
domèstic *adj.* domestic
dominant *adj.* dominant
dominar *v.* dominate
domini *n.m.* domain
dòmino *n.m.* dominoes
dona *n.f.* wife; woman
donació *n.f.* donation
donant *n.* donor
donar *v.* donate, give
donar a llum *v.* give birth (to)
donar feina *v.* employ
donar un cop de peu *v.* kick
donar un cop de puny *v.* punch

dones *n.f.* women
dònut *n.m.* doughnut
donzell *n.m.* wormwood
dorment *n.* sleeper
dormida *n.f.* sleep
dormir *v.* sleep
dormisquejar *v.* doze
dormitori *n.m.* dormitory, bedroom
dos *num.* two
dosi *n.f.* dosage, dose
dot *n.m.* dowry
dotzè *adj.* twelfth
dotze *num.* twelve
dotzena *n.f.* dozen
dragar *v.* dredge
drama *n.m.* drama
dramàtic *adj.* dramatic
dramàticament *adv.* dramatically
drap de cuina *n.m.* dish cloth
drecera *n.f.* shortcut
dret *adj.* right, straight
dret de retenció *n.m.* lien
drets civils *n.m.* civil rights
drets d'autor *n.m.* copyright
drets humans *n.m.* human rights
drets iguals *n.m.* equal rights
droga *n.f.* drug
duana *n.f.* customs
dubtar *v.* doubt
dubte *n.m.* doubt
dues *num.* two
dues vegades *adv.* twice
dumpling *n.m.* dumpling
d'un sol ús *adj.* disposable
dur *adj.* hard, tough
durant *prep.* during
durant la nit *adv.* overnight
durian *n.m.* durian
dutxa *n.f.* shower
dutxar-se *v.* shower
DVD *n.m.* DVD

E

eclair *n.* éclair
eclipsar *v.* eclipse, outshine
eclipsi *n.m.* eclipse
eco *n.m.* echo
economia *n.f.* economy, economics
econòmic *adj.* economic
economista *n.* economist
ecosistema *n.m.* ecosystem
edamame *n.* edamame
edat *n.f.* age
edició *n.f.* edition; publishing
edifici *n.m.* building
edifici d'aparcament *n.m.*
  parking garage
edifici d'oficines *n.m.* office
  building
edifici històric *n.m.* historic
  building
editar *v.* edit
editor *n.* publisher
edredó *n.m.* duvet
educació *n.f.* education
educar *v.* educate
educat *adj.* educated
edulcorant *n.m.* sweetener
efecte *n.m.* effect | *adv.* en ~
  indeed
eficaç *adj.* effective
eficàcia *n.f.* effectiveness
eficaçment *adv.* effectively
eficiència *n.f.* efficiency
eficient *adj.* efficient
eficientment *adv.* efficiently
eglefí *n.m.* haddock
ego *n.m.* ego

egoista *adj.* selfish
egotisme *n.m.* egotism
eina *n.f.* tool
eix *n.m.* axis
eixugar *v.* wipe
el *def. art.* the
el que *pron.* whatever
El Salvador *n.f.* El Salvador
elaborar *v.* elaborate
elàstic *adj.* elastic
elecció *n.f.* election
eleccions generals *n.f.* general
  election
electiu *adj.* elective
electorat *n.m.* electorate
elèctric *adj.* electric, electrical
electricitat *n.f.* electricity
electró *n.m.* electron
electròlit *n.m.* electrolyte
electrònic *adj.* electronic
electrònica *n.f.* electronics
elegància *n.f.* elegance
elegant *adj.* elegant
elegir *v.* choose, elect
element *n.m.* element
elevar *v.* raise *(height)*
elf *n.m.* elf
eliminació *n.f.* elimination,
  removal
eliminar *v.* eliminate, remove, rid
elixir *n.m.* elixir
ell *pron.* he, him
ell mateix *pron.* himself
ella *pron.* she; her
ella mateixa *pron.* herself

elles *pron.* they
elles mateixes *pron.* themselves
ells *pron.* they
ells mateixos *pron.* themselves
eloqüència *n.f.* eloquence
eloqüent *adj.* eloquent
els *def. art.* the *(plural)*
emancipació *n.f.* emancipation
emancipar *v.* emancipate
embaràs *n.m.* pregnancy
embarassada *adj.* pregnant
embarcador *n.m.* pier
embarcament *n.m.* boarding
embassament *n.m.* reservoir
embolcall *n.m.* wrapping
embolicar *v.* wrap
embolicat *adj.* wrapped
emboscar *v.* ambush
embotellat *adj.* bottled
embragatge *n.m.* clutch
embrió *n.m.* embryo
emergència *n.f.* emergency
emergent *adj.* emergent
emergir *v.* emerge, surface
èmfasi *n.m.* emphasis
emfatitzar *v.* emphasize
emigració *n.f.* emigration
emigrar *v.* emigrate
emissari *n.* emissary
emissió *n.f.* emission; broadcast
emmagatzemar *v.* store
emmanillar *v.* handcuff
emoció *n.f.* emotion; excitement, thrill
emocional *adj.* emotional
emocionalment *adv.* emotionally
emocionant *adj.* exciting, thrilling
emocionar *v.* excite, thrill
emocionat *adj.* excited, thrilled
empaquetar *v.* pack

empassada *n.f.* swallow
empassar *v.* swallow
empenta *n.f.* push, boost
empènyer *v.* push
emperadriu *n.f.* empress
empleat *n.* employee
emprendre *v.* undertake
empresa *n.f.* enterprise, undertaking
empresonament *n.m.* incarceration
empresonar *v.* incarcerate
emulsió *n.f.* emulsion
en *prep.* on, upon
en algun lloc *adv.* somewhere
en altre lloc *adv.* elsewhere
en blanc *adj.* blank
en comptes *adv.* instead
en conjunt *adv.* altogether
en conserva *adj.* preserved
en contrast *adj.* contrasting
en efecte *adv.* indeed
en general *adv.* overall, broadly
en gran part *adv.* largely
en línia *adj.* online
en lloc de *prep.* instead of
en part *adv.* partly
en pols *adj.* powdered
en privat *adv.* privately
en veu alta *adv.* aloud
enagos *n.m.* petticoat
encaixar *v.* fit
encaixonar *v.* encase
encaixonat *adj.* encased
encantador *adj.* charming, delightful, glamorous
encantar *v.* charm
encantat *adj.* delighted
encants *n.m.* flea market
encara *adv.* still, yet
encara que *conj.* although, though, albeit

encarregat *n.m.* foreman
encendre *v.* light, ignite
encenedor *n.m.* lighter
enciam *n.m.* lettuce
enciam iceberg *n.m.* iceberg
lettuce
enciam romà *n.m.* romaine
lettuce
encontrar *v.* encounter
encontre *n.m.* encounter
encoratjament *n.m.* encouragement
encoratjar *v.* encourage
encreuament *n.m.* crossing
endarrere *adv.* back
endarrerit *adj.* backward; overdue
endavant *adj.* forward
endevinador *n.* psychic, fortune
teller
endevinalla *n.f.* puzzle, riddle
endevinar *v.* guess
endívia *n.f.* endive
endoll *n.m.* plug, socket *(electrical)*
endormiscat *adj.* sleepy
enemic *n.m.* enemy
enemiga *n.f.* enemy
enemistat *n.f.* enmity, feud
energia *n.f.* energy
energia nuclear *n.f.* nuclear energy
enèrgic *adj.* forceful
enfadat *adj.* angry
enfarinada *adj.* floured
enfilat *adj.* skewered
enfilar *v.* thread; skewer
enfocar *v.* focus
enfonsar *v.* sink
enfrontar-se a *v.* cope (with)
enganxar *v.* paste, stick

enganxat *adj.* stuck
enganxós *adj.* sticky
engany *n.m.* delusion
enganyar *v.* trick, bluff
engegar *v.* switch on
enginy *n.m.* wit
enginyer *n.* engineer
enginyeria *n.f.* engineering
engolir *v.* engulf
engrandir *v.* enlarge
engruna *n.f.* crumb
enllaç *n.m.* link
enllaçar *v.* link
enllaunat *adj.* canned
enlloc *adv.* nowhere
ennuegar-se *v.* choke
ennuvolat *adj.* cloudy, overcast
enorme *adj.* enormous
enquesta *n.f.* poll
enrotllar *v.* reel
ensenyament *n.m.* teaching
ensenyar *v.* teach
ensucrat *adj.* candied
entabanar *v.* cajole
entalladura *n.* carving
entendre *v.* understand
enter *adj.* entire
enterament *adv.* entirely
enterrar *v.* bury
entomologia *n.f.* entomology
entorns *n.m.* environs
entrada *n.f.* entrance, entry; input
entrada il·legal *n.f.* illegal entry
entrant *n.m.* entree
entrar *v.* enter; **no** ~ keep out
entre *prep.* among, between
entreacte *n.m.* intermission
entremaliadura *n.f.* mischief
entremaliat *adj.* mischievous,
naughty

entremetre's *v.* intrude
entrenador *n.* trainer
entrenament *n.m.* training
entrenar *v.* train
entrenat *adj.* trained
entrepà *n.m.* sandwich
entreteniment *n.m.* entertainment; hobby
entretenir *v.* entertain
entreveure *v.* glimpse
entrevista *n.f.* interview
entrevistar *v.* interview
entusiasme *n.m.* enthusiasm
entusiasta *adj.* enthusiastic
envair *v.* invade
envelliment *adj.* aging
enviar *v.* send, ship
enviar un fax *v.* fax
envoltar *v.* surround
enyorar *v.* miss *(emotion)*
enzim *n.m.* enzyme
ep *interj.* hey
epicuri *adj.* epicurean
epidèmia *n.f.* epidemic
epilèptic *adj.* epileptic
episodi *n.m.* episode
època *n.f.* epoch
equació *n.f.* equation
Equador *n.m.* Ecuador
equilibrar *v.* poise
equilibri *n.m.* equilibrium, poise, balance
equip *n.m.* team; outfit; kit
equipament *n.m.* equipment
equipatge *n.m.* luggage, baggage
equipatge de mà *n.m.* carry-on, hand baggage
equitació *n.f.* riding
equitat *n.f.* equity
equivalent *adj.* equivalent

equivocació *n.f.* misconception
equivocat *adj.* mistaken
era *n.f.* era
erradicar *v.* eradicate
eriçó de mar *n.m.* sea urchin
erigir *v.* erect
erigit *adj.* erected
erm *n.m.* moor
eròtic *adj.* erotic
error *n.m.* error, mistake
erudit *n.* scholar
erupció *n.f.* rash
és clar *phr.* of course
esbandir *v.* rinse
esborrany *n.m.* draft
esborrar *v.* delete, expunge
esbós *n.m.* sketch
esbossar *v.* sketch
esbufec *n.m.* pant *(breath)*
esbufegar *v.* pant
escacs *n.m.* chess
escala *n.f.* ladder; stair, staircase, stairway, stairwell; scale
escala mecànica *n.f.* escalator
escalada *n.f.* climbing
escalar *v.* escalate; scale
escaldar *v.* scald
escaldat *adj.* scalding
escalfador *n.m.* heater
escalfar *v.* warm
escalfat *adj.* poached
escalunya *n.f.* shallot
escama *n.f.* scale *(fish)*
escamós *adj.* flaky
escamot *n.m.* platoon
escandalós *adj.* outrageous
escàndol *n.m.* scandal
escanejar *v.* scan
escàner *n.m.* scanner
escapolir *v.* abscond

escarabat *n.m.* beetle
escassetat *n.f.* shortage
escatar *v.* scale *(fish)*
escena *n.f.* scene
escenari *n.m.* stage *(theater)*
esclop *n.m.* clog
Escòcia *n.f.* Scotland
escola *n.f.* school
escola secundària *n.f.* high school
escoltar *v.* listen
escombrar *v.* sweep
escombraries *n.f.* garbage, trash, rubbish, litter
escopir *v.* spit
escorça *n.f.* bark
escorpí *n.m.* scorpion; Scorpio
escórrer *v.* drain
escriptor *n.* writer
escriptori *n.m.* desk
escriptura *n.f.* writing
escrit *adj.* written
escriure *v.* write
escull *n.m.* reef
esculpir *v.* carve
escultor *n.* sculptor
escultura *n.f.* sculpture
escuma de cabells *n.f.* hair mousse
escumós *adj.* sparkling
escuradents *n.m.* toothpick
escut *n.m.* shield
esdeveniment *n.m.* event
esdevenir *v.* become
esfèric *adj.* spherical
esfondrar-se *v.* collapse
esforç *n.m.* effort
esglaó *n.m.* step *(stairs)*
església *n.f.* church
esgotat *adj.* exhausted
esgrima *n.f.* fencing *(sport)*
Eslovàquia *n.f.* Slovakia

Eslovènia *n.f.* Slovenia
esmalt *n.m.* enamel
esmentar *v.* mention
esmicolar *v.* crumble
esmorteir *v.* muffle
esmorzar *n.m.* breakfast
espaguetis *n.m.* spaghetti
espai *n.m.* space
espantar *v.* frighten, scare
espantar-se *v.* panic
espantat *adj.* frightened
espantós *adj.* frightening
Espanya *n.f.* Spain
espanyol *adj./n.m.* Spanish
espàrrec *n.m.* asparagus
espasa *n.f.* sword
espatlla *n.f.* shoulder
espatllat *adj.* damaged
espàtula *n.f.* spatula
espècia *n.f.* spice
especial *adj.* special
especialista *n.* specialist
especialitat *n.f.* specialty
especialitzar-se *v.* specialize
especialitzat *adj.* specialized
especialment *adv.* specially, especially
especiar *v.* spice
espècie *n.f.* species
espècie amenaçada *n.f.* endangered species
específic *adj.* specific
especificació *n.f.* specification
específicament *adv.* specifically
especificar *v.* specify
espècimen *n.m.* specimen
espectacle *n.m.* show
espectador *n.* spectator, onlooker, viewer
espectre *n.m.* spectrum

especulador *n.m.* profiteer
espelma *n.f.* candle
esperança *n.f.* hope
esperançat *adj.* hopeful
esperar *v.* wait, hope, expect, look forward to
esperat *adj.* expected
esperit *n.m.* spirit
espermatozoide *n.m.* sperm
espès *adj.* thick
espiar *v.* pry
espinacs *n.m.* spinach
espinada *n.f.* spine
espiritual *adj.* spiritual
espoliar *v.* plunder
esponja *n.f.* sponge
esport *n.m.* sport
esports *n.m.* sports
esprai *n.m.* spray
esprémer *v.* squeeze
esquelet *n.m.* skeleton
esquema *n.m.* outline
esquematitzar *v.* outline
esquena *n.f.* back
esquerda *n.f.* crack
esquerdat *adj.* cracked
esquerra *adj.* left-wing | *n.f.* left
esquerrà *adj.* left-wing
esquí *n.m.* ski
esquí alpí *n.m.* downhill skiing
esquí aquàtic *n.m.* water-skiing
esquiar *v.* ski
esquinç *n.m.* tear *(rip)*
esquinçar *v.* tear
esquirol *n.m.* squirrel
esquitxar *v.* sprinkle
essència *n.f.* essence
essencial *adj.* essential
essencialment *adv.* essentially
ésser *v.* be | *n.m.* being

est *n.m.* east
estable *adj.* steady, stable
establement *adv.* steadily
estables *n.m.* stables
establiment *n.m.* establishment, settlement
establir *v.* establish
estaca *n.f.* stake
estació *n.f.* station; season *(of the year)*
estació de metro *n.f.* metro station
estació de tren *n.f.* train station
estació de metro *n.f.* subway station
estació terminal *n.f.* terminus
estacional *adj.* seasonal
estadi *n.m.* stadium
estadístic *adj.* statistical
estadística *n.f.* statistic
estafar *v.* cheat, swindle
estalvis *n.m.* savings
estàndard *adj./n.m.* standard
estany *n.m.* pond; tin *(metal)*
estar *v.* be
estar abatut *v.* mope
estar dempeus *v.* stand
estat *n.m.* state; status
estat d'emergència *n.m.* state of emergency
Estats Units d'Amèrica *n.m.* United States of America
estàtua *n.f.* statue
estatueta *n.f.* figurine
estatut *n.m.* statute
estatutari *adj.* statutory
estavellar-se *v.* crash
estel polar *n.m.* lodestar
estella *n.f.* splinter
estendre *v.* extend, spread

estèril *adj.* sterile
esterilitzar *v.* sterilize
esterilitzat *adj.* sterilized
estès *adj.* widespread
estètic *adj.* aesthetic
estil *n.m.* style
estil gòtic *n.m.* Gothic style
estilístic *adj.* stylistic
estimació *n.f.* estimate
estimar *v.* estimate
estimat *adj.* dear
estímul *n.m.* stimulus
estimular *v.* stimulate
estirada *n.f.* stretch
estirar *v.* pull, stretch, strain
estiu *n.m.* summer
estoc *n.m.* stock *(monetary)*
estofat *adj.* stewed | *n.m.* stew,
  ragout
estómac *n.m.* stomach
Estònia *n.f.* Estonia
estora *n.f.* mat
estovalles *n.f.* tablecloth
estragó *n.m.* tarragon
estranger *adj.* foreign | *n.* alien,
  foreigner | *adv.* **a l'estranger**
  abroad
estrany *adj.* strange, odd, weird,
  bizarre, alien
estranyament *adv.* strangely,
  oddly
estratègia *n.f.* strategy
estratègic *adj.* strategic
estratègicament *adv.* strategically
estrella *n.f.* star
estrella de mar *n.f.* starfish
estrena *n.f.* premiere, opening
  night
estrenar *v.* premiere
estrès *n.m.* stress

estressant *adj.* stressful
estressat *adj.* stressed
estret *adj.* narrow, tight
estretament *adv.* tightly
estri *n.m.* utensil
estrictament *adv.* strictly
estricte *adj.* strict
estripar *v.* rip, shred
estripat *adj.* torn
estrofa *n.f.* stanza
estruç *n.m.* ostrich
estructura *n.f.* structure
estructural *adj.* structural
estructuralment *adv.* structurally
estudi *n.m.* study, studio
estudiant *n.* student
estudiar *v.* study
estufa *n.f.* stove
estufa de querosè *n.f.* kerosene
  stove
estúpid *adj.* stupid, dumb
esturió *n.m.* sturgeon
et al. *abbr.* et al.
etapa *n.f.* stage *(level)*
etcètera *abbr.* etc.
etern *adj.* everlasting
ètic *adj.* ethical
ètica *n.f.* ethics
etiqueta *n.f.* etiquette; label, tag
ètnic *adj.* ethnic
EUA *n.m.* USA
eunuc *n.m.* eunuch
euro *n.m.* euro
Europa *n.f.* Europe
europeu *adj.* European
evacuació *n.f.* evacuation
evacuar *v.* evacuate
evangeli *n.m.* gospel
evaporat *adj.* evaporated
evidència *n.f.* evidence

evident *adj.* evident, noticeable

evitar *v.* avoid

evolució *n.f.* evolution

evolucionar *v.* evolve

evolutiu *adj.* evolutionary

ex- *prefix* ex-

exactament *adv.* exactly, accurately

exacte *adj.* exact, accurate

exageració *n.f.* exaggeration

exagerar *v.* exaggerate

exagerat *adj.* exaggerated, overdone

examen *n.m.* examination, exam

examinar *v.* examine

excedent *adj./n.m.* surplus

excedir *v.* exceed, outdo

excel·lent *adj.* excellent, terrific

excepció *n.f.* exception

excepcional *adj.* outstanding

excepte *prep.* except, excluding

excés *n.f.* excess

excessiu *adj.* excessive

exclamació *n.f.* exclamation

excloure *v.* exclude

exclusió *n.f.* exclusion

exclusiu *adj.* exclusive

exclusivament *adv.* exclusively

excursió *n.f.* excursion, outing, hike, trek

excusa *n.f.* excuse

excusar *v.* excuse

execució *n.f.* execution

executant *n.* performer

executiu *n.* executive

exempció *n.f.* exemption

exemple *n.m.* example

exempt *adj.* exempt

exercici *n.m.* exercise, workout | *v.* **fer** ~ workout

exercir *v.* exercise; ply

exèrcit *n.m.* army

exhaurit *adj.* out-of-print

exhaustiu *adj.* thorough

exhaustivament *adv.* thoroughly

exhibició *n.f.* exhibition

exhibir *v.* display

exigent *adj.* picky

exigir *v.* demand

existència *n.f.* existence

existir *v.* exist

èxit *n.m.* success

exonerar *v.* exonerate

exòtic *adj.* exotic

expandir *v.* expand

expansió *n.f.* expansion

expectació *n.f.* expectation

expel·lir *v.* flush

experiència *n.f.* experience

experiment *n.m.* experiment

experimental *adj.* experimental

experimentar *v.* experiment; experience

experimentat *adj.* experienced

expert *adj./n.* expert, skilled

expiació *n.f.* atonement

expiració *n.f.* expiration

explicació *n.f.* explanation

explicar *v.* explain

exploració *n.f.* exploration

explorar *v.* explore

explosió *n.f.* explosion

explotació *n.f.* exploitation

explotar *v.* explode; exploit

exportació *n.f.* export

exportar *v.* export

exposar *v.* expose, exhibit

exposició *n.f.* exposure

exposímetre *n.m.* exposure meter

expressar *v.* express

expressió *n.f.* expression
expulsar *v.* oust
èxtasi *n.m.* rapture
extens *adj.* extensive
extensió *n.f.* extension
exterior *adj.* outer
extern *adj.* external
extintor *n.m.* fire extinguisher
extra *adj.* extra
extracte *n.m.* extract
extraordinari *adj.* extraordinary, stunning

extraordinàriament *adv.* unusually
extravagant *adj.* extravagant, outlandish
extrem *adj.* extreme
extremadament *adv.* extremely
extreure *v.* extract
extrovertit *adj.* outgoing

F

fàbrica *n.f.* factory
fabricació *n.f.* manufacturing
fabricant *n.* manufacturer, maker
fabricar *v.* manufacture
facial *adj.* facial
fàcil *adj.* easy
facilitat *n.f.* ease
fàcilment *adv.* easily, readily
factible *adj.* feasible
factor *n.m.* factor
factura *n.f.* bill, invoice
factura detallada *n.f.* itemized bill
facturació *n.f.* turnover
fahrenheit *adj.* Fahrenheit
faisà *n.m.* pheasant
fajol *n.m.* buckwheat
falàfel *n.m.* falafel
falcó *n.m.* falcon
faldilla *n.f.* skirt
fal·làcia *n.f.* fallacy
fallida *n.f.* bankruptcy
fals *adj.* false
falsificació *n.f.* forgery
falsificar *v.* forge
falta *n.f.* foul
fam *n.m.* hunger
fama *n.f.* fame
família *n.f.* family
familiar *adj.* familiar
famós *adj.* famous
fang *n.m.* mud
fangós *adj.* muddy
fantasia *n.f.* fantasy
fantasma *n.f.* phantom

fantàstic *adj.* fantastic, great | *phr.* Great!
far *n.m.* headlight
farcir *v.* stuff
farcit *adj.* stuffed | *n.m.* stuffing, filling; pad
farigola *n.f.* thyme
farina *n.f.* flour
farina de blat de moro *n.f.* cornmeal
farinetes *n.f.* mush, gruel
farinetes de civada *n.f.* porridge
farmacèutic *n.* pharmacist
farmàcia *n.f.* pharmacy, drugstore
fascinació *n.f.* fascination
fascinant *adj.* fascinating
fascinar *v.* fascinate
fascinat *adj.* fascinated
fase *n.f.* phase
fàstic *n.m.* disgust
fastigós *adj.* disgusting
fatigar *v.* exhaust
fatigós *adj.* tiring
fauna *n.f.* wildlife
favor *n.m.* favor
favorit *adj.* favorite
fax *n.m.* fax
fe *n.f.* faith
feble *adj.* weak, flimsy
febre *n.f.* fever
febrer *n.m.* February
Federació Russa *n.f.* Russian Federation
federal *adj.* federal
feina de casa *n.f.* housework

feliç *adj.* happy
felicitació *n.f.* congratulation
felicitar *v.* congratulate
felicitat *n.f.* happiness
Felicitats! *interj.* Congratulations!
feliçment *adv.* happily
fems *n.m.* manure
femella *n.f.* female
femení *adj.* female, feminine
feminisme *n.m.* feminism
feminista *adj./n.* feminist
fenc *n.m.* hay
fenomen *n.m.* phenomenon
fenomenal *adj.* phenomenal
fer *v.* do, make, render
fer autoestop *v.* hitchhike
fer broma *v.* joke
fer exercici *v.* workout
fer girar *v.* spin
fer gresca *v.* revel
fer picor *v.* itch
fer senderisme *v.* hike
fer surf *v.* surf
fer un blau *v.* bruise
fer un descans *v.* recess
fer una incursió *v.* raid
fer una pausa *v.* pause
fer una trucada *v.* make a phone call
fer vaga *v.* strike *(protest)*
fer vibrar *v.* rattle
fer xantatge a algú *v.* blackmail
fer-se adult *v.* grow up
ferida *n.f.* injury, wound
ferir *v.* hurt, wound
ferit *adj.* wounded
ferm *adj.* firm
fermall *n.m.* brooch
fermentar *v.* ferment
ferotge *adj.* fierce

ferro *n.m.* iron *(metal)*
ferro colat *n.m.* cast iron
ferrocarril *n.m.* railroad
ferros *n.m.* braces
fervent *adj.* fervent
fervor *n.m.* fervor
fes-ho tu mateix *n.m.* do-it-yourself
festa *n.f.* party
festa d'aniversari *n.f.* birthday party
festí *n.m.* feast
festival *n.m.* festival
fet *adj.* made | *n.m.* fact | *adv.* **de ~** actually
fet a casa *adj.* homemade
fet a mà *adj.* handmade
fetge *n.m.* liver
feudal *adj.* feudal
fi *adj.* fine | *n.f.* end, ending
fiança *n.f.* bail, bail bond
fiasco *n.m.* fiasco
fibra *n.f.* fiber
fibrós *adj.* stringy
ficció *n.f.* fiction, figment
fictici *adj.* fictional
fidel *adj.* faithful
fidelment *adv.* faithfully
fideu *n.m.* noodle
fiduciari *n.m.* fiduciary
figa *n.f.* fig
figura *n.f.* figure
figura de cera *n.f.* waxwork
figuratiu *adj.* figurative
fil *n.m.* thread; wire | *adj.* **sense ~** wireless
fil dental *n.m.* dental floss
fila *n.f.* row
filantrop *n.* philanthropist
filantropia *n.f.* philanthropy
filantròpic *adj.* philanthropic

filet *n.m.* fillet; sirloin
filet de llonzes *n.m.* chuck steak
filial *n.m.* subsidiary
fill *n.m.* son
filla *n.f.* daughter
filòleg *n.* philologist
filologia *n.f.* philology
filològic *adj.* philological
filòsof *n.* philosopher
filosofia *n.f.* philosophy
filtrar *v.* filter
filtrat *adj.* filtered
filtre *n.m.* filter
filtre d'oli *n.m.* oil filter
final *adj.* final; eventual
finalitzar una sessió *v.* log out/off
finalment *adv.* finally, ultimately, eventually
finament *adv.* finely
finançar *v.* finance
financer *adj.* financial
finances *n.f.* finance
finca *n.f.* estate
finestra *n.f.* window
fingir *v.* pretend
Finlàndia *n.f.* Finland
fins *prep.* until
fins a *prep.* till
fins i tot *adv.* even
firmar *v.* sign
fiscal *adj.* fiscal | *n.* prosecutor
físic *adj.* physical | *n.* physicist
física *n.f.* physics
física nuclear *n.f.* nuclear physics
físicament *adv.* physically
fisonomia *n.f.* physiognomy
fita *n.f.* landmark, milestone
fitar *v.* peer
fitxa *n.f.* token
fitxer *n.m.* file

fix *adj.* fixed
flaix *n.m.* flash
flam *n.m.* flan, custard
flama *n.f.* flame
flamarada *n.f.* flare
flambé *n.f.* flambé
flanc *n.m.* flank
flauta *n.f.* flute
fleca *n.f.* bakery
fletxa *n.f.* arrow
flexibilitat *n.f.* flexibility
flexible *adj.* flexible
floc *n.m.* flake
flor *n.f.* flower
Florida *n.* Florida
florir *v.* flourish
florista *n.* florist
florit *adj.* moldy | *n.m.* mold *(fungus)*
flotar *v.* float
fluid *adj.* fluent | *n.m.* fluid
fluïdesa *n.f.* fluency
fluir *v.* flow
foc *n.m.* fire
foc artificial *n.m.* firecracker
focs artificials *n.m.* fireworks
fogós *adj.* fiery
foie-gras *n.m.* foie gras
folrat *adj.* lined
fomentar *v.* foster
fonamental *adj.* fundamental
fonda *n.f.* inn
fondre *v.* melt
fonètica *n.f.* phonetics
fongs *n.m.* fungus
fonoll *n.m.* fennel
fons *n.m.* funding, fund; bottom; background
font *n.f. (water)* fountain, font, spring, source

font termal *n.f.* hot spring
fora *adv.* outside, out
fora de joc *adj.* offside
foradar *v.* pierce
foraster *n.* outsider
forat *n.m.* hole
força *n.f.* force, strength, might
forma *n.f.* shape
formació *n.f.* formation; array
formal *adj.* formal
formalment *adv.* formally
formar *v.* shape
format *adj.* shaped | *n.m.* layout, format
formatar *v.* format
formatge *n.m.* cheese
formatge fresc *n.m.* cottage cheese
formiga *n.f.* ant
fórmula *n.f.* formula
formular *v.* formulate
formulari *n.m.* form
forn *n.m.* oven, furnace
forn torradora *n.m.* toaster oven
fornejar *v.* bake
fornejat *adj.* baked
forner *n.* baker
fornir *v.* cater
fornit *adj.* chunky
forquilla *n.f.* fork
fort *adj.* strong
fortalesa *n.f.* fortress
fortament *adv.* strongly
fortificat *adj.* fortified
fortuna *n.f.* fortune
fòrum *n.m.* forum; message board
fos *adj.* molten
fosc *adj.* dark; **més ~** darker
fòsfor *n.m.* phosphorous
fossat *n.m.* moat
fòssil *n.m.* fossil

foto *n.f.* photo
foto de passaport *n.f.* passport photo
fotocòpia *n.f.* photocopy
fotocopiadora *n.f.* photocopier
fotògraf *n.* photographer
fotografia *n.f.* photograph; photography
fotografia amb flaix *n.f.* flash photography
fotòmetre *n.m.* light meter
fracàs *n.m.* failure
fracassar *v.* fail
fracció *n.f.* fraction
fractura *n.f.* fracture
fragància *n.f.* fragrance
fragant *adj.* fragrant
fragment *n.m.* fragment
franc *adj.* outspoken
França *n.f.* France
francès *adj./n.* French
frankfurt *n.m.* hot dog
franqueig *n.m.* postage
franqueig pagat *n.m.* postage paid
franquícia *n.f.* franchise
frase *n.f.* phrase, sentence *(gram.)*
fraseologia *n.f.* phraseology
frau *n.m.* fraud
fraudulent *adj.* fraudulent
fre *n.m.* brake
fre de mà *n.m.* handbrake
fred *adj.* cold, chilly, freezing
fredament *adv.* coldly
fregar *v.* rub
fregir *v.* fry
fregit *adj.* fried
frenètic *adj.* frantic
freqüència *n.f.* frequency
freqüent *adj.* frequent

freqüentment *adv.* frequently
fresa *n.f.* roe
fresc *adj.* fresh; lush; cool | *n.m.*
  fresco
front *n.m.* front; forehead
frontera *n.f.* border
frotis de Papanicolau *n.m.* pap
  smear
fructosa *n.f.* fructose
frugal *adj.* frugal
fruita *n.f.* fruit
fuet *n.m.* whip
fuetejar *v.* whip
fuga *n.f.* leak
fugir *v.* escape
full *n.m.* sheet
full de càlcul *n.m.* spreadsheet
fulla de llorer *n.f.* bay leaf
fulla *n.f.* leaf; blade
fullatge *n.m.* foliage
fullet *n.m.* booklet, brochure,
  pamphlet
fum *n.m.* fume, smoke

fumador *n.* smoker; **no ~**
  non-smoker | *adj.* **de no ~** non-
  smoking
fumar *v.* smoke | *n.m.* smoking
fumat *adj.* smoked
funció *n.f.* function
funcional *adj.* functional
funcionalitat *n.f.* functionality
funcionament *n.m.* running
fundació *n.f.* foundation
fundar *v.* found
funeral *n.m.* funeral
furgoneta *n.f.* van
furt *n.m.* theft, larceny, shoplifting
fuselatge *n.m.* fuselage
fusible *n.m.* fuse
fusió *n.f.* fusion
fusionar *v.* merge, meld
fusta *n.f.* wood | *adj.* **de ~**
  wooden
futbol *n.m.* football, soccer
futur *n.m.* future

G

gàbia *n.f.* cage
gabinet *n.m.* cabinet
gai *adj.* gay
gairebé *adv.* nearly
galàxia *n.f.* galaxy
galeria *n.f.* gallery
galeta *n.f.* cracker, cookie, biscuit
Galícia *n.* Galicia
gall *n.m.* rooster
gall dindi *n.m.* turkey
gallec *adj./n.* Galician
galleda *n.f.* pail
Gal·les *n.m.* Wales
gallina *n.f.* hen
gallina de Guinea *n.f.* guinea
  fowl
galó *n.m.* gallon
galta *n.f.* cheek
galteres *n.f.* mumps
gamba *n.f.* prawn
gambeta *n.f.* shrimp
gambit *n.m.* gambit
gana *n.f.* appetite
ganga *n.f.* bargain
ganivet *n.m.* knife
ganxo *n.m.* hook
garantia *n.f.* guarantee, warranty
garantir *v.* guarantee
garatge *n.m.* garage
garbellar *v.* sift
gàrgola *n.f.* gargoyle
garrofó *n.m.* lima beans
garsa *n.f.* magpie
gasa *n.f.* gauze
gasolina *n.f.* gasoline, gas, petrol

gasolina amb plom *n.f.* leaded
  gasoline
gasolinera *n.f.* gas station
gastar *v.* spend
gasteròpode *n.m.* gastropod
gastritis *n.f.* gastritis
gastroenteritis *n.f.* gastroenteritis
gastronomia *n.f.* gastronomy
gat *n.m.* cat
gat salvatge *n.m.* wildcat
gatet *n.m.* kitten
gaudir de *v.* enjoy, relish
gebrat *adj.* frosted
gebre *n.m.* frost
gegant *adj.* huge | *n.* giant
gel *n.m.* ice; gel
geladeria *n.f.* ice cream parlor
gelat *adj.* icy | *n.m.* ice cream
gelat de neula *n.m.* ice cream cone
gelatina *n.f.* gelatin, jello
gelea *n.f.* jelly
gelós *adj.* jealous
gemma *n.f.* gemstone, gem
gen *n.m.* gene
gendre *n.m.* son-in-law
gener *n.m.* January
generació *n.f.* generation
generador *n.m.* generator
general *adj.* general | *adv.* **en ~**
  overall, broadly
generalment *adv.* generally
generar *v.* generate
gènere *n.m.* gender; genre
generós *adj.* generous
generosament *adv.* generously

generositat *n.f.* generosity
genet *n.* rider
genètic *adj.* genetic
genètica *n.f.* genetics
genèticament *adv.* genetically
geni *n.* genius
genitals *n.m.* genitals
genoll *n.m.* knee
gent *n.f.* people, folk
genuí *adj.* genuine
geografia *n.f.* geography
geòleg *n.* geologist
geologia *n.f.* geology
geològic *adj.* geological
Geòrgia *n.f.* Georgia
gerd *n.m.* raspberry
gerent *n.* manager
germà *n.m.* brother, sibling
germana *n.f.* sister
germandat *n.m.* brotherhood
germen *n.m.* germ
germen de blat *n.m.* wheat germ
germicida *n.m.* germicide
gerra *n.f.* jug, carafe
gerret *n.m.* picarel
gerro *n.m.* vase, pitcher
gerundi *n.m.* gerund
gessamí *n.m.* jasmine
gest *n.m.* gesture
gibrella *n.f.* basin
gimnàs *n.m.* gymnasium, gym
gimnasta *n.* gymnast
gimnàstica *n.f.* gymnastics
ginebra *n.f.* gin
ginebre *n.m.* juniper
ginecòleg *n.* gynecologist
gingebre *n.m.* ginger
ginkgo *n.m.* ginkgo
gintònic *n.m.* gin and tonic
gir *n.m.* turn

gir postal *n.m.* money order
gira-sol *n.m.* sunflower
girafa *n.f.* giraffe
girar *v.* turn; **fer ~** spin
girar al descobert *v.* overdraw
gla *n.f.* acorn
glacejat *adj.* iced | *n.m.* icing, frosting
glacera *n.f.* glacier
glàndula *n.f.* gland
glicerina *n.f.* glycerin
global *adj.* global
globalització *n.f.* globalization
globus *n.m.* balloon
globus ocular *n.m.* eyeball
glopada *n.f.* mouthful
glòria *n.f.* glory
glossari *n.m.* glossary
glucosa *n.f.* glucose
gluten *n.m.* gluten
gofra *n.f.* waffle
gol *n.m.* goal
gola *n.f.* throat
golf *n.m.* golf
gominola *n.f.* gumdrop
góndola *n.f.* gondola
gorra *n.f.* cap
gos *n.m.* dog
gos pigall *n.m.* guidedog
gossada *n.f.* kennel
gota *n.f.* drip, drop
gotejar *v.* drip
govern *n.m.* government
governador *n.* governor
governant *n.* ruler *(government)*
governar *v.* govern, rule
gra *n.m.* grain; pimple
gràcies *phr.* thanks
gradient *n.m.* gradient
gradual *adj.* gradual

gradualment *adv.* gradually
graduat *n.* graduate
graella *n.f.* grill | *adj.* **a la ~** charcoal-grilled, grilled
gràfic *adj.* graphic | *n.m.* graph
gràfica *n.f.* chart
gràfics *n.m.* graphics
gram *n.m.* gram
gramàtica *n.f.* grammar
gran *adj.* big, large, great, grand; **més ~** bigger; senior | *adv.* **en ~ part** largely
Gran Bretanya *n.f.* Great Britain
gran magatzem *n.m.* department store
granat *n.m.* garnet
granger *n.* farmer
granja *n.f.* farm
granola *n.f.* granola
granota *n.f.* frog
grànul *n.m.* granule
granulat *adj.* granulated
gras *adj.* fat, fatty
grassó *adj.* chubby
grassonet *adj.* plump
gratis *adj.* free, free of charge
grau *n.m.* grade, degree, extent, rank
grau Celsius *n.m.* Celsius
gravació *n.f.* recording
gravadora *n.m.* recorder
gravar *v.* record; tax; engrave
gravat *n.m.* engraving
gravetat *n.f.* gravity
gravitacional *adj.* gravitational
Grècia *n.f.* Greece
greix *n.m.* grease, fat
gresca *n.f.* revelry | *v.* **fer ~** revel
greuge *n.m.* grievance
grip *n.f.* influenza, flu

gripau *n.m.* toad
gris *adj.* gray, grey
groc *adj.* yellow
grollerament *adv.* rudely
gronxar *v.* swing
gropa *n.f.* rump
grosella *n.f.* currant
grosella negra *n.f.* black currant
gruix *n.m.* thickness
grup *n.m.* group, band
grup sanguini *n.m.* blood type
guaiaba *n.f.* guava
Guaiana *n.f.* Guyana
guant *n.m.* glove
guant de cuina *n.m.* oven mitt
guany *n.m.* profit
guanyador *adj.* winning | *n.* winner
guanyar *v.* win; earn, gain, profit
guanys *n.m.* earnings
guarda-roba *n.m.* closet, cloakroom
guardabosc *n.* ranger
guardar *v.* save, keep
guàrdia *n.f.* guard
guarnició *n.f.* trimming, topping
Guatemala *n.f.* Guatemala
guatlla *n.f.* quail
guerra *n.f.* war
guia *n.f.* guide; guidebook; guidance
guia telefònica *n.f.* phone book
guiar *v.* guide
guió *n.m.* hyphen; dash; script
guió il·lustrat *n.m.* storyboard
guitarra *n.f.* guitar
guitarrista *n.* guitarist
guix *n.m.* plaster
gust *n.m.* taste, flavor

H

habilitar *v.* enable
habilitat *n.f.* skill
hàbit *n.m.* habit
habitació *n.f.* room
habitació privada *n.f.* private room
hàbitat *n.m.* habitat
habitatge *n.m.* housing
habitual *adj.* usual
habitualment *adv.* usually
Haití *n.f.* Haiti
haixix *n.m.* hashish
halibut *n.m.* halibut
ham *n.m.* fishhook
hamaca *n.f.* hammock
hamburguesa *n.f.* hamburger, burger, hamburger patty
hàmster *n.m.* hamster
handicap *n.m.* handicap *(in golf)*
harmonia *n.f.* harmony
haver *n.m.* asset
haver de *v.* must, ought to
Hawaii *n.* Hawaii
helicòpter *n.m.* helicopter
hemorroides *n.f.* hemorrhoids
herba *n.f.* herb; grass
herbívor *n.m.* herbivore
hèrnia *n.f.* hernia
heroi *n.m.* hero
heroïna *n.f.* heroin, heroine
heterosexual *adj.* heterosexual
hibernació *n.f.* hibernation
hibernar *v.* hibernate
híbrid *adj./n.m.* hybrid
hidrogen *n.m.* hydrogen

higienista *n.* hygienist
himne *n.m.* anthem
himne nacional *n.m.* national anthem
hipermetropia *n.f.* far-sightedness
hípica *n.* horseback riding
hipnotisme *n.m.* hypnotism
hipnotitzar *v.* hypnotize
hipoteca *n.f.* mortgage
hipòtesi *n.m.* hypothesis
histèria *n.f.* hysteria
histèric *adj.* hysterical
història *n.f.* story; history
historiador *n.* historian
històric *adj.* historic, historical
historietes *n.f.* comics
hivern *n.m.* winter
ho sento *phr.* I'm sorry
hola *interj.* hello, hi
holocaust *n.m.* holocaust
home *n.m.* man, guy
homeopatia *n.f.* homeopathy
homicidi *n.m.* homicide, manslaughter
homogeneïtzat *adj.* homogenized
homosexual *adj.* homosexual
Hondures *n.f.* Honduras
honest *adj.* honest
honestament *adv.* honestly
Hongria *n.f.* Hungary
honor *n.m.* honor
honoraris *n.m.* fee
hoquei *n.m.* hockey
hoquei sobre gel *n.m.* ice hockey
hora *n.f.* hour; **més d'hora** earlier

hora de dinar *n.f.* lunchtime
horari *n.m.* schedule, timetable
hores extraordinàries *n.f.*
  overtime
horitzontal *adj.* horizontal
horrible *adj.* horrible
horror *n.m.* horror
hort *n.m.* orchard
hospital *n.m.* hospital
hospitalitat *n.f.* hospitality
hostal *n.m.* guesthouse
hostil *adj.* hostile
hotel *n.m.* hotel

humà *adj.* human
humil *adj.* humble
humiliació *n.f.* humiliation
humiliar *v.* humiliate
humilitat *n.f.* humility
humit *adj.* damp
humitat *n.f.* humidity
humitejar *v.* moisten
humor *n.m.* humor, mood
humorístic *adj.* humorous
humus *n.m.* hummus
hurra *interj.* hooray

I

i *conj.* and
iarda *n.f.* yard *(measurement)*
iceberg *n.m.* iceberg
icterícia *n.f.* jaundice
Idaho *n.* Idaho
idea *n.f.* idea
ideal *adj.* ideal
idealisme *n.m.* idealism
idealista *adj.* idealistic | *n.* idealist
idealment *adv.* ideally
idèntic *adj.* identical
identificació *n.f.* identification
identificar *v.* identify
ideològic *adj.* ideological
idil·li *n.m.* romance
idioma *n.m.* language; idiom
idiota *n.* fool
igni *adj.* igneous
ignició *n.f.* ignition
ignorància *n.f.* ignorance
ignorant *adj.* ignorant
igual *adj.* equal, matching | *n.m.*
  match, peer
igualar *v.* match
igualment *adv.* equally
igualtat *n.f.* equality
illa *n.f.* island
il·legal *adj.* illegal
il·legalment *adv.* illegally
il·legibilitat *n.f.* illegibility
il·legible *adj.* illegible
il·legítim *adj.* illegitimate
Illes Canàries *n.f.* Canary Islands
il·limitat *adj.* unlimited
Illinois *n.* Illinois

il·luminació *n.f.* illumination,
  lighting
il·luminar *v.* illuminate
il·lustració *n.f.* illustration
il·lustrar *v.* illustrate
imaginació *n.f.* imagination
imaginar *v.* imagine
imaginari *adj.* imaginary
imaginatiu *adj.* imaginative
imant *n.m.* magnet
imatge *n.f.* image, picture
imatges *n.f.* imagery
imitació *n.f.* imitation
imitar *v.* imitate, impersonate
immadur *adj.* unripe
immediat *adj.* immediate
immediatament *adv.* immediately
immigració *n.f.* immigration
immigrant *n.* immigrant
immoble *n.m.* property *(owner-*
  ship)
immoral *adj.* immoral
immund *adj.* filthy
immundícia *n.f.* filth
immune *adj.* immune
immunitat *n.f.* immunity
immunització *n.f.* immunization
impaciència *n.f.* impatience
impacient *adj.* impatient
impacientment *adv.* impatiently
impacte *n.m.* impact
imperatiu *adj.* imperative
imperi *n.m.* empire
impermeable *adj.* waterproof |
  n.m. raincoat

implacable *adj.* relentless
implementació *n.f.* implementation
implementar *v.* implement
implicació *n.f.* implication
implicar *v.* imply
importació *n.f.* import
importància *n.f.* importance
important *adj.* important | *adv.* importantly
imposar *v.* impose
impossible *adj.* impossible
impost *n.m.* tax, sales tax
impost sobre la renda *n.m.* income tax
impostor *n.* impostor
impostos *n.m.* taxation
impostura *n.f.* imposture
impressió *n.f.* impression; printing
impressionant *adj.* impressive
impressionar *v.* impress
impressionat *adj.* impressed
impressora *n.f.* printer
imprimir *v.* print
improbable *adj.* unlikely
impuls *n.m.* urge; momentum
inacceptable *adj.* unacceptable
inaccessible *adj.* inaccessible
inaguantable *adj.* unbearable
incapaç *adj.* unable
incapacitat *n.f.* inability
incendi *n.m.* blaze, fire
incendi provocat *n.m.* arson
incentiu *n.m.* incentive
incert *adj.* uncertain
incertesa *n.f.* uncertainty
incidència *n.f.* incidence
incident *n.m.* incident
incloent *prep.* including
inclòs *adj.* included

incloure *v.* include
inclusiu *adj.* inclusive
incòmode *adj.* uncomfortable, awkward
incompetent *adj.* incompetent
inconscient *adj.* unconscious; oblivious
incorporat *adj.* incorporated
incorporar *v.* incorporate
incorrectament *adv.* incorrectly, wrongly
incorrecte *adj.* incorrect, wrong
incórrer en *v.* incur
increïble *adj.* incredible
incriminar *v.* incriminate
incrustat *adj.* encrusted, embedded
incubar *v.* incubate
incursió *n.f.* raid | *v.* **fer una ~** raid
indeleble *adj.* colorfast
independència *n.f.* independence
independent *adj.* independent
independentment *adv.* independently
índex *n.m.* index
indi *adj.* Indian
Índia *n.f.* India
Indiana *n.* Indiana
indicació *n.f.* indication
indicador *n.m.* gauge
indicador de combustible *n.m.* fuel gauge, gas gauge
indicar *v.* indicate
indiferència *n.f.* nonchalance
indiferent *adj.* nonchalant
indigestió *n.f.* indigestion
indignació *n.f.* outrage
indirectament *adv.* indirectly
indirecte *adj.* indirect

individual *adj.* individual
indubtablement *adv.* undoubtedly
inducció *n.f.* induction
induir *v.* induce
indulgència *n.f.* leniency
indulgent *adj.* lenient
indústria *n.f.* industry
industrial *adj.* industrial
inesperadament *adv.* unexpectedly
inesperat *adj.* unexpected
inestable *adj.* unstable, unsteady
inevitable *adj.* inevitable
inevitablement *adv.* inevitably
infància *n.f.* childhood
infant *n.m.* infant
infanteria *n.f.* infantry
infecció *n.f.* infection
infecciós *adj.* infectious
infectar *v.* infect
infectat *adj.* infected
infeliç *adj.* unhappy
infelicitat *n.f.* unhappiness
infermer *n.* nurse
infermeria *n.f.* infirmary
infern *n.m.* hell
infinitiu *n.m.* infinitive
inflació *n.f.* inflation
inflamació *n.f.* inflammation
inflamatori *adj.* inflammatory
inflar *v.* swell
inflat *adj.* bloated, swollen
inflor *n.f.* swelling
influència *n.f.* influence
influir *v.* influence
informació *n.f.* information
informal *adj.* informal, casual
informar *v.* inform
informàtica *n.f.* computing
informe *n.m.* report
infracció *n.f.* infraction

infraestructura *n.f.* infrastructure
infraroig *adj.* infrared
infringir *v.* breach
infructuós *adj.* unsuccessful
infusió *n.f.* infusion
ingenu *adj.* naive
ingredient *n.m.* ingredient
ingrés *n.m.* deposit
ingressar *v.* deposit
ingressos *n.m.* income, revenue
inicial *adj.* initial
inicialment *adv.* initially
iniciar una sessió *v.* log in/on
iniciativa *n.f.* initiative
ininterromput *adj.* uninterrupted
injecció *n.f.* injection
injectar *v.* inject
injunció *n.f.* injunction
injust *adj.* unfair
injustament *adv.* unfairly
innat *adj.* innate
innecessari *adj.* unnecessary
innocent *adj.* innocent
innovació *n.f.* innovation
innovar *v.* innovate
inoculació *n.f.* inoculation
inofensiu *adj.* harmless
inquilí *n.* tenant
insatisfet *adj.* unsatisfied
insecte *n.m.* insect
insegur *adj.* unsafe
inserir *v.* insert
insignificant *adj.* unimportant
insípid *adj.* bland
insistència *n.f.* insistence
insistir *v.* insist
insolació *n.f.* sunstroke
insolvent *adj.* bankrupt
insomni *n.m.* insomnia
inspecció *n.f.* inspection, survey

inspeccionar *v.* inspect, survey
inspiració *n.f.* inspiration
inspirar *v.* inspire
instal·lació *n.f.* installation;
facility
instal·lar *v.* install
instància *n.f.* instance
instantani *adj.* instant
instar *v.* urge
instigació *n.f.* instigation
instigar *v.* instigate
instint *n.m.* instinct
institució *n.f.* institution
institucional *adj.* institutional
institut *n.m.* institute
institut d'educació secundària
n.m. junior high school
instrucció *n.f.* instruction
instructiu *adj.* instructional
instructor *n.* instructor
instrument *n.m.* instrument
instrument musical *n.m.*
musical instrument
instrumental *adj.* instrumental
insuficient *adj.* insufficient
insulina *n.f.* insulin
insult *n.m.* insult
insultant *adj.* insulting
insultar *v.* insult
integració *n.f.* integration
integrar *v.* integrate
integrat *adj.* integrated
intel·lectual *adj.* intellectual
intel·ligència *n.f.* intelligence
intel·ligent *adj.* intelligent, smart
intenció *n.f.* intention
intens *adj.* intense
intensitat *n.f.* intensity
intensiu *adj.* intensive
intent *n.m.* attempt

intentar *v.* intend
interacció *n.f.* interaction
interaccionar *v.* interact
interactiu *adj.* interactive
intercanvi *n.m.* exchange
intercanviar *v.* exchange
intercedir *v.* mediate
interès *n.m.* interest
interessant *adj.* interesting
interessat *adj.* interested
interferència *n.f.* interference
interior *adj.* inner, indoor,
interior
intermedi *adj.* intermediate
intern *adj.* internal
internacional *adj.* international
Internet *n.* Internet
intèrpret *n.* interpreter
interpretació *n.f.* interpretation
interpretar *v.* interpret
interrogar *v.* quiz
interrompre *v.* interrupt
interrupció *n.f.* interruption
interruptor *n.m.* switch *(electric)*
intersecció *n.f.* intersection
interval *n.m.* interval; range
intervenció *n.f.* intervention;
audit
intervenir *v.* intervene; audit
interventor *n.* interventor;
auditor
intestí *n.m.* bowel
íntim *adj.* intimate
intimitat *n.f.* intimacy
intrínsec *adj.* intrinsic
introducció *n.f.* introduction
introduir *v.* introduce
introspecció *n.f.* introspection
intrús *n.* intruder
intrusió *n.f.* intrusion

inundació *n.f.* flood
inútil *adj.* useless, moot
invàlid *adj.* disabled
invalidar *v.* void
invenció *n.f.* invention, fabrication
inventar *v.* invent, fabricate,
  make (something) up
inversió *n.f.* reversal; investment
inversor *n.* investor
invertir *v.* invest; reverse
investigació *n.f.* investigation,
  inquiry
investigador *n.* researcher
investigar *v.* investigate, probe,
  research
invitació *n.f.* invitation
invitar *v.* invite
involucrar *v.* involve
ió *n.m.* ion
io-io *n.m.* yo-yo
iode *n.m.* iodine
ioga *n.m.* yoga
iogurt *n.m.* yogurt
iot *n.m.* yacht
Iowa *n.* Iowa

ira *n.f.* anger
Iran *n.m.* Iran
iranià *adj./n.* Iranian
Iraq *n.m.* Iraq
iraquià *adj./n.* Iraqi
Irlanda *n.f.* Ireland
Irlanda del Nord *n.f.* Northern
  Ireland
irlandès *adj./n.* Irish
ironia *n.f.* irony
irònic *adj.* ironic
irraonable *adj.* unreasonable
irregular *adj.* irregular
irritabilitat *n.f.* petulance
irritant *adj.* irritating
irritar *v.* irritate
irritat *adj.* irritated, annoyed
islam *n.m.* Islam
islàmic *adj.* Islamic
Islàndia *n.f.* Iceland
Israel *n.m.* Israel
israelià *adj./n.* Israeli
Itàlia *n.f.* Italy
itinerari *n.m.* itinerary

J

ja *adv.* already
jalapeño *n.m.* jalapeño
Japó *n.m.* Japan
japonès *adj./n.* Japanese
jaqueta *n.f.* jacket, windbreaker
jardí *n.m.* garden
jardí botànic *n.m.* botanical garden
jardí d'infants *n.m.* nursery
jardineria *n.f.* gardening
jarret *n.m.* shank
jazz *n.m.* jazz
jeep *n.m.* jeep
jersei *n.m.* pullover
Jerusalem *n.m.* Jerusalem
jet *n.m.* jet
jeure *v.* lie down
jo *pron.* I
joc *n.m.* game; gambling
joc d'arcade *n.m.* arcade game
joc d'escacs *n.m.* chess set
joc de paraules *n.m.* pun
joc del milió *n.m.* pinball machine
Jocs Olímpics *n.m.* Olympic Games
jogging *n.m.* jogging
joguina *n.f.* toy
joia *n.f.* jewel
joier *n.* jeweler
joies *n.f.* jewelry
joquei *n.m.* jockey

jordà *adj./n.* Jordanian
Jordània *n.f.* Jordan
jove *adj.* young
joventut *n.f.* youth
jubilació *n.f.* retirement
jubilar-se *v.* retire
jubilat *adj.* retired
judici *n.m.* trial; judgement
judici nul *n.m.* mistrial
judicial *n.* judiciary
jueu *adj.* Jewish | *n.* Jew
jugador *n.* player; gambler
jugar *v.* play, romp; gamble
juliol *n.m.* July
julivert *n.m.* parsley
jungla *n.f.* jungle
junta *n.f.* joint
juntament *adv.* together
juny *n.m.* June
jurament *n.m.* oath
jurar *v.* vow, swear
jurat *n.m.* jury
jurisdicció *n.f.* jurisdiction
jurisprudència *n.f.* jurisprudence, case law
just *adj./adv.* just, righteous
justícia *n.f.* justice
justificar *v.* justify
justificat *adj.* justified
jutge *n.* judge

K

Kansas *n.* Kansas
karaoke *n.m.* karaoke
karate *n.m.* karate
Kazakhstan *n.m.* Kazakhstan
kebab *n.m.* kebab
Kentucky *n.* Kentucky
kilobyte *n.m.* kilobyte
kiwi *n.m.* kiwi

L

la *def. art.* the
laberint *n.m.* maze
laboratori *n.m.* laboratory
laca *n.f.* lacquer; hair spray
lactància materna *n.f.* breast-feeding
lactis *n.m.* dairy
lactosa *n.f.* lactose
laic *n.* lay person
lamentable *adj.* lamentable
lamentació *n.f.* lamentation
lamentar *v.* lament, mourn, rue, regret
lampista *n.* plumber
làpida sepulcral *n.f.* gravestone
lapse *n.m.* lapse
laringitis *n.f.* laryngitis
lasanya *n.f.* lasagna
làser *n.m.* laser
latitud *n.f.* latitude
lava *n.f.* lava
lavabo *n.m.* restroom, washroom, lavatory, toilet; sink
lavabos femenins *n.m.* ladies restroom
lavanda *n.f.* lavender
laxant *n.m.* laxative
lector *n.* reader
lector de CD *n.m.* CD-player
lectura *n.f.* reading
lectura detallada *n.f.* perusal
legal *adj.* legal
legalització *n.f.* legalization
legalitzar *v.* legalize
legalment *adv.* legally

legislació *n.f.* legislation
legislador *n.* legislator
legislatiu *adj.* legislative
legislatura *n.m.* legislature
lema *n.m.* motto
lent *adj.* slow | *n.f.* lens
lent de contacte *n.f.* contact lens
lentament *adv.* slowly
les *def. art. pl.* the
lesbiana *n.f.* lesbian
lesionar *v.* injure
lesionat *adj.* injured
letargia *n.f.* lethargy
Letònia *n.f.* Latvia
li *pron.* him; her *(see page 8)*
licor *n.m.* liquor, liqueur
líder *n.* leader
lideratge *n.m.* leadership
Liechtenstein *n.m.* Liechtenstein
lilà *n.m.* lilac
límit *n.m.* limit, boundary
límit de velocitat *n.m.* speed limit
limitació *n.f.* limitation
limitar *v.* limit
limitat *adj.* limited
limúlid *n.m.* horseshoe crab
limusina *n.f.* limousine
lineal *adj.* linear; **no** ~ nonlinear
lingüista *n.* linguist
lingüística *n.f.* linguistics
línia *n.f.* line | *adj.* **en** ~ online
línia elèctrica *n.f.* power line
liofilitzat *adj.* freeze-dried
liquadora *n.f.* blender
liquar *v.* liquefy

líquid *n.m.* liquid
liquidació *n.f.* liquidation
liquidar *v.* liquidate
liquiditat *n.f.* liquidity
líric *adj.* lyrical
literal *adj.* literal
literari *adj.* literary
literatura *n.f.* literature
litigar *v.* litigate
litigi *n.m.* litigation
litre *n.m.* liter
Lituània *n.f.* Lithuania
llac *n.m.* lake
lladre *n.* thief, robber
llagosta *n.f.* lobster; locust
llàgrima *n.f.* tear
llambordí *n.m.* paving stone
llaminadura *n.f.* confection
llamp *n.m.* lightening
llana *n.f.* wool
llança *n.f.* lance
llançador *n.* pitcher
llançament *n.m.* toss
llançar *v.* launch, pitch, toss
llançar escombraries *v.* litter
llangardaix *n.m.* lizard
llanguir *v.* languish
llanterna *n.f.* flashlight
llanxa *n.f.* motorboat
llapis *n.m.* pencil
llapis de llavis *n.m.* lipstick
llar *n.f.* home | *adj.* **sense ~**
  homeless
llar d'infants *n.f.* daycare
llar de foc *n.f.* fireplace
llard *n.m.* lard
llarg *adj.* long; **més ~** longer |
  prep. **al ~ de** throughout, along
llarg termini *adj.* long-term
llarga distància *adj.* long-distance

llargada *n.f.* length
llàstima *n.f.* pity
llastimós *adj.* pitiful, pitiable,
  piteous, sorry
llauna *n.f.* can, tin *(container)*
llaurar *v.* plow
llautó *n.m.* brass
llavi *n.m.* lip
llavor *n.f.* seed
llavors *adv.* then
llebre *n.m.* hare
llegenda *n.f.* legend
llegir *v.* read
llegir detalladament *v.* peruse
llegum *n.m.* legume
llei *n.f.* law
lleial *adj.* loyal
lleialtat *n.f.* loyalty, allegiance
lleig *adj.* ugly
lleixa *n.f.* ledge
lleixiu *n.m.* bleach
llençar *v.* flip
llenceria *n.f.* lingerie
llengua *n.f.* tongue
llengua estrangera *n.f.* foreign
  language
llenguatge *n.m.* parlance
llentia *n.f.* lentil
llenya *n.f.* firewood
lleó *n.m.* lion; Leo
lleopard *n.m.* leopard
llesca *n.f.* slice
llescar *v.* slice
llest *adj.* ready; clever
llet *n.f.* milk
llet de mantega *n.f.* buttermilk
llet de soja *n.f.* soy milk
llet desnatada *n.f.* skim milk
llet maternitzada *n.f.* infant
  formula

lletra *n.f.* letter *(alphabet)*
lletrejar *v.* spell
lleuger *adj.* slight
lleugerament *adv.* slightly, lightly
llevadora *n.f.* midwife
llevat *n.m.* yeast, leavening, baking powder
llevat que *conj.* unless
llevataps *n.m.* corkscrew
lli *n.m.* linen; flax
llibertat *n.f.* freedom
llibertat condicional *n.f.* parole
llibertat vigilada *n.f.* probation
llibre *n.m.* book
llibre de cuina *n.m.* cookbook
llibre de frases *n.m.* phrase book
llibreria *n.f.* bookstore
llicència *n.f.* license
llicència de pesca *n.f.* fishing license
lliçó *n.f.* lesson
lliga *n.f.* league
lligar *v.* tie, bind
lligat *adj.* bound
llima *n.f.* file *(tool)*; lime
llimar *v.* file *(with a tool)*
llimona *n.f.* lemon
llimonada *n.f.* lemonade
llinatge *n.m.* lineage
lliri *n.m.* lily
llis *adj.* smooth
lliscar *v.* slide
llissa *n.f.* mullet
llista *n.f.* list
llit *n.m.* bed
llitera *n.f.* stretcher; berth
lliura esterlina *n.f.* sterling
lliurament *n.m.* delivery
lliurar *v.* deliver
lliure d'impostos *adj.* duty-free

lliurement *adv.* freely
lloable *adj.* laudable, praiseworthy
lloança *n.f.* praise
lloar *v.* praise
llobarro *n.m.* sea bass
lloc *n.m.* location, place, spot, site, venue | *adv.* **en altre ~** elsewhere | *prep.* **en ~ de** instead of
lloc d'avançada *n.m.* outpost
lloc de diaris *n.m.* newsstand
lloc de naixement *n.m.* place of birth
lloc de reunió *n.m.* gathering place
lloc de trobada *n.m.* meeting place
lloc històric *n.m.* historic site
lloc web *n.m.* website
llogar *v.* rent
lloguer *n.m.* rent, rental
llom *n.m.* tenderloin
llom de porc *n.m.* pork loin
llop *n.m.* wolf
llorer *n.m.* laurel
lloro *n.m.* parrot
lluç *n.m.* hake *(fish)*
lluç de riu *n.m.* pike *(fish)*
llúdriga *n.f.* otter
lluita *n.f.* fight, struggle, fighting
lluitador *n.* fighter
lluitar *v.* fight, struggle
llum *n.f.* lamp, light
llum antiboira *n.f.* fog light
llum de querosè *n.m.* kerosene lamp
llum del sol *n.f.* sunlight, sunshine
lluminós *adj.* luminous
lluna *n.f.* moon
lluna de mel *n.f.* honeymoon
llunàtic *n.* lunatic
lluny *adv.* far; away, off; **més ~** farther, further; **més ~à** farthest, furthest

llúpol *n.m.* hops
llustre *n.m.* glaze, gloss
local *adj.* local | *n.m.* premises
localitzar *v.* locate, spot
localment *adv.* locally
loció *n.f.* lotion
loció postafaitat *n.f.* aftershave
locomotora *n.f.* locomotive
locutor *n.* announcer
lògic *adj.* logical
lògica *n.f.* logic
lona *n.f.* canvas
Londres *n.m.* London

longevitat *n.f.* longevity
longitud *n.f.* longitude
loteria *n.f.* lottery
Louisiana *n.* Louisiana
lubricació *n.f.* lubrication
lubricant *n.m.* lubricant
lubricar *v.* lubricate
lucratiu *adj.* lucrative
l'un a l'altre *phr.* one another
luxe *n.m.* luxury
Luxemburg *n.m.* Luxembourg
luxúria *n.f.* lust

M

mà *n.f.* hand
maça *n.f.* mallet
macarrons *n.m.* macaroni
Macedònia *n.f.* Macedonia
macerar *v.* macerate
maçó *n.m.* ram
maçonar *v.* ram
Madrid *n.m.* Madrid
maduixa *n.f.* strawberry
madur *adj.* mature; ripe
maduresa *n.f.* maturity
mag *n.* magician
magatzem *n.m.* store; warehouse, depot
màgia *n.f.* magic
magnesi *n.m.* magnesium
magnètic *adj.* magnetic
magnetisme *n.m.* magnetism
magnífic *adj.* magnificent, superb, striking
magnitud *n.f.* magnitude
magrana *n.f.* pomegranate
magre *adj.* meager, lean
mai *adv.* never
maig *n.m.* May
Maine *n.* Maine
mainell *n.m.* mullion
maionesa *n.f.* mayonnaise
major *adj.* major
majordoma *n.f.* housekeeper
majoria *n.f.* majority
mal *adj.* bad | *n.m.* malady
mal d'estómac *n.m.* stomachache
mal d'orella *n.m.* earache
mal de cap *n.m.* headache

mal de queixal *n.m.* toothache
mal educat *adj.* rude
mala conducta *n.f.* misconduct
malalt *adj.* ill, sick, ailing
malaltia *n.f.* illness, sickness, ailment, disease
malament *adv.* badly
malària *n.f.* malaria
maldestrament *adv.* awkwardly
malenconia *n.f.* melancholy
malentès *n.m.* misunderstanding
maleta *n.f.* suitcase
maleter *n.m.* trunk *(car)*
malgastador *adj.* profligate
malgastar *v.* waste
malgrat *prep.* despite
malhumorat *adj.* bad-tempered, moody
malícia *n.f.* malice
maliciós *adj.* malicious
maligne *adj.* malignant
malles *n.f.* leggings
malmetre *v.* spoil
malnutrició *n.f.* malnutrition
malparit *n.m.* bastard
malsà *adj.* unhealthy
malson *n.m.* nightmare
Malta *n.f.* Malta
maltejat *adj.* malted
maluc *n.m.* hip
malvat *adj.* evil
mama *n.f.* mom
mamífer *n.m.* mammal
mamut *n.m.* mammoth
manat *n.m.* bunch

mancar *v.* lack

mandarina *n.f.* mandarin orange; tangerine

mandat *n.m.* power of attorney; mandate

mandíbula *n.f.* jaw

mandonguilla *n.f.* meatball

mandrós *adj.* lazy

manera *n.f.* manner, way *(method)*

mango *n.m.* mango

mania *n.f.* mania

manicura *n.f.* manicure

manifest *n.m.* manifesto

manifestació *n.f.* rally

màniga *n.f.* sleeve

manillar *n.m.* handlebar

manilles *n.f.* handcuffs

maniquí *n.f.* mannequin

manllevar *v.* borrow

manta *n.f.* blanket

mantega *n.f.* butter

manteniment *n.m.* maintenance

mantenir *v.* maintain

manual *adj./n.m.* manual

manuscrit *n.m.* manuscript

maó *n.m.* brick

mapa *n.m.* map

mapa de carreteres *n.m.* road map

maquillatge *n.m.* makeup

màquina *n.f.* machine

màquina d'afaitar *n.f.* razor

màquina de cosir *n.f.* sewing machine

màquina de fax *n.f.* fax machine

maquinari *n.m.* hardware

maquinària *n.f.* machinery

maquineta d'afaitar *n.f.* shaver

mar *n.* sea

maracujà *n.m.* passion fruit

maragda *n.f.* emerald

marató *n.f.* marathon

marbre *n.m.* marble

març *n.m.* March

marc *n.m.* mark; framework, frame

marca *n.f.* brand

marcapassos *n.m.* pacemaker

marcar *v.* mark, score; dial

marcat *adj.* marked

marcir *v.* wither

marduix *n.m.* marjoram

mare *n.f.* mother; parent

marea *n.f.* tide

marejat *adj.* seasick; dizzy

maresme *n.m.* marsh

margalló *n.m.* heart of palm

margarina *n.f.* margarine

marge *n.m.* margin

marginat *n.* outcast

marí *adj.* marine

marihuana *n.f.* marijuana

marina *n.f.* navy

marinada *n.f.* marinade

marinat *adj.* marinated

mariner *n.* sailor

marisc *n.m.* seafood, shellfish

mariscal *n.m.* marshal

marit *n.m.* husband

màrqueting *n.m.* marketing

marrà *n.m.* ram *(animal)*

marró *adj.* brown

Mart *n.m.* Mars

martell *n.m.* hammer

màrtir *n.* martyr

marxa *n.f.* gear

marxar *v.* march

Maryland *n.* Maryland

màscara *n.f.* mask

mascota *n.f.* mascot

mascle *n.m.* male

masculí *adj.* masculine, male
massa *adv.* too
Massachusetts *n.* Massachusetts
massapà *n.m.* marzipan
massatge *n.m.* massage
massatgista *n.m.* masseur
massiu *adj.* massive
mastegar *v.* chew, munch
masticable *adj.* chewable
masturbar-se *v.* masturbate
matalàs *n.m.* mattress
matança *n.f.* killing, massacre
matar *v.* kill
mateix *adj.* self, same
matemàtiques *n.f.* mathematics
matèria *n.f.* material, matter
maternitat *n.f.* motherhood
matí *n.m.* morning | *adv.* **del ~** a.m.
matinada *n.f.* morning *(early)* |
  adv. **de la ~** a.m. *(early morning)*
matinal *n.m.* matinée
matís *n.m.* shade
matrícula *n.f.* registration;
  license plate, number plate;
  license plate number
matriculació *n.f.* matriculation
matricular *v.* matriculate
matrimoni *n.m.* marriage
matriu *n.f.* matrix
matrona *n.f.* matron
mausoleu *n.m.* mausoleum
màxim *adj.* maximum
màxima *n.f.* maxim
maximitzar *v.* maximize
mecànic *adj.* mechanical | *n.*
  mechanic
mecànica *n.f.* mechanics
mecanisme *n.m.* mechanism
medalla *n.f.* medal
medi ambient *n.m.* environment

mediació *n.f.* mediation
mediador *n.* mediator
mèdic *adj.* medical
medicament *n.m.* medication
medicina *n.f.* medicine
medieval *adj.* medieval
mediocre *adj.* mediocre
mediocritat *n.f.* mediocrity
meditació *n.f.* meditation
Mediterrani *adj.* Mediterranean
Mediterrània *n.f.* Mediterranean
medul·la *n.f.* marrow
medusa *n.f.* jellyfish
megabyte *n.m.* megabyte
meitat *n.f.* half
mel *n.m.* honey
melassa *n.f.* molasses
melic *n.m.* navel
melmelada *n.f.* marmalade, jam
meló *n.m.* melon, honeydew
melodia *n.f.* melody, tune
melsa *n.f.* spleen
membrana *n.f.* membrane
membre *n.m.* member
memoràndum *n.m.* memo,
  memorandum
memòria *n.f.* memory
memorial *n.m.* memorial
memòries *n.f.* memoir
mena *n.f.* ore; sort
meningitis *n.f.* meningitis
menjador *n.m.* dining room
menjar *n.m.* food | *v.* eat
menjar per emportar *n.m.*
  take-out food
menopausa *n.f.* menopause
menor *n.* minor | *adj.* minor,
  smaller; junior
menstruació *n.f.* menstruation
mensual *adj.* monthly

ment *n.f.* mind
menta *n.f.* mint, peppermint
mental *adj.* mental
mentalment *adv.* mentally
mentida *n.f.* lie
mentider *n.* liar
mentir *v.* lie
mentol *n.m.* menthol
mentre *conj.* while
mentre que *conj.* whereas
mentrestant *adv.* meanwhile
menú *n.m.* menu
menuts *n.m.* offal, giblets
menys *adv.* less | *pron.* least
menyspreable *adj.* despicable
mer *adj.* mere
meravellós *adj.* marvelous, wonderful
mercaderia *n.f.* commodity
mercaderies *n.f.* merchandise
mercat *n.m.* market, marketplace
mercat de productes *n.m.* produce market
mercuri *n.m.* mercury, quicksilver
merèixer *v.* deserve
merenga *n.f.* meringue
meridià *n.m.* meridian
merlet *n.m.* battlement
mes *n.m.* month | *adv.* **mes que ve** next month
més *adj.* more | *conj.* plus | *adv.* else; **a ~** furthermore, moreover
més aviat *adv.* rather
més baix *adj.* lower
més barat *adj.* cheaper
més calent *adj.* warmer
més d'hora *adj.* earlier
més enllà *adv.* beyond
més fosc *adj.* darker
més gran *adj.* bigger; senior

més llarg *adj.* longer
més lluny *adv.* farther, further
més llunyà *adj.* farthest, furthest
més proper *adj.* nearest
més ràpida *adj.* quickest
més recent *adj.* latest
més sorollós *adv.* louder
més tard *adv.* later
més tranquil *adj.* quieter
mesc *n.m.* musk
mesquita *n.f.* mosque
mestre *n.* teacher
mestressa de casa *n.f.* housewife
mestressa *n.f.* mistress
mesura *n.f.* measurement
mesurar *v.* measure
metabòlic *adj.* metabolic
metabolisme *n.m.* metabolism
metàfora *n.f.* metaphor
metall *n.m.* metal
meteor *n.m.* meteor
meteoròleg *n.* meteorologist
meteorologia *n.f.* meteorology
metge *n.* doctor, physician, medic
meticulós *adj.* painstaking
mètode *n.m.* method
metre *n.m.* meter, metre
metro *adj.* metro | *n.m.* metro, subway
metròpoli *n.f.* metropolis
metropolità *adj.* metropolitan
meu *pos. adj.* my | *pron.* mine
meus *pos. adj.* my | *pron.* mine
meva *pos. adj.* my | *pron.* mine
meves *pos. adj.* my | *pron.* mine
Mèxic *n.m.* Mexico
mexicà *adj./n.* Mexican
miàlgia *n.f.* myalgia
Michigan *n.* Michigan
micròfon *n.m.* microphone

microones *n.m.* microwave;
microwave oven
microscopi *n.m.* microscope
microscòpic *adj.* microscopic
mida *n.f.* size
midó *n.m.* starch
midó de blat de moro *n.m.*
cornstarch
mig *adj.* half | *n.m.* middle
migdia *n.m.* noon, midday
migranya *n.f.* migraine
mil *num.* thousand
mil milions *n.m.* billion
milfulles *n.f.* yarrow
milió *num.* million
milionari *n.* millionaire
militar *adj.* military
milla *n.f.* mile
mil·lèsim *adj.* thousandth
mil·ligram *n.m.* milligram
mil·límetre *n.m.* millimeter
millor *adj.* best, better
millora *n.f.* improvement
millorar *v.* improve, enhance
millorat *adj.* improved, enhanced
mim *n.m.* mime
minaret *n.m.* minaret
mineral *n.m.* mineral
miniatura *n.f.* miniature
minibar *n.m.* minibar
mínim *adj.* minimum
minimitzar *v.* minimize
ministeri *n.m.* ministry
ministre *n.* minister
Minnesota *n.* Minnesota
minoria *n.f.* minority
minúscul *adj.* minuscule
minúscul *adj.* tiny
minusvàlid *adj.* handicapped
minut *n.m.* minute

miopia *n.f.* near-sightedness,
myopia
mirall *n.m.* mirror
mirar *v.* look, watch
mirar al voltant *v.* look around
mirar amb insinuació *v.* ogle
mirar des de dalt *v.* overlook
mirar fixament *v.* stare
misèria *n.f.* pittance
missa *n.f.* mass
missatge *n.m.* message
missatger *n.* messenger
míssil *n.m.* missile
missioner *n.* missionary
Mississipí *n.* Mississippi
Missouri *n.* Missouri
misteri *n.m.* mystery
misteriós *adj.* mysterious
místic *n.* mystic | *adj.* mystical,
mystic
misticisme *n.m.* mysticism
mistos *n.m.* matches
mite *n.m.* myth
mitges *n.f.* stockings
mític *adj.* mythical
mitjà *adj.* medium | *n.m.* means
mitjana *adj.* average
mitjanit *n.f.* midnight
mitjans de comunicació *n.m.*
media
mitjans de vida *n.m.* livelihood
mitjó *n.m.* sock
mitologia *n.f.* mythology
mòbil *adj.* mobile | *n.m.* cellphone,
mobile phone
mobilitat *n.f.* mobility
moblar *v.* furnish
moblat *adj.* furnished
mobles *n.m.* furniture | *adj.*
sense ~ unfurnished

moc *n.m.* mucus

mocador *n.m.* handkerchief, tissue

moda *n.f.* mode, fashion | *adj.* **de ~** fashionable

modal *adj.* modal

mode *n.m.* mode

model *n.m.* model, paragon

mòdem *n.m.* modem

modern *adj.* modern

modest *adj.* modest

modificació *n.f.* modification

modificar *v.* modify

Moldàvia *n.f.* Moldova

moldre *v.* grind

molècula *n.f.* molecule

molecular *adj.* molecular

molest *adj.* annoying

molestar *v.* annoy, bother, disturb

molèstia *n.f.* nuisance

molí de vent *n.m.* windmill

moll *n.m.* dock

molla *n.f.* spring *(device)*

molsa *n.f.* moss

molt *adj.* much | *adv.* most, very, highly, greatly

molts *pron.* many | *phr.* a lot of

moment *n.m.* moment; momentum

momentani *adj.* momentary

mòmia *n.f.* mummy

món *n.m.* world

mona *n.f.* monkey

Mònaco *n.m.* Monaco

monarca *n.* monarch

monarquia *n.f.* monarchy

moneda *n.f.* currency, coin

moneda estrangera *n.f.* foreign currency

moneder *n.m.* purse

monestir *n.m.* monastery

monetari *adj.* monetary

mongeta *n.f.* kidney bean, bean

mongetes verdes *n.f.* green beans

moniato *n.m.* sweet potato

monitor *n.m.* monitor

monja *n.f.* nun

monogàmia *n.f.* monogamy

monòleg *n.m.* monologue

mononucleosi infecciosa *n.f.* infectious mononucleosis

monopoli *n.m.* monopoly

monsó *n.m.* monsoon

Montana *n.* Montana

Montenegro *n.m.* Montenegro

monument *n.m.* monument

monumental *adj.* monumental

mora *n.f.* blackberry

moral *adj./n.m.* moral

moralista *n.* moralist

moralment *adv.* morally

mòrbid *adj.* morbid

morbositat *n.f.* morbidity

mordacitat *n.f.* poignancy

morena *adj.* brunette

morfina *n.f.* morphine

moribund *adj.* dying

morir *v.* die

morro *n.m.* muzzle

mort *adj.* dead | *n.f.* death

mortal *adj./n.* mortal

mortalitat *n.f.* mortality

morter *n.m.* mortar

mortificar *v.* mortify

mos *n.m.* morsel

mosaic *n.m.* mosaic

Moscou *n.m.* Moscow

mosquet *n.m.* musket

mosqueter *n.m.* musketeer

mosquit *n.m.* mosquito

mosquitera *n.f.* mosquito net

mossegada *n.f.* nibble
mossegar *v.* bite, nibble
mostassa *n.f.* mustard
mostassa bruna *n.f.* mustard greens
mostra *n.f.* sample
mostrar *v.* show
motel *n.m.* motel
motí *n.m.* mutiny
motiu *n.m.* motive, motif
motivació *n.f.* motivation
motivar *v.* motivate
motivat *adj.* motivated
motlle *n.m.* mold *(for shaping)*
moto d'aigua *n.f.* jet-ski
motocicleta *n.f.* motorcycle, motorbike
motor *n.m.* motor, engine
motor de cerca *n.m.* search engine
motor dièsel *n.m.* diesel engine
motxilla *n.f.* backpack, knapsack, rucksack
moure *v.* move
mousse *n.f.* mousse
movible *adj.* movable
moviment *n.m.* movement, motion
muffin *n.m.* muffin
mul *n.m.* mule
mullat *adj.* wet
multa *n.f.* fine
multicinemes *n.m.* multiplex cinema
multilateral *adj.* multilateral
multimèdia *adj.* multimedia
multinacional *adj.* multinational
múltiple *adj.* multiple
multiplicació *n.f.* multiplication
multiplicar *v.* multiply
multiplicitat *n.f.* multiplicity

multitud *n.f.* multitude, crowd
mundà *adj.* mundane
mundial *adj.* worldwide
municions *n.f.* munitions
municipal *adj.* municipal
municipi *n.m.* municipality
munífic *adj.* munificent
muntanya *n.f.* mountain
muntanyenc *n.* mountaineer
muntanyisme *n.m.* mountain climbing
muntanyós *adj.* mountainous, hilly
mural *n.m.* mural
murmurar *v.* murmur, mutter
murmurejar *v.* whisper
murmuri *n.m.* murmur, whisper
musa *n.f.* muse
musclo *n.m.* mussel
múscul *n.m.* muscle
muscular *adj.* muscular
museu *n.m.* museum
músic *n.* musician
música *n.f.* music
música clàssica *n.f.* classical music
música pop *n.f.* pop music
música tradicional *n.f.* folk music
musical *adj.* musical
musli *n.m.* muesli
mussitar *v.* mumble
mussol *n.m.* owl
mussolina *n.f.* muslin
musulmà *adj./n.* Muslim
mut *adj.* mute
mutació *n.f.* mutation
mutant *adj.* mutant
mutilació *n.f.* mutilation
mutilar *v.* mutilate
mutu *adj.* mutual

N

nabiu *n.m.* blueberry
nabiu de grua *n.f.* cranberry
nació *n.f.* nation
nacional *adj.* national
nacionalisme *n.m.* nationalism
nacionalitat *n.f.* nationality
nacionalització *n.f.* nationalization
nacionalitzar *v.* nationalize
Nadal *n.m.* Christmas; **nit de ~**
  n.f. Christmas Eve
nadiu *adj./n.* native
nafra *n.f.* sore
naixement *n.m.* birth
naixent *adj.* nascent
nansa *n.f.* handle
nap *n.m.* turnip
narcisisme *n.m.* narcissism
narcisista *n.* narcissist
narcosi *n.f.* narcosis
narcòtic *n.m.* narcotic
narguil *n.m.* hookah
narrador *n.* narrator
narrativa *n.f.* narrative
nas *n.m.* nose
nascut *adj.* born
nata *n.f.* cream
natació *n.f.* swimming
natilles *n.f.* custard
natura *n.f.* nature
natural *adj.* natural; plain
naturalment *adv.* naturally
nau *n.f.* nave
nàusea *n.f.* nausea
nauseabund *adj.* nauseous
naval *adj.* naval

navalla *n.f.* penknife
navegació *n.f.* navigation, sailing
navegador *n.m.* browser
navegant *n.* navigator
navegar *v.* navigate, sail; browse
neboda *n.f.* niece
nebot *n.m.* nephew
Nebraska *n.* Nebraska
nebulosa *n.f.* nebula
necessari *adj.* necessary, required,
  requisite
necessàriament *adv.* necessarily
necessitar *v.* need
nèctar *n.m.* nectar
nectarina *n.f.* nectarine
nedar *v.* swim
negar *v.* deny
negatiu *adj.* negative
negligència *n.f.* negligence,
  malpractice
negligent *adj.* careless
negligentment *adv.* carelessly
negligir *v.* neglect
negoci *n.m.* business
negociació *n.f.* negotiation
negociar *v.* negotiate
negre *adj.* black
nen *n.m.* child, kid
nena *n.f.* child, kid
nens *n.m.* children
neolític *adj.* neolithic
nepotisme *n.m.* nepotism
Neptú *n.m.* Neptune
nervi *n.m.* nerve
nerviós *adj.* nervous

nerviosament *adv.* nervously
nét *n.m.* grandson; *n.* grandchild
neta *n.f.* granddaughter
neteja *n.f.* cleaning
netejar *v.* clean; clear
neu *n.f.* snow
neuròleg *n.* neurologist
neurologia *n.f.* neurology
neurosi *n.f.* neurosis
neutral *adj.* neutral
neutralitzar *v.* neutralize
neutre *adj.* neuter
neutró *n.m.* neutron
Nevada *n.* Nevada
nevar *v.* snow
nevera *n.f.* refrigerator, fridge
ni *adv.* neither | *conj.* nor
Nicaragua *n.f.* Nicaragua
nicotina *n.f.* nicotine
nihilisme *n.m.* nihilism
niló *n.m.* nylon
nimbe *n.m.* nimbus
nina *n.f.* doll
ningú *pron.* nobody, no one
nínxol *n.m.* alcove
nit *n.f.* night
nit de cap d'any *n.m.* New Year's
  Eve
nit de Nadal *n.f.* Christmas Eve
nitrogen *n.m.* nitrogen
niu *n.m.* nest
nivell *n.m.* level, tier
no *adv.* no, not
no entrar *v.* keep out
no fer cas *v.* ignore
no fumador *n.* non-smoker
no importa *phr.* never mind
no lineal *adj.* nonlinear
no obstant *adv.* nevertheless
no retornable *adj.* nonreturnable

no-ficció *n.f.* non-fiction
noble *adj.* noble | *n.m.* nobleman
noblesa *n.f.* nobility
noció *n.f.* notion
node *n.m.* node
nodrir *v.* nourish
noi *n.m.* boy, lad
noia *n.f.* girl
nom *n.m.* name
nom d'usuari *n.m.* username
nombrós *adj.* numerous
nomenar *v.* appoint
només *adv.* only
nominació *n.f.* nomination
nominal *adj.* nominal
nora *n.f.* daughter-in-law
noranta *num.* ninety
norantè *adj.* ninetieth
nord *n.m.* north | *adj.* **del ~**
  northern
nord-americà *adj.* North American
nord-est *adj./n.m.* northeast
nord-oest *adj./n.m.* northwest
norma *n.f.* norm
normal *adj.* normal
normalitzar *v.* normalize
normalment *adv.* normally
normes *n.f.* rules
Noruega *n.f.* Norway
nosaltres *pron.* us, we
nosaltres mateixos *pron.* ourselves
nostàlgia *n.f.* nostalgia
nostra *pos. adj.* our | *pron.* ours
nostre *pos. adj.* our | *pron.* ours
nostres *pos. adj.* our | *pron.* ours
nota *n.f.* note
notable *adj.* notable, noteworthy,
  remarkable
notablement *adv.* notably

notació *n.f.* notation
notar *v.* notice
notari *n.* notary
notícies *n.f.* news
notificació *n.f.* notification
notificar *v.* notify
notori *adj.* notorious
notorietat *n.f.* notoriety
nou *adj.* new; **de ~** nutty | *num.* nine | *n.f.* nut, walnut | *adj.* **de ~** again
nou del Brasil *n.f.* Brazil nut
Nou Hampshire *n.* New Hampshire
Nou Mèxic *n.* New Mexico
nou moscada *n.f.* nutmeg
Nova Jersey *n.* New Jersey
Nova York *n.* New York
Nova Zelanda *n.f.* New Zealand
novè *adj.* ninth
novel·la *n.f.* novel

novel·lista *n.* novelist
novembre *n.m.* November
novetat *n.f.* novelty
nu *adj.* naked, nude
nuclear *adj.* nuclear
nucli *n.m.* kernel; nucleus
numerador *n.m.* numerator
número *n.m.* number
número de telèfon *n.m.* phone number
nupcial *adj.* bridal
nus *n.m.* knot
nutrició *n.f.* nutrition
nutrient *n.m.* nutrient
nutritiu *adj.* nutritious
nuvi *n.m.* bridegroom
núvia *n.f.* bride
núvol *n.m.* cloud; marshmallow
nyam *n.m.* yam

O

o *conj.* or
oasi *n.m.* oasis
obeir *v.* obey
obert *adj.* open
obertament *adv.* openly
obertura *n.f.* opening
obès *adj.* obese
obesitat *n.f.* obesity
obituari *n.m.* obituary
objecció *n.f.* objection
objectable *adj.* objectionable
objectar *v.* object
objecte *n.m.* object
objectes de valor *n.m.* valuables
objectiu *n.m.* objective, target, aim
oblació *n.f.* oblation
oblia *n.f.* wafer
oblic *adj.* oblique
oblidadís *adj.* forgetful
oblidar *v.* forget
obligació *n.f.* obligation
obligar *v.* oblige
obligatori *adj.* obligatory, mandatory
oblit *n.m.* oblivion
obliteració *n.f.* obliteration
obliterar *v.* obliterate
obra d'art *n.f.* artwork
obra mestra *n.f.* masterpiece
obrir *v.* open, unlock
obrir la cremallera *v.* unzip
obrir-se *v.* open up
obscè *adj.* obscene
obscenitat *n.f.* obscenity

obscur *adj.* obscure
obscuritat *n.f.* obscurity
observació *n.f.* observation
observador *n.* observer
observança *n.f.* observance
observar *v.* observe
observatori *n.m.* observatory
obsessió *n.f.* obsession
obsessionar *v.* obsess
obsolet *adj.* obsolete
obstacle *n.m.* obstacle
obstinació *n.f.* obstinacy
obstinat *adj.* headstrong
obstinat *adj.* obstinate
obstrucció *n.f.* obstruction, blockage
obstructiu *adj.* obstructive
obstruir *v.* obstruct
obstruït *adj.* blocked
obtenció *n.f.* procurement
obtenir *v.* obtain, get, procure
obturador *n.m.* shutter *(camera)*
obtús *adj.* obtuse
obvi *adj.* obvious
òbviament *adv.* obviously
oca *n.f.* goose
ocasió *n.f.* occasion
occidental *adj.* western
oceà *n.m.* ocean
Oceà Pacífic *n.m.* Pacific Ocean
Oceania *n.f.* Oceania
ocell *n.m.* bird
ocell de corral *n.m.* fowl
oci *n.m.* leisure
ociós *adj.* idle

ocórrer *v.* occur
ocra *n.f.* okra
octàgon *n.m.* octagon
octubre *n.m.* October
ocular *adj./n.m.* ocular
oculista *n.* oculist
ocult *adj.* occult
ocultar *v.* conceal
ocupació *n.f.* occupation, employment, occupancy
ocupada *adj.* occupied
ocupant *n.* occupant
ocupar *v.* occupy
ocupat *adj.* busy, engaged
ocurrència *n.f.* occurrence
oda *n.f.* ode
odi *n.m.* hate, hatred, odium
odiar *v.* hate, loathe
odiós *adj.* odious, loathsome
odissea *n.f.* odyssey
oest *n.m.* west
ofegar-se *v.* drown
ofendre *v.* offend
ofensiu *adj.* offensive
oferir *v.* offer, bid
oferta *n.f.* offer
ofici *n.m.* craft
oficial *adj.* official | *n.* officer
oficialment *adv.* officially
oficiar *v.* officiate
oficina *n.f.* office
oficina d'informació *n.f.* information office
oficina d'objectes perduts *n.f.* lost and found office
oficina de canvi *n.f.* exchange office
oficina de correus *n.f.* post office
oficinista *n.* clerk
oficiós *adj.* officious

ofrena *n.f.* offering
oftalmòleg *n.* opthalmologist
Ohio *n.* Ohio
oïda *n.f.* hearing
oient *n.* listener
Oklahoma *n.* Oklahoma
oli *n.m.* oil
oli d'oliva *n.m.* olive oil
oli de càrtam *n.m.* safflower oil
oli de gira-sol *n.m.* sunflower oil
oli de llavors de raïm *n.m.* grapeseed oil
oli de palma *n.m.* palm oil
oligarquia *n.f.* oligarchy
oliós *adj.* oily
oliva *n.f.* olive
olla *n.f.* pot
olla de vapor *n.f.* steamer *(food)*
olor *n.m.* odor, smell
olorar *v.* smell
olorós *adj.* odorous
ombra *n.f.* shadow, shade
ombrejat *adj.* shady
ometre *v.* omit, leave out
ominós *adj.* ominous
omissió *n.f.* omission
omnipotència *n.f.* omnipotence
omnipotent *adj.* omnipotent
omnipresència *n.f.* omnipresence
omnipresent *adj.* omnipresent
omnisciència *n.f.* omniscience
omniscient *adj.* omniscient
omnívor *adj.* omnivorous
omplir *v.* fill
on *adv.* where
onada *n.f.* wave
onades *n.f.* surf
oncle *n.m.* uncle
oncòleg *n.* oncologist
oncologia *n.f.* oncology

onerós *adj.* onerous
ònix *n.m.* onyx
onzè *adj.* eleventh
onze *num.* eleven
opac *adj.* opaque
opacitat *n.f.* opacity
òpal *n.m.* opal
opció *n.f.* option
opcional *adj.* optional
òpera *n.f.* opera
operació *n.f.* operation
operador *n.* operator
operar *v.* operate
operatiu *adj.* operational
opi *n.m.* opium
opiaci *n.m.* opiate
opinió *n.f.* opinion
oponent *n.* opponent
oportunisme *n.m.* opportunism
oportunitat *n.f.* chance
oportunitat *n.f.* opportunity
oposar *v.* oppose
oposat *adj.* opposite
opressió *n.f.* oppression
opressor *n.* oppressor
oprimir *v.* oppress
òptic *adj.* optical | *n.* optician
òptim *adj.* optimum
optimisme *n.m.* optimism
optimista *adj.* optimistic | *n.* optimist
optometrista *n.* optometrist
opulència *n.f.* opulence
opulent *adj.* opulent
or *n.m.* gold
oració *n.f.* prayer
oracle *n.m.* oracle
orador *n.* orator
oral *adj.* oral
oralment *adv.* orally

oratòria *n.f.* oratory
òrbita *n.f.* orbit
orbitar *v.* orbit
ordalia *n.f.* ordeal
ordenança *n.f.* ordinance
ordenar *v.* sort; command
ordenat *adj.* orderly, tidy
ordi *n.m.* barley
ordinador *n.m.* computer
ordinador personal *n.m.* personal computer (PC)
ordinal *n.* ordinal
ordinari *adj.* ordinary
ordre *n.m.* order; warrant, writ
ordre de detenció *n.m.* bench warrant
ordre de registre *n.m.* search warrant
ordre del dia *n.m.* agenda
Oregon *n.* Oregon
orella *n.f.* ear
oreneta *n.f.* swallow *(bird)*
orenga *n.f.* oregano
orfe *n.* orphan
orfenat *n.m.* orphanage
òrgan *n.m.* organ
orgànic *adj.* organic
organisme *n.m.* organism
organització *n.f.* organization
organitzar *v.* organize, arrange
organitzatiu *adj.* organizational
orgasme *n.m.* orgasm
orgull *n.m.* pride
orgullós *adj.* proud
orgullosament *adv.* proudly
oriental *adj.* eastern, oriental
orientar *v.* orientate
origen *n.m.* origin
original *adj.* original
originalment *adv.* originally

orina *n.f.* urine
orinar *v.* urinate
ornament *n.m.* ornament
orquestra *n.f.* orchestra
orquestral *adj.* orchestral
ortiga *n.f.* nettle
ortodox *adj.* orthodox
ortografia *n.f.* spelling
os *n.m.* bone; bear
oscil·lació *n.f.* oscillation; swing
oscil·lar *v.* oscillate
osset de peluix *n.m.* teddy bear
ostatge *n.* hostage

ostra *n.f.* oyster
ostracisme *n.m.* ostracism
ou *n.m.* egg
ou dur *n.m.* hard-boiled egg
ovació *n.f.* ovation
oval *adj.* oval
ovari *n.m.* ovary
ovella *n.f.* sheep
oxidació *n.f.* oxidation
oxigen *n.m.* oxygen
ozó *n.m.* ozone

P

p. ex. *abbr.* e.g.

pa *n.m.* bread; loaf

pa de blat de moro *n.m.* cornbread

pa de pessic *n.m.* sponge cake

pa de sègol *n.m.* pumpernickel bread

pa ratllat *n.m.* breadcrumbs

pacana *n.f.* pecan

paciència *n.f.* patience

pacient *adj./n.* patient

pacífic *adj.* pacific, peaceful

pacificar *v.* pacify

pacte *n.m.* deal

paella *n.f.* frying pan, skillet

pagable *adj.* payable

pagament *n.m.* payment

pagar *v.* pay

pagaré *n.m.* promissory note

pagat *adj.* paid

pàgina inicial *n.f.* homepage

pàgina *n.f.* page

pàgina web *n.f.* webpage

pagoda *n.f.* pagoda

país *n.m.* country

paisatge *n.m.* landscape, scenery

Països Baixos *n.m.* Netherlands

pal *n.m.* pole, stick

pal de fregar *v.* mop

pal de golf *n.m.* golf club

pal indicador *n.m.* signpost

pala *n.f.* shovel, spade

palaia *n.f.* flounder

palanca de canvis *n.f.* gearshift lever

palanquí *n.m.* palanquin

palau *n.m.* palace

palau de justícia *n.m.* courthouse

paleta *n.f.* palette

palla *n.f.* straw

pallasso *n.m.* clown

pàl·lid *adj.* pale

palma *n.f.* palm *(tree)*

palmell *n.m.* palm *(of the hand)*

palpable *adj.* palpable

palpitació *n.f.* palpitation

palpitar *v.* palpitate

panacea *n.f.* panacea

Panamà *n.m.* Panama

pàncrees *n.m.* pancreas

panegíric *n.m.* panegyric

panerola *n.f.* cockroach

panerola *n.f.* roach

panet *n.m.* bun

pànic *n.m.* panic

panorama *n.m.* panorama

pansa *n.f.* raisin

pantà *n.m.* swamp

pantalla *n.f.* screen

pantaló *n.m.* pant *(clothing)*

pantalons *n.m.* pants, trousers

pantalons curts *n.m.* shorts

pantera *n.f.* panther

panti *n.m.* pantyhose

pantis *n.m.* tights

pantomima *n.f.* pantomime

paó *n.m.* peacock

papa *n.m.* dad

Papa *n.m.* Pope

papaia *n.f.* papaya

papallona *n.f.* butterfly
paper *n.m.* paper; role
paper higiènic *n.m.* toilet paper
paper pergamí *n.m.* parchment paper
paperera *n.f.* garbage can, bin
papereta *n.f.* ballot
paquet *n.m.* packet, package, parcel
para-sol *n.m.* parasol, sunshade
para-xocs *n.m.* bumper
paràbola *n.f.* parable
parabrisa *n.f.* windshield
paracaigudes *n.m.* parachute
paradís *n.m.* paradise
paradoxa *n.f.* paradox
parafang *n.m.* fender
parafina *n.f.* paraffin
parafrasejar *v.* paraphrase
paràgraf *n.m.* paragraph
Paraguai *n.m.* Paraguay
paraigua *n.f.* umbrella
paràlisi *n.f.* paralysis, palsy
paralitzar *v.* paralyse
paral·lel *adj.* parallel
paràmetre *n.m.* parameter
paranoic *adj.* paranoid
paraplègic *adj./n.* paraplegic
paràsit *n.m.* parasite
paraula clau *n.f.* keyword
paraula *n.f.* word
parc *n.m.* park
parc infantil *n.m.* playground
parcel·la *n.f.* plot *(land)*
parcial *adj.* partial
parcialment *adv.* partially
pare *n.m.* father; parent
parell *n.m.* pair
parella *n.f.* couple, partner *(relationship)*

parent *n.* relative
parèntesi *n.m.* parenthesis, bracket
parentiu *n.m.* kinship
paret *n.f.* wall
París *n.m.* Paris
paritat *n.f.* parity
parlament *n.m.* parliament
parlant *n.* speaker
parlar *v.* talk, speak
parlat *adj.* spoken
parmesà *n.m.* parmesan cheese
paròdia *n.f.* parody
parpella *n.f.* eyelid
parpellejar *v.* blink, flicker
parquímetre *n.m.* parking meter
parrac *n.m.* rag
parròquia *n.f.* parish
part *n.f.* part | *adv.* **a ~** apart, aside; **en ~** partly | *prep.* **a ~ de** part from
part superior *n.m.* top
partenariat *n.m.* partnership
partició *n.f.* partition
participació *n.f.* involvement
participant *n.* participant
participar *v.* participate
participi *n.m.* participle
partícula *n.f.* particle
particular *adj.* particular
particularment *adv.* particularly
partidari *n.* supporter
partidista *adj./n.* partisan
pàrvul *n.* kindergartener
parvulari *n.m.* kindergarten
pas *n.m.* pass; pace; step *(phase)*
pas a nivell *n.m.* level crossing
Pasqua *n.f.* Easter
passadís *n.m.* aisle
passaport *n.m.* passport

passar *v.* pass
passarel·la *n.f.* walkway
passat *adj.* gone | *n.m.* past
passat de moda *adj.* old-fashioned
passatemps *n.m.* pastime
passatge *n.m.* passage
passatger *n.* passenger
passeig *n.m.* ride
passejada *n.f.* walk, stroll
passejar *v.* stroll; ramble
passió *n.f.* passion
passiu *adj.* passive
pasta *n.f.* paste; pasta; pastry; dough
pasta de dents *n.f.* toothpaste
pasta fullada *n.f.* puff-pastry
pastanaga *n.f.* carrot
pastar *v.* knead
pastel *adj./n.m.* pastel
pasteuritzat *adj.* pasteurized
pastilla *n.f.* pill, lozenge
pastilla per dormir *n.f.* sleeping pill
pastís *n.m.* cake; pie, torte, tart
pastura *n.f.* pasture
pasturar *v.* graze
patata *n.f.* potato
patates fregides *n.f.* french fries
patates xips *n.f.* potato chips
paté *n.m.* paté
patent *n.f.* patent
patentat *adj.* proprietary, patented
patètic *adj.* pathetic
patetisme *n.m.* pathos
pati *n.m.* courtyard, yard *(of a house)*
patí *n.m.* skate
patiment *n.m.* suffering
patinar *v.* skate
patinar sobre gel *v.* ice skate

patir *v.* suffer
pàtria *n.f.* homeland
patrimoni *n.m.* heritage
patriota *n.* patriot
patriòtic *adj.* patriotic
patriotisme *n.m.* patriotism
patró *adj./n.m.* patron; pattern | *n.* employer
patrocinador *n.* sponsor
patrocinar *v.* patronize, sponsor
patrocini *n.m.* patronage
patrulla *n.f.* patrol
patrullar *v.* patrol
pau *n.f.* peace
pausa *n.f.* respite | *v.* **fer una ~** pause
pavelló *n.m.* pavilion
paviment *n.m.* pavement
peatge *n.m.* toll
pebre *n.m.* pepper *(spice)*
pebre de caiena *n.m.* cayenne pepper
pebre vermell *n.m.* paprika
pebrot *n.m.* pepper *(vegetable)*; bell pepper; pimiento; capsicum
pebrot de morro de bou *n.m.* green pepper
peça de recanvi *n.f.* spare part
pecar *v.* sin
pecat *n.m.* sin
peculiar *adj.* peculiar
pedaç *n.m.* patch
pedagogia *n.f.* pedagogy
pedal *n.m.* pedal
pedant *adj.* pedantic | *n.* pedant
pedanteria *n.f.* pedantry
pedestal *n.m.* pedestal
pediatre *n.* pediatrician
pedigrí *n.m.* pedigree
pedra *n.f.* stone

pedra angular *n.f.* cornerstone
pedregós *adj.* pebbly
pedrer *n.m.* gizzard
pedrera *n.f.* quarry
pegar *v.* hit; beat
peix *n.m.* fish
peix espasa *n.m.* swordfish
peixater *n.* fishmonger
Peixos *n.m.* Pisces
pel que fa a *prep.* regarding
pela *n.f.* peel
pelar *v.* peel
pelat *adj.* peeled
pelegrí *n.* pilgrim
pell *n.f.* skin; fur; rind
pell de llimona *n.f.* zest
pell de taronja *n.f.* orange peel
pel·lícula *n.f.* movie, film
peltre *n.m.* pewter
pena *n.f.* penalty
penalitzar *v.* penalize
pendent *adj.* pending | *n.m.* slope, incline
pèndol *n.m.* pendulum
penediment *n.m.* repentance
penedir-se *v.* repent
penetració *n.f.* penetration
penetrar *v.* penetrate, pervade
penic *n.m.* penny
penics *n.m.* pence
península *n.f.* peninsula
penis *n.m.* penis
penja-robes *n.m.* hanger
penjar *v.* hang
Pennsilvània *n.* Pennsylvania
pensament *n.m.* thought, thinking
pensar *v.* think
pensió *n.f.* pension; allowance
pensió alimentària *n.f.* alimony
pensionista *n.* pensioner

pentàgon *n.m.* pentagon
pentinar-se *v.* brush *(~ one's hair)*
pentinat *n.m.* haircut, hairdo
penya-segat *n.f.* cliff
per *prep.* by, per; for
per això *adv.* hence
per cent *n.* percent
per exemple *phr.* for example, for instance
per mal camí *adv.* astray
per què *adv.* why
per sempre *adv.* forever
per separat *adv.* separately
per tant *adv.* therefore
pera *n.f.* pear
perca *n.f.* perch
percebre *v.* perceive
percentatge *n.m.* percentage
percepció *n.f.* perception
perceptible *adj.* perceptible
perceptiu *adj.* perceptive
perdedor *n.* loser
perdiu *n.f.* partridge
perdó *n.m.* pardon
perdonar *v.* pardon, forgive
perdoni *phr.* excuse me *(for attention)*
perdre *v.* lose, miss
perdre el camí *v.* lose one's way
perdre sang *v.* lose blood
pèrdua *n.f.* loss
pèrdua de pilota *n.f.* fumble
perdut *adj.* lost, missing
peregrinació *n.f.* pilgrimage
perfecció *n.f.* perfection
perfectament *adv.* perfectly
perfecte *adj.* perfect
perfídia *n.f.* perfidy
perfil *n.m.* profile
perfum *n.m.* perfume

pergamí *n.m.* parchment
perible *adj.* perishable
perícia *n.f.* expertise
perill *n.m.* peril, danger, hazard
perillós *adj.* perilous, dangerous
període *n.m.* period *(menstrual)*
periòdica *adj.* periodic
periodisme *n.m.* journalism
periodista *n.* journalist, reporter
perir *v.* perish
perjudicial *adj.* harmful
perjuri *n.m.* perjury
perla *n.f.* pearl
permanent *adj.* permanent | *n.f.* perm *(hair)*
permanentment *adv.* permanently
permès *adj.* permitted, allowed
permetre *v.* permit, allow, afford
permís *n.m.* permission, permit
permutació *n.f.* permutation
perniciós *adj.* pernicious
pernil *n.m.* ham
però *conj.* but | *adv.* however
perpendicular *adj.* perpendicular
perpetu *adj.* perpetual
perpetuar *v.* perpetuate
perplexitat *n.f.* perplexity
perquè *conj.* because
perruquer *n.* hairdresser
perruqueria *n.f.* hair salon
persecució *n.f.* persecution; pursuit
perseguir *v.* pursue, chase; persecute
perseverança *n.f.* perseverance
perseverar *v.* persevere
persistència *n.f.* persistence
persistent *adj.* persistent
persistir *v.* persist
persona *n.f.* person
persona de negocis *n.f.* businessperson

persona sense llar *n.f.* homeless person
personal *adj.* personal | *n.m.* personnel, staff
personalitat *n.f.* personality
personalitzar *v.* customize
personalment *adv.* personally
personatge *n.m.* personage, character
personificació *n.f.* personification
perspectiva *n.f.* perspective, outlook, prospect
perspicàcia *n.f.* insight
persuadir *v.* persuade
persuasió *n.f.* persuasion
pertànyer *v.* pertain; belong
pertinent *adj.* pertinent, relevant
pertorbador *adj.* disturbing, upsetting
Perú *n.m.* Peru
pervers *adj.* perverse
perversió *n.f.* perversion
perversitat *n.f.* perversity
pervertir *v.* pervert
pervertit *n.* pervert
pes *n.m.* weight
pes net *n.m.* net weight
pesadament *adv.* heavily
pesar *v.* weigh
pesat *adj.* heavy
pesca *n.f.* fishing
pescador *n.* fisherman
pèsol *n.m.* pea
pessic *n.m.* pinch
pessigar *v.* pinch
pessimisme *n.m.* pessimism
pessimista *adj.* pessimistic | *n.* pessimist
pesta *n.f.* pest
pestanya *n.f.* eyelash

pesticida *n.m.* pesticide
pestilència *n.f.* pestilence
pètal *n.m.* petal
petició *n.f.* petition, plea
petit *adj.* small, little
petó *n.m.* kiss
petroli *n.m.* oil *(fuel)*
peu *n.m.* foot; **a ~** *phr.* on foot
peu de pàgina *n.m.* footer *(book)*
pH *n.m.* pH
pi *n.m.* pine
piano *n.m.* piano
PIB (producte interior brut) *n.m.*
  GDP (Gross Domestic Product)
pic *n.m.* pickaxe
picada *n.f.* sting, insect bite;
  nibble *(of a fish)*; hash
picada de mosquit *n.f.* mosquito
  bite
picant *adj.* piquant, pungent,
  spicy, tangy
picar *v.* sting; mince; knock
pícnic *n.m.* picnic
picor *n.f.* itch | *v.* **fer ~** itch
pietós *adj.* pious
pigment *n.m.* pigment
pigmeu *n.* pygmy
pijama *n.f.* pajamas
pila *n.f.* battery, pile
pilaf *n.* pilaf
pilar *n.m.* pillar
pilot *n.* pilot | *n.m.* pilot light
pilota *n.f.* ball
pilota de golf *n.f.* golf ball
pilotar *v.* pilot
pinacle *n.m.* pinnacle
pinces *n.f.* tweezers
píndola *n.f.* pill
píndola del dia després *n.f.*
  morning-after pill

ping-pong *n.m.* ping pong
pinta *n.f.* pint; comb
pintar *v.* paint
pintor *n.* painter
pintoresc *adj.* picturesque
pintura *n.f.* paint, painting
  (activity)
pintura a l'oli *n.f.* oil painting
pinya *n.f.* pineapple
pioner *n.* pioneer
pipa *n.f.* pipe *(tobacco)*
piquet *n.m.* picket
pira *n.f.* pyre
piràmide *n.m.* pyramid
piràmide dels aliments *n.f.* food
  pyramid
piranya *n.f.* piranha
pirata *n.m.* pirate
pirateria *n.f.* piracy
piruleta *n.f.* lollipop
piscina *n.f.* swimming pool, pool
piscina coberta *n.f.* indoor pool
piscina infantil *n.f.* paddling pool
pista *n.f.* track; hint
pistatxo *n.m.* pistachio
pistó *n.m.* piston
pistola *n.f.* pistol
pit *n.m.* chest, breast, bosom
pita *n.f.* pita bread
pitet *n.m.* bib
pitjor *adj.* worse, worst
pitó *n.m.* python
piular *v.* peep
pivotar *v.* pivot
pizza *n.f.* pizza
pizzeria *n.f.* pizzeria
pla *adj.* flat | *n.m.* plan, scheme
placa *n.f.* plate, platter
plaça *n.f.* square *(city)*
plaça principal *n.f.* main square

placar *v.* tackle
placebo *n.m.* placebo
plàcid *adj.* placid
plaer *n.m.* pleasure, enjoyment
plafó *n.m.* panel
plaga *n.f.* plague, pest
plana *n.f.* plain
planador *n.m.* glider
planeta *n.m.* planet
planificació *n.f.* planning
planta *n.f.* floor; *(botanical)* plant
planta baixa *n.f.* ground floor
plantació *n.f.* plantation, planting
plantar *v.* plant
planxa *n.f.* iron *(appliance)*
planxar *v.* iron
plasma *n.m.* plasma
plàstic *n.m.* plastic
plat *n.m.* dish
plat principal *n.m.* main course
plata *n.f.* silver | *adj.* **de** ~ silver
plataforma *n.f.* platform
plàtan *n.m.* banana, plantain
platet *n.m.* saucer
platí *n.m.* platinum
platja *n.f.* beach
platja nudista *n.f.* nudist beach
platònic *adj.* platonic
ple *adj.* full
plebiscit *n.m.* plebiscite
plegar *v.* fold
plenament *adv.* fully
plet *n.m.* lawsuit
ploma *n.f.* feather
plomar *v.* pluck
plomí *n.m.* nib
plorar *v.* cry
ploure *v.* rain
plovisquejar *v.* drizzle
plugim *n.m.* drizzle

pluja *n.f.* rain
plujós *adj.* rainy
plural *adj./n.m.* plural
pneumàtic *n.m.* tire
pneumònia *n.m.* pneumonia
població *n.f.* population
poble *n.m.* village
pobre *adj.* poor | *n.* pauper
pobresa *n.f.* poverty
poc amable *adj.* unkind
poc disposat *adj.* reluctant
poc profund *adj.* shallow
pocs *adj.* few
poder *v.* can *(be able)* | *n.m.* power
poderós *adj.* powerful
podrir *v.* rot
podrit *adj.* rotten, rotted
poema *n.m.* poem
poesia *n.f.* poetry
poeta *n.* poet
poètic *adj.* poetic
poètica *n.f.* poetics
polar *adj.* polar
policia *n.f.* police | *n.* police officer
polièster *n.m.* polyester
polígam *adj.* polygamous
poligàmia *n.f.* polygamy
poliglot *n.* polyglot
poliment *n.m.* polish
polir *v.* polish
pòlissa d'assegurança *n.f.*
  insurance policy
polític *adj.* political | *n.* politician
política *n.f.* policy; politics
políticament *adv.* politically
politja *n.f.* pulley
pollastre *n.m.* chicken
pol·len *n.m.* pollen
polls *n.m.* lice
polo *n.m.* polo

Polònia *n.f.* Poland
polpa *n.f.* pulp
pols *n.f.* dust, powder; pulse | *adj.* **en** ~ powdered
polsar *v.* pulse
polsegós *adj.* powdery
polsim *n.m.* pinch *(measure)*
polzada *n.f.* inch
polze *n.m.* thumb
poma *n.f.* apple
pompa *n.f.* pomp, pageantry
pompós *adj.* pompous
pompositat *n.f.* pomposity
poncem *n.m.* citron
ponderar *v.* ponder
poni *n.m.* pony
pont *n.m.* bridge
pont llevadís *n.m.* drawbridge
pop *n.m.* octopus
popular *adj.* popular
popularitat *n.f.* popularity
populós *adj.* populous
pòquer *n.m.* poker
por *n.f.* fear | *adj.* **de** ~ scary
porc *n.m.* pig
porcellana *n.f.* porcelain
porció *n.f.* portion
porro *n.m.* leek
port *n.m.* port, harbor
porta *n.f.* door, doorway, gate
porta d'entrada *n.f.* front door
portada *n.f.* front page
portador *n.m.* carrier
portal *n.m.* portal
portar *v.* bring, carry, fetch; wear
portàtil *adj.* portable | *n.m.* laptop
porter *n.* gate keeper; goalkeeper; porter
pòrtic *n.m.* portico
porticó *n.m.* shutter

Portugal *n.m.* Portugal
porus *n.m.* pore
porxo *n.m.* porch
posar *v.* pose, set, put, lay
posar-se *v.* perch
posició *n.f.* position
positiu *adj.* positive
posseir *v.* possess, own
possessió *n.f.* possession, holding
possessiu *adj.* possessive
possibilitat *n.f.* possibility
possible *adj.* possible, prospective
possiblement *adv.* possibly
post *n.m.* post *(position)*; board
posta del sol *n.f.* sunset
postdata *n.f.* postscript
posterior *adj.* rear
posteritat *n.f.* posterity
postrat *adj.* prostrate
postres *n.f.* dessert
postura *n.f.* posture
pot *n.m.* jar
pota *n.f.* paw
pota davantera *n.f.* foreleg
potable *adj.* potable
potència *n.f.* potency
potencial *adj.* potential
potser *adv.* maybe, perhaps
pràctic *adj.* practical
pràctica *n.f.* practice
practicabilitat *n.f.* practicability
pràcticament *adv.* practically
practicar *v.* practice
pragmàtic *adj.* pragmatic
pragmatisme *n.m.* pragmatism
praliné *n.m.* praline
prat *n.m.* meadow
preàmbul *n.m.* preamble
precaució *n.f.* precaution
precedència *n.f.* precedence

precedent *n.m.* precedent
precedir *v.* precede
precepte *n.m.* precept
preciós *adj.* precious, lovely
precís *adj.* precise
precisament *adv.* precisely
precisió *n.f.* precision
precursor *n.m.* precursor, fore-runner
predecessor *n.* predecessor
predestinació *n.f.* predestination
predeterminar *v.* predetermine
predicador *n.* preacher
predicar *v.* preach
predicció *n.f.* prediction
predir *v.* predict
predominant *adj.* predominant, prevalent
predominar *v.* predominate, prevail
predomini *n.m.* predominance, prevalence
preeminència *n.f.* preeminence
preeminent *adj.* preeminent
prefaci *n.m.* preface
prefecte *n.m.* prefect
preferència *n.f.* preference
preferir *v.* prefer
prefix *n.m.* prefix
pregunta *n.f.* question, query
preguntar *v.* ask, question, query
preguntar-se *v.* wonder
prehistòric *adj.* prehistoric
prejudici *n.m.* prejudice, bias
prelat *n.m.* prelate
preliminar *adj.* preliminary
preludi *n.m.* prelude
prematur *adj.* premature
premeditar *v.* premeditate
premeditat *adj.* premeditated

prémer *v.* press
premi *n.m.* prize, award
premonició *n.f.* premonition
premsa *n.f.* press
prendre *v.* take
preocupació *n.f.* concern
preocupació *n.f.* preoccupation
preocupant *adj.* worrying
preocupar *v.* preoccupy, worry
preocupat *adj.* worried, concerned
preparació *n.f.* preparation
preparar *v.* prepare
preparat *adj.* prepared
preponderància *n.f.* preponderance
preponderar *v.* preponderate
preposició *n.f.* preposition
prerrogativa *n.f.* prerogative
pres *n.* prisoner
presa *n.f.* prey
presa de corrent elèctric *n.f.* electrical outlet
presagi *n.m.* omen
presagiar *v.* portend
prescient *adj.* prescient
prescriure *v.* prescribe
presència *n.f.* presence
presenciar *v.* witness
present *n.m.* present
presentació *n.f.* presentation
presentar *v.* submit
presentar-se *v.* introduce oneself
president *n.* president; chairperson
presó *n.m.* prison, jail
pressa *n.f.* rush
préssec *n.m.* peach
pressió *n.f.* pressure
pressionar *v.* pressurize
pressuposar *v.* presuppose
pressuposició *n.f.* presupposition
pressupost *n.m.* budget

prestador *n.* lender
prestar *v.* loan, lend
prestatari *n.* borrower
prestatge *n.m.* shelf, rack
préstec *n.m.* loan
prestigi *n.m.* prestige
prestigiós *adj.* prestigious
presumiblement *adv.* presumably
presumir *v.* presume
presumpció *n.f.* presumption
pretensió *n.f.* pretence, pretension
pretensiós *adj.* pretentious
pretext *n.m.* pretext
pretzel *n.m.* pretzel
preu *n.m.* price
preu de mercat *n.m.* market price
preu fix *n.m.* fixed price
preu per litre *n.m.* price per liter
prevenció *n.f.* prevention
prevenir *v.* prevent
preventiu *adj.* preventive, precautionary
previsió *n.f.* foresight
prim *adj.* thin, slim
prima *n.f.* premium; bonus
prima facie *adj.* prima facie
primari *adj.* primary
primavera *n.f.* spring *(season)*
primer *adj.* first, foremost
primer lloc *n.m.* first place
primer ministre *n.* prime minister, premier
primera classe *adj.* first class
primera dama *n.f.* first lady
primers auxilis *n.m.* first aid
primigeni *adj.* primeval
primitiu *adj.* primitive
príncep *n.m.* prince
princesa *n.f.* princess
principal *adj.* principal, main, leading, prime

principalment *adv.* principally, mostly, primarily, mainly
principi *n.m.* principle; beginning, outset
principiant *n.* beginner
prioritat *n.f.* priority
prioritzar *v.* prioritize
privació *n.f.* privation
privadesa *n.f.* privacy
privat *adj.* private | *adv.* **en ~** privately
privatització *n.f.* privatization
privilegi *n.m.* privilege
probabilitat *n.f.* probability, odds
probable *adj.* probable, likely
probablement *adv.* probably
problema *n.m.* problem, trouble
problemàtic *adj.* problematic
procediment *n.m.* proceeding, procedure
procedir *v.* proceed
procés *n.m.* process
processat *adj.* processed
processador *n.m.* processor
processament *n.m.* indictment
processament de textos *n.m.* word processing
processar *v.* process; prosecute, indict
processó *n.f.* procession
proclamació *n.f.* proclamation
proclamar *v.* proclaim
proclivitat *n.f.* proclivity
pròdig *adj.* prodigal
prodigalitat *n.f.* prodigality
producció *n.f.* production
producte *n.m.* product, produce
producte interior brut (PIB) *n.m.* Gross Domestic Product (GDP)

productivitat *n.f.* productivity
productor *n.* producer
produir *v.* produce
profà *adj.* profane
profecia *n.f.* prophecy
professar *v.* profess
professió *n.f.* profession
professional *adj./n.* professional, practitioner
professor *n.* professor
profeta *n.m.* prophet
profètic *adj.* oracular
profetitzar *v.* prophesy
profiterol *n.m.* cream puff
profund *adj.* profound, deep
profundament *adv.* deeply
profunditat *n.f.* profundity, depth
profús *adj.* profuse
profusió *n.f.* profusion
programa *n.m.* program
programari *n.m.* software
progrés *n.m.* progress
progressiu *n.* progressive
prohibició *n.f.* prohibition
prohibir *v.* prohibit, ban
prohibit *adj.* prohibited, forbidden
projecció *n.f.* projection
projectar *v.* project
projecte *n.m.* project
projectil *n.m.* projectile
projector *n.m.* projector
prole *n.f.* progeny
pròleg *n.m.* prologue
proliferació *n.f.* proliferation
proliferar *v.* proliferate
prolífic *adj.* prolific
prolongació *n.f.* prolongation
prolongar *v.* prolong
promès *n.m.* fiancé
promesa *n.f.* promise, pledge; fiancée

prometedor *adj.* promising
prometre *v.* promise, pledge
prominència *n.f.* prominence
prominent *adj.* prominent
promoció *n.f.* promotion
promoure *v.* promote
pronom *n.m.* pronoun
pronòstic *n.m.* forecast
pronosticar *v.* forecast
pronúncia *n.f.* utterance
pronunciació *n.f.* pronunciation
pronunciar *v.* pronounce
prop: *adv.* **de** ~ closely | *prep.* **a** ~ **de** close to
propagació *n.f.* propagation
propaganda *n.f.* propaganda
propagandista *n.* propagandist
propagar *v.* propagate
propens *adj.* prone
proper *adj.* near, nearby; **més** ~ nearest
propi *adj.* own; fitting
propici *adj.* auspicious
propietari *n.* proprietor, owner, landlord
propietat *adj.* propriety, ownership, property *(a quality)*
propietat intel·lectual *n.f.* intellectual property
propietat privada *n.f.* private property
propina *n.f.* gratuity, tip
proporció *n.f.* proportion
proporcional *adj.* proportional
proporcionar *v.* provide
proposar *v.* propose, propound
proposició *n.f.* proposition
propòsit *n.m.* purpose
proposta *n.f.* proposal
propulsar *v.* propel

prosa *n.f.* prose
prosaic *adj.* prosaic
prosòdia *n.f.* prosody
prospecte *n.m.* prospectus
pròsper *adj.* prosperous
prosperar *v.* prosper
prosperitat *n.f.* prosperity
prostitució *n.f.* prostitution
prostituta *n.f.* prostitute
prostració *n.f.* prostration
protagonista *n.* protagonist
protecció *n.f.* protection
protector solar *n.m.* sunblock
protegir *v.* protect
protegit *adj.* protected
proteïna *n.f.* protein
protesta *n.f.* protest
protestant *adj./n.* Protestant
protestar *v.* protest
protó *n.m.* proton
protocol *n.m.* protocol
prototip *n.m.* prototype
prou *adj.* enough, plenty
prova *n.f.* proof; test
provar *v.* prove, try
proveïdor *n.* provider, supplier
proverbi *n.m.* proverb
providencial *adj.* providential
provident *adj.* provident
província *n.f.* province
provincialisme *n.m.* provincialism
provisió *n.f.* provision
provisional *adj.* interim
provisionalitat *n.f.* provisionality
provisionalment *adv.* provisionally
provocació *n.f.* provocation
provocar *v.* provoke
provocar aldarulls *v.* riot
provocatiu *adj.* provocative

pròxim *adj.* next, proximate
Pròxim Orient *n.m.* Middle East
proximitat *n.f.* proximity
prudència *n.f.* prudence
prudent *adj.* prudent, wise
pruna *n.f.* plum, prune
pseudònim *n.m.* pseudonym
psicòleg *n.* psychologist
psicològic *adj.* psychological
psicòpata *n.* psychopath
psicoteràpia *n.f.* psychotherapy
psicòtic *adj.* psychotic
psique *n.f.* psyche
psiquiatre *n.* psychiatrist
psiquiatria *n.f.* psychiatry
pub *n.m.* pub
pubertat *n.f.* puberty
públic *adj.* public
publicació *n.f.* publication
públicament *adv.* publicly
publicar *v.* publish
publicitat *n.f.* publicity, advertising
puça *n.f.* flea
púding *n.m.* pudding
pueril *adj.* puerile
Puerto Rico *n.m.* Puerto Rico
pujar *v.* climb, rise, mount
pujol *n.m.* mound
pulcrament *adv.* neatly
pulcre *adj.* neat
pulmó *n.m.* lung
púlpit *n.m.* pulpit
pulsació *n.f.* pulsation
punt *n.m.* point, dot, period; stitch
punt de control *n.m.* checkpoint
punt de llibre *n.m.* bookmark
punt de vista *n.m.* point of view, viewpoint
punt i coma *n.m.* semicolon
punta *n.f.* tip, point *(sharp)*; lace *(material)*

punta del dit *n.f.* fingertip
puntal *n.m.* prop
puntcom *n.f.* dotcom
puntuació *n.f.* punctuation
puntual *adj.* punctual, prompt
puntualitat *n.f.* punctuality
puntualment *adv.* promptly
puntuar *v.* punctuate
punxada *n.f.* puncture; flat tire
punxar *v.* puncture, pop, prick
punxegut *adj.* pointed
puny *n.m.* fist
pupil·la *n.f.* pupil
pur *adj.* pure
purament *adv.* purely
puré *n.m.* puree

puré de patates *n.m.* mashed potatoes
puresa *n.f.* purity
purga *n.f.* purge
purgació *n.f.* purgation
purgant *adj.* purgative
purgar *v.* purge
purgatori *n.m.* purgatory
purificació *n.f.* purification
purificar *v.* purify
purista *n.* purist
purità *adj./n.* puritan
púrpura *adj./n.f.* purple
pus *n.m.* pus
puzle *n.m.* puzzle

Q

quadern *n.m.* notebook
quadra *n.f.* stable
quadrangle *n.m.* quadrangle
quadrat *n.m.* square
quadre *n.m.* painting *(fine art)*
quadre de distribució *n.m.* fuse
  box
quàdruple *adj.* quadruple
qualificació *n.f.* qualification
qualificar *v.* qualify
qualificat *adj.* qualified
qualitat *n.f.* quality
quallada *n.f.* curd
quallar *v.* curdle
qualsevol *adj.* any | *pron.* anyone;
  either, whoever | *adv.* **a ~ lloc**
  anywhere, wherever
qualsevol cosa *pron.* anything
quan *adv.* when, whenever
quant? *phr.* how much?
quantitat *n.f.* quantity, amount
quants? *phr.* how many?
quaranta *num.* forty
quarantè *adj.* fortieth
quarantena *n.f.* quarantine
Quaresma *n.f.* Lent
quart *adj.* fourth | *n.m.* quarter
  (quantity) | *adj.* **a ~s** quartered
quasi *adv.* almost
quatre *num.* four
què *pron.* what
que *conj.* than; *rel. pron.* that
que engreixa *adj.* fattening

que parla anglès *adj.* English-
  speaking
que treballa *adj.* working
quedar-se *v.* stay
queixa *n.f.* complaint, grouse
queixal *n.m.* molar
queixar-se *v.* complain
querellant *n.* complainant
querosè *n.m.* kerosene
qüestionable *adj.* questionable
qüestionari *n.m.* questionnaire
quètxup *n.m.* ketchup
qui *pron.* who, whom | *adj.* **de ~**
  whose
quiche *n.f.* quiche
quiet *adj.* still
quilogram *n.m.* kilogram
quilometratge *n.m.* mileage
quilòmetre *n.m.* kilometer
químic *adj.* chemical | *n.* chemist
química *n.f.* chemistry
quin(a) *adj.* what | *pron.* which
quinoa *n.f.* quinoa
quinzè *adj.* fifteenth
quinze *num.* fifteen
quinzena *n.f.* fortnight
quiromància *n.f.* palmistry
quiromàntic *n.* palmist
quiropràctic *n.* chiropractor
quist *n.m.* cyst
quixotesc *adj.* quixotic
quòrum *n.m.* quorum
quota *n.f.* quota

R

rabí *n.m.* rabbi
ràbia *n.f.* rage
raça *n.f.* race
racial *adj.* racial
ració *n.f.* ration, serving
racional *adj.* rational
racionalitat *n.f.* rationality
racionalitzar *v.* rationalize
racionar *v.* ration
racisme *n.m.* racism
racó *n.m.* corner
radi *n.m.* radius
radiació *n.f.* radiation
radiador *n.m.* radiator
radiant *adj.* radiant
radiar *v.* radiate
radical *adj.* radical
radicalisme *n.m.* radicalism
ràdio *n.f.* radio
ragú *n.m.* ragout
raig *n.m.* ray, beam; spoke
raig X *n.m.* x-ray
rail *n.m.* rail
raïm *n.m.* grape
raima *n.f.* ream
rajola *n.f.* tile
RAM *n.f.* RAM
rampa *n.f.* ramp; cramp
rampell *n.m.* outburst
rampinyar *v.* pilfer
ranci *adj.* stale, musty
rancor *n.m.* rancor
raó *n.f.* reason
raonable *adj.* reasonable
raonablement *adv.* reasonably

raonament *n.m.* rationale
rap *n.m.* angler fish
ràpel *n.m.* rappeling
ràpid *adj.* rapid, quick, fast; **més ràpida** quickest
ràpidament *adv.* rapidly, quickly
ràpids *n.m.* rapids
raqueta *n.f.* racket
raquitisme *n.m.* rickets
rar *adj.* rare, unusual
rarament *adv.* rarely
raspall de cabells *n.m.* hairbrush
raspall de dents *n.m.* toothbrush
raspallar-se *v.* brush one's teeth
raspar *v.* scrape
rastre *n.f.* trace
rata *n.f.* rat
ratificar *v.* ratify
ràtio *n.f.* ratio
ratlla *n.f.* stripe
ratllador *n.m.* grater
ratllar *v.* grate, scratch
ratllat *adj.* grated; striped
ratolí *n.m.* mouse
rat-penat *n.m.* bat
rave *n.m.* radish
rave picant *n.m.* horseradish
reacció *n.f.* reaction
reaccionar *v.* react
reaccionari *adj./n.* reactionary
reactor *n.m.* reactor
real *adj.* real, actual
realisme *n.m.* realism
realista *adj.* realistic | *n.* realist
realitat *n.f.* reality

realitat virtual *n.f.* virtual reality
realització *n.f.* realization
realitzar *v.* realize; perform
realment *adv.* really
rebaixa *n.f.* rebate
rebel *adj.* rebellious | *n.* rebel
rebel·lar *v.* rebel
rebel·lió *n.f.* rebellion
rebentar *v.* burst
rebost *n.m.* pantry
rebosteria *n.f.* pastry shop
rebot *n.m.* rebound
rebotar *v.* rebound
rebre *v.* receive
rebuf *n.m.* rebuff
rebuig *n.m.* rejection; by-product
rebut *n.m.* sales receipt, receipt
rebutjar *v.* reject, refuse
recanvi: de ~ *adj.* spare
recaptar *v.* levy
recaiguda *n.f.* relapse
recaptació *n.f.* levy
recaptació de fons *n.f.* fundraiser
recaure *v.* relapse
recel *n.m.* misgiving
recent *adj.* recent; **més ~** latest
recentment *adv.* recently, freshly,
   newly
recepció *n.f.* reception, front desk
recepcionista *n.* receptionist
recepta *n.f.* recipe; prescription
receptar *v.* prescribe *(medical)*
receptor *n.m.* receiver, receptor |
   n. recipient
recerca *n.f.* research; quest
recessió *n.f.* recession
reciclable *adj.* recyclable
reciclar *v.* recycle
reciclatge *n.m.* recycling
recipient *n.m.* container

recíproc *adj.* reciprocal
reciprocar *v.* reciprocate
recitació *n.f.* recitation
recital *n.m.* recital
recitar *v.* recite
reclamació *n.f.* reclamation,
   claim
reclamar *v.* reclaim, claim
reclús *n.* recluse
recluta *n.* recruit
reclutament *n.m.* recruitment
reclutar *v.* recruit
recobert *adj.* coated
recollir *v.* collect, reap, pick up
recomanació *n.f.* recommendation
recomanar *v.* recommend
recomanat *adj.* recommended
recompensa *n.f.* recompense,
   reward
recomptar *v.* recount
reconciliació *n.f.* reconciliation
reconciliar *v.* reconcile
reconeixement *n.m.* recognition
reconèixer *v.* recognize,
   acknowledge
reconstruir *v.* rebuild
reconstruït *adj.* rebuilt
record *n.m.* souvenir
recordança *n.f.* remembrance
recordar *v.* remember, recollect;
   remind
recordatori *n.m.* reminder
recórrer *v.* rove
recrear *v.* recreate
rectangle *n.m.* rectangle
recte *n.m.* rectum
rectificació *n.f.* rectification
rectificar *v.* rectify
rector *n.m.* parson
recuperació *n.f.* recovery, salvage

recuperar *v.* recoup, recover, retrieve, salvage
recurrència *n.f.* recurrence
recurrent *adj.* recurrent
recurs *n.m.* recourse; resource
redactor *n.* editor
redempció *n.f.* redemption
redimir *v.* redeem
redirigir *v.* redirect
reducció *n.f.* reduction
reduir *v.* reduce
reduït *adj.* reduced
redundància *n.f.* redundancy, redundance
redundant *adj.* redundant
reeixit *adj.* successful
reemborsament *n.m.* repayment, reimbursement, refund
reemborsar *v.* reimburse, refund
reemplaçament *n.m.* replacement
reemplaçar *v.* replace
reescalfar *v.* re-heat
reestructuració *n.f.* restructuring
reestructurar *v.* restructure
referència *n.f.* reference
referèndum *n.m.* referendum
referent a *prep.* concerning
referir-se a *v.* refer to
refinar *v.* refine
refinat *adj.* refined
refineria *n.f.* refinery
reflectir *v.* reflect
reflector *n.m.* reflector
reflex *n.m.* reflex, reflection
reflexiu *adj.* reflexive
reforçament *n.m.* reinforcement
reforçar *v.* reinforce
reforma *n.f.* reform
reformació *n.f.* reformation
reformador *n.* reformer

reformar *v.* reform
reformatori *n.m.* reformatory
refredar *v.* chill
refredat *adj.* chilled
refrenar *v.* curb, restrain
refresc *n.m.* refreshment
refrescant *adj.* refreshing
refrigeració *n.f.* refrigeration
refugi *n.m.* refuge
refugiat *n.* refugee
refús *n.m.* refusal
refutació *n.f.* refutation
refutar *v.* refute
regal *n.m.* gift
regalar *v.* give (something) away
regalèssia *n.f.* licorice
regany *n.m.* rebuke
reganyar *v.* rebuke
regatge *n.m.* irrigation
regeneració *n.f.* regeneration
regenerar *v.* regenerate
regi *adj.* regal
regicidi *n.m.* regicide
règim *n.m.* regime
regiment *n.m.* regiment
regió *n.f.* region
regional *adj.* regional
registrar *v.* register
registre *n.m.* registry
regla *n.f.* rule
regle *n.m.* ruler
regnar *v.* reign
regnat *n.m.* reign
regne *n.m.* realm
Regne Unit *n.m.* United Kingdom (UK)
regulació *n.f.* regulation
regulador *adj.* regulatory | *n.* regulator
regular *adj.* regular | *v.* regulate

regularment *adv.* regularly
rehabilitació *n.f.* rehabilitation
rehabilitar *v.* rehabilitate
rei *n.m.* king
reial *adj.* royal
reialesa *n.f.* royalty
reimpressió *n.f.* reprint
reina *n.f.* queen
reintegració *n.f.* reinstatement
reintegrar *v.* reinstate
reiteració *n.f.* reiteration
reiterar *v.* reiterate
rejoveniment *n.m.* rejuvenation
rejovenir *v.* rejuvenate
relació *n.f.* relationship, relation
relacionat amb *adj.* related (to)
relacions *n.f.* relations
relatar *v.* report; relate
relatiu *adj.* relative
relativament *adv.* relatively
relaxació *n.f.* relaxation
relaxat *adj.* relaxed
relaxar *v.* relax
religió *n.f.* religion
religiós *adj.* religious
relíquia *n.f.* relic
relleu *n.m.* relay
rellevància *n.f.* relevance
relliscar *v.* slip
rellotge *n.m.* watch, clock
rellotger *n.* watchmaker
rem *n.m.* paddle, rowing
remar *v.* paddle
remei *n.m.* remedy, cure
remenar *v.* scramble, stir
remenat *adj.* scrambled
remesa *n.f.* remittance
remetre *v.* remit
reminiscència *n.f.* reminiscence
reminiscent *adj.* reminiscent

remissió *n.f.* remission
remitent *n.* sender
remolatxa *n.f.* beet, beetroot
remolcar *v.* tow
remordiment *n.m.* remorse
remot *adj.* remote
remuneració *n.f.* remuneration
remunerar *v.* remunerate
ren *n.m.* reindeer
renaixement *n.m.* rebirth,
  Renaissance
rendibilitat *n.f.* profitability
rendible *adj.* profitable
rendir *v.* yield, surrender
renom *n.m.* renown
renombrado *adj.* renowned
renovació *n.f.* renovation, renewal
renovar *v.* renovate, renew
rentable a la rentadora *adj.*
  machine washable
rentadora *n.f.* washing machine
rentamans *n.m.* washbasin
rentaplats *n.m.* dishwasher
rentar *v.* wash
rentaülls *n.m.* medical eyewash
  station
renúncia *n.f.* renunciation; waiver
renunciar *v.* renounce
reomplir *v.* replenish
reparable *adj.* reparable
reparació *n.f.* repair
reparador *n.* repairman
reparar *v.* repair
repatriació *n.f.* repatriation
repatriar *v.* repatriate
repel·lent *adj./n.m.* repellent
repel·lent d'insectes *n.m.* insect
  repellant
repel·lir *v.* repel, repulse
repercussió *n.f.* repercussion

repetició *n.f.* repetition, repeat
repetidament *adv.* repeatedly
repetir *v.* repeat, recur
repetit *adj.* repeated
replet *adj.* replete
rèplica *n.f.* replica; rejoinder, retort
rèplica ràpida *n.f.* repartee
replicar *v.* retort
repòs *n.m.* repose
repositori *n.m.* repository
reprendre *v.* reprimand; resume
reprensió *n.f.* reproof
represa *n.f.* resumption
represàlia *n.f.* retaliation
represaliar *v.* retaliate
representació *n.f.* representation; play *(theater)*
representant *n.* representative
representar *v.* represent, portray, depict
repressió *n.f.* repression
reprimenda *n.f.* reprimand
reprimir *v.* repress
reproducció *n.f.* reproduction
reproductiu *adj.* reproductive
reproduir *v.* reproduce
reproduir-se *v.* breed
reprotxar *v.* reproach
reprotxe *n.m.* reproach
rèptil *n.m.* reptile
republicà *adj./n.* republican
república *n.f.* republic
República Dominicana *n.f.* Dominican Republic
República Txeca *n.f.* Czech Republic
repudi *n.m.* repudiation
repudiar *v.* repudiate
repugnància *n.f.* repugnance

repugnant *adj.* repugnant, nasty revolting
repulsió *n.f.* repulsion
repulsiu *adj.* repulsive
reputació *n.f.* reputation, repute
reputar *v.* repute
requeriment *n.m.* requisition
requerir *v.* require
requisit *n.m.* requirement, prerequisite
res *pron.* nothing
resar *v.* pray
rescat *n.m.* rescue; ransom
rescatar *v.* rescue
reserva *n.f.* reservation; booking
reserva natural *n.f.* nature reserve
reservar *v.* reserve
reservat *adj.* reserved
residència *n.f.* hall *(residence)*
resident *n.* resident
residir *v.* reside
residu *n.m.* residue
resistència *n.f.* resistance
resistir *v.* resist
resoldre *v.* resolve, solve, settle
resolució *n.f.* resolution
resolut *adj.* resolute
respectar *v.* respect
respecte *n.m.* respect, regard
respectiu *adj.* respective
respectivament *adv.* respectively
respectuós *adj.* respectful
respiració *n.f.* respiration, breathing
respirar *v.* breathe
resplendor *n.f.* radiance
respondre *v.* respond, reply
responsabilitat *n.f.* responsibility, liability
responsable *adj.* responsible, liable

resposta *n.f.* response, answer, reply

ressaca *n.f.* hangover

ressonar *v.* resound

ressorgiment *n.m.* resurgence

resta *n.f.* remainder

restant *adj.* remaining

restauració *n.f.* restoration

restaurat *adj.* restored

restaurant *n.m.* restaurant, eatery

restaurar *v.* restore

restes *n.f.* remains

restrenyiment *n.m.* constipation

restret *adj.* constipated

restricció *n.f.* restriction, constraint

restringir *v.* restrict

restringit *adj.* restricted

resultat *n.m.* result, outcome; score

resum *n.m.* resumé; summary

retallar *v.* trim

retard *n.m.* delay

retard mental *n.m.* mental retardation

retardar *v.* retard

retardat *adj.* delayed

retenció *n.f.* retention

retenir *v.* retain

retentiu *adj.* retentive

reticència *n.f.* reticence

reticent *adj.* reticent, unwilling

retina *n.f.* retina

retir *v.* retreat

retirada *n.f.* withdrawal

retirar *v.* recall, withdraw

retocar *v.* retouch

retolador *n.m.* marker

retòric *adj.* rhetorical

retòrica *n.f.* rhetoric

retornable *adj.* returnable; **no ~** nonreturnable

retrat *n.m.* portrait

retrocedir *v.* recede, recoil; retrace

retrospecció *n.f.* retrospection, retrospect

reumàtic *adj.* rheumatic

reumatisme *n.m.* rheumatism

reunir-se *v.* gather

revelació *n.f.* revelation, disclosure

revelar *v.* reveal, disclose

reverència *n.f.* reverence, awe

reverencial *adj.* reverential

reverenciar *v.* revere

revertir *v.* revert

revés *n.m.* backhand | *adv.* **al ~** upside down

revifalla *n.f.* revival

revisar *v.* revise, review; revive

revisió *n.f.* revision

revista *n.f.* journal, periodical, magazine; review

revocable *adj.* revocable

revocació *n.f.* revocation

revocar *v.* revoke

rèvola *n.f.* turbot

revolució *n.f.* revolution

revolucionari *adj.* revolutionary

Rhode Island *n.* Rhode Island

riba *n.f.* shore

ribera *n.f.* seashore

ric *adj.* wealthy, rich

rickshaw *n.m.* rickshaw

ridícul *adj.* ridiculous

ridiculitzar *v.* ridicule

rierol *n.m.* rivulet

rifle *n.m.* rifle

rígid *adj.* rigid, stiff

rígidament *adv.* stiffly

rigor *n.m.* rigor
rigorós *adj.* rigorous
rima *n.f.* rhyme
rimar *v.* rhyme
rímel *n.m.* mascara
rinitis al·lèrgica *n.f.* hay fever, allergic rhinitis
rinoceront *n.m.* rhinoceros
rínxol *n.m.* ringlet
riquesa *n.f.* wealth
ris *n.m.* ripple, curl
risc *n.m.* risk
ritme *n.m.* rhythm
rítmic *adj.* rhythmic
ritual *n.m.* ritual
riu *n.m.* river
riure *v.* laugh | *n.m.* laughter, laugh
rival *n.* rival
rivalitat *n.f.* rivalry
roba *n.f.* clothing, clothes
roba de llit *n.f.* bedding
roba interior *n.f.* underwear
robar *v.* steal, rob
robat *adj.* stolen, robbed
robatori *n.m.* robbery, stealing
robí *n.m.* ruby
robot *n.m.* robot
roca *n.f.* rock
roda *n.f.* wheel
rodar *v.* roll
rodera *n.f.* rut
rodet *n.m.* reel
rom *n.m.* rum
Roma *n.f.* Rome
romandre *v.* remain
romaní *n.m.* rosemary
Romania *n.f.* Romania
romàntic *adj.* romantic
romanticisme *n.m.* Romanticism

roncar *v.* snore
ronyó *n.m.* kidney
ros *adj.* blonde
rosa *adj.* pink | *n.f.* rose
rosella *n.f.* poppy
rostes de Santa Teresa *n.f.* french toast
rostidoria *n.m.* rotisserie
rostir *v.* roast, broil
rostit *adj.* roasted | *n.m.* pot roast
rostit de porc *n.m.* pork roast
rotació *n.f.* rotation
rotatori *adj.* rotary
rotlle *n.m.* roll
rotonda *n.f.* roundabout
roure *n.m.* oak
rovell *n.m.* rust; yolk
rovellat *adj.* rusty
ruc *n.m.* donkey
ruca *n.f.* arugula
rudiment *n.m.* rudiment
rudimentari *adj.* rudimentary
rufià *n.* ruffian
rugbi *n.m.* rugby
rugir *v.* roar
ruibarbre *n.m.* rhubarb
ruïnes *n.f.* ruins
ruixar *v.* spray
rumiar *v.* ponder
rumor *n.m.* rumor, hearsay
runes *n.f.* rubble
rural *adj.* rural
rus *adj./n.* Russian
rusc *n.m.* beehive
Rússia *n.f.* Russia
rústic *adj.* rustic
rusticitat *n.f.* rusticity
ruta *n.f.* route
rutina *n.f.* routine

S

sabata *n.f.* shoe
sabatilla *n.f.* sneaker; slipper
saber *v.* know *(knowledge)*
sabó *n.m.* soap
saborós *adj.* palatable
sabotatge *n.m.* sabotage
sabotejar *v.* sabotage
sac *n.m.* sack
sac de dormir *n.m.* sleeping bag
sacarina *n.f.* saccharin
sacerdot *n.* priest
sacrilegi *n.m.* sacrilege
sacsejar *v.* shake, jerk
sadisme *n.m.* sadism
safata *n.f.* tray
safata de sortida *n.f.* outbox
safata de forn *n.f.* baking sheet
safir *n.m.* sapphire
safrà *n.m.* saffron
sagaç *adj.* sagacious
sagacitat *n.f.* sagacity
Sagitari *n.m.* Sagittarius
sagnar *v.* bleed
sagrament *n.m.* sacrament
sagrat *adj.* holy, sacred
sal *n.f.* salt
sala *n.f.* room, parlor, hall *(events)*
sala d'urgències *n.f.* emergency room
sala d'estar *n.f.* living room, lounge
salari *n.m.* wage
salat *adj.* salty, salted, savory
saliva *n.f.* saliva, spit
salm *n.m.* psalm

salmó *n.m.* salmon
salmorra *n.f.* brine
saló *n.m.* salon
salsa *n.f.* sauce, gravy
salsa de soja *n.f.* soy sauce
salsa picant *n.f.* hot sauce
salsa tàrtara *n.f.* tartar sauce
salsitxa *n.f.* sausage
salsitxa de porc *n.f.* pork sausage
salt de pont *n.m.* bungee-jumping
saltador *n.* jumper
saltar *v.* jump, leap; stir-fry
saltat *adj.* sautéed
saludable *adj.* healthy
saludar *v.* greet, salute
salut *n.f.* health, fitness
Salut! *interj.* Cheers!
salutació *n.f.* greeting, salutation, salute
salvació *n.f.* salvation
salvador *n.* saviour
salvatge *adj.* wild, savage
salvatgement *adv.* wildly
sàlvia *n.f.* sage
samarreta *n.f.* t-shirt
San Marino *n.m.* San Marino
sanatori *n.m.* sanatorium
sanció *n.f.* sanction
sandàlia *n.f.* sandal
sanejament *n.m.* sanitation
sang *n.f.* blood
sangonera *n.f.* leech
sanitari *adj.* sanitary
sant *n.* saint
santificació *n.f.* sanctification

santificar *v.* sanctify
santuari *n.m.* sanctuary, shrine
saquejar *v.* ransack
sarcasme *n.m.* sarcasm
sarcàstic *adj.* sarcastic
sardina *n.f.* sardine
sastre *n.m.* tailor
Satanàs *n.* Satan
satèl·lit *n.m.* satellite
sàtira *n.f.* satire
satisfacció *n.f.* satisfaction
satisfactori *adj.* satisfying, all right
satisfer *v.* satisfy
satisfet *adj.* satisfied
saturació *n.f.* saturation
saturar *v.* saturate
saturat *adj.* saturated
sauna *n.f.* sauna
saviesa *n.f.* wisdom
sec *adj.* dry, dried
secció *n.f.* section
secret *adj./n.m.* secret
secretament *adv.* secretly
secretari *n.* secretary
secretisme *n.m.* secrecy
sector *n.m.* sector
secular *adj.* secular
secundari *adj.* secondary
seda *n.f.* silk
sedant *n.m.* sedative
sediment *n.m.* sediment
seductor *adj.* alluring
segador *n.* reaper
segar *v.* reap
segell *n.m.* seal, stamp
segellar *v.* seal, stamp
segle *n.m.* century
segment *n.m.* segment
segó *n.m.* bran

sègol *n.m.* rye
segon *adj./n.m.* second | *adj.* **de segona mà** secondhand
segona opinió *n.f.* second opinion
segons *prep.* depending on
segrest *n.m.* abduction
segrestador *n.* kidnapper
segrestar *v.* sequester, kidnap
següent *adj.* following
seguici *n.m.* retinue
seguir *v.* follow
segur *adj.* secure, safe; sure
segurament *adv.* surely
seguretat *n.f.* security, safety
seient *n.m.* seat
seient davanter *n.m.* front seat
seixanta *num.* sixty
seixantè *adj.* sixtieth
selecció *n.f.* selection, choice
seleccionar *v.* select
sella *n.f.* saddle
semblança *n.f.* resemblance
semblar *v.* seem
semblar-se *v.* resemble
sembra *n.f.* sowing
sembrar *v.* sow
seminari *n.m.* seminar
sèmola *n.f.* grits
sempre *adv.* always, ever
sempre que *adv.* whenever; provided
senador *n.* senator
senat *n.m.* senate
sender *n.m.* path, footpath, nature trail
senderisme: fer ~ *v.* hike
sensació *n.f.* feeling *(physical)*
sensat *adj.* sensible
sense *prep.* without
sense alcohol *adj.* non-alcoholic

sense cafeïna *adj.* caffeine-free
sense fil *adj.* wireless
sense llar *adj.* homeless
sense mobles *adj.* unfurnished
sense ossos *adj.* boneless
sense parar *adj.* nonstop
sense perill *adv.* safely
sense plom *adj.* lead-free
sense sucre *adj.* sugar-free
sensibilitat *n.f.* sensitivity
sensible *adj.* sensitive
sentència *n.f.* sentence *(legal)*
sentiment *n.m.* feeling *(emotion)*
sentimental *adj.* sentimental
sentir per casualitat *v.* overhear
sentir *v.* feel, sense; hear
sentit *n.m.* sense
senyal *n.m.* signal, sign
senyor *n.m.* sir, gentleman; lord
senyora *n.f.* madam, lady
senyoreta *n.f.* Miss, Ms.
senzill *adj.* simple
senzillament *adv.* simply
separació *n.f.* separation
separar *v.* separate, detach
separat *adj.* separated, separate
seqüència *n.f.* sequence
seqüencial *adj.* sequential
sequera *n.f.* drought
ser *v.* be
Sèrbia *n.f.* Serbia
sèrie *n.f.* series
seriós *adj.* serious
seriosament *adv.* seriously
serp *n.f.* snake
serra *n.f.* mountain range, mountain chain; saw
sèrum *n.m.* serum
sèrum de llet *n.m.* whey
servei *n.m.* service; amenity; **de ~** *phr.* on duty

servei d'àpats *n.m.* catering
servei d'habitacions *n.m.* room service
servei de bugaderia *n.m.* laundry service
servei inicial *n.m.* kick-off
servei militar *n.m.* military service
servei *n.m.* service
servidor *n.* server
servir *v.* serve
sèsam *n.m.* sesame
sessió *n.f.* session
set *num.* seven | *n.f.* thirst | *n.m.* set
setanta *num.* seventy
setantè *adj.* seventieth
setè *adj.* seventh
setembre *n.m.* September
setí *n.m.* satin
setmana *n.f.* week
setmana que ve *adv.* next week
setmanal *adj.* weekly
setzè *adj.* sixteenth
setze *num.* sixteen
seu *pos. adj.* her, his, its, their | *pron.* hers, his, its, theirs
seure *v.* sit
seus *pos. adj.* her, his, its, their; *pron.* hers, his, its, theirs
seva *pos. adj.* her, his, its, their | *pron.* hers, his, its, theirs
sever *adj.* severe
severament *adv.* severely
seves *pos. adj.* her, his, its, their | *pron.* hers, his, its, theirs
sexe *n.m.* sex
sexisme *n.m.* sexism
sexual *adj.* sexual
sexualitat *n.f.* sexuality
sexualment *adv.* sexually
sí *adv.* yes | *interj..* yeah
si *conj.* if, whether

si mateix *pron.* itself
si us plau *phr.* please
sibilació *n.f.* wheezing
SIDA *n.f.* AIDS
sidra *n.f.* cider
signar *v.* sign
signatura *n.f.* signature
signe d'exclamació *n.m.*
  exclamation point
significació *n.f.* significance
significar *v.* mean
significat *n.m.* meaning
significatiu *adj.* significant
significativament *adv.* significantly
silenci *n.m.* silence
silenciador *n.m.* muffler
silenciós *adj.* silent
silenciosament *adv.* quietly
síl·laba *n.f.* syllable
silvicultura *n.f.* forestry
símbol *n.m.* symbol
simetria *n.f.* symmetry
similar *adj.* similar
similaritat *n.f.* similarity
símptoma *n.f.* symptom
sinagoga *n.f.* synagogue
sincer *adj.* sincere
sincerament *adv.* sincerely,
  genuinely
síndria *n.f.* watermelon
síndrome *n.f.* syndrome
síndrome premenstrual (SPM)
  n.f. premenstrual syndrome (PMS)
simfonia *n.f.* symphony
singlot *n.m.* hiccup
singular *adj.* singular
síntesi *n.f.* synthesis
sintètic *adj.* synthetic
sirena *n.f.* siren
sis *num.* six

sisè *adj.* sixth
sistema *n.f.* system
sistema circulatori *n.m.* circulatory system
sistema immunitari *n.m.* immune
  system
sistema nerviós *n.m.* nervous
  system
sistema operatiu *n.m.* operating
  system
sistema respiratori *n.f.* respiratory system
situació *n.f.* situation
situat *adj.* located
smoothie *n.m.* smoothie
snack *n.m.* snack
sobrant *adj.* leftover
sobre *adj.* over | *prep.* on, onto |
  adv. about | *n.m.* envelope
sobrecarregar *v.* overload
sobredosi *n.f.* overdose
sobreescalfar *v.* overheat
sobregiro *n.m.* overdraft
sobrenom *n.m.* nickname
sobrepès *adj.* overweight
sobreviure *v.* survive, outlive,
  outlast
sobtat *adj.* sudden
socarrar *v.* char, singe
soci *n.* partner *(business)*
sociable *adj.* sociable
social *adj.* social
socialista *adj./n.* socialist
socialment *adv.* socially
societat *n.f.* society
societat anònima *n.f. (Br.)*
  Public Limited Company (PLC);
  (U.S.) Publicly Traded Company
socorrista *n.* lifeguard
soda *n.f.* soda, soft drink

sodi *n.m.* sodium
sofisticat *adj.* sophisticated
sogra *n.f.* mother-in-law
sogre *n.m.* father-in-law
soja *n.f.* soy, soya, soybean
sojorn *n.m.* sojourn
sol *adj.* alone, single; lonely, lonesome | *n.m.* sun
sòl *n.m.* soil
sola *n.f.* sole
solar *adj.* solar
soldat *n.* soldier
sòlid *adj.* solid
solista *n.* soloist
sol·licitar *v.* request
sol·licitud *n.f.* request; application
solo *n.m.* solo
solt *adj.* loose
solter *adj.* single, unmarried | *n.m.* bachelor
soltera *n.f.* bachelorette
solució *n.f.* solution
somiar *v.* dream
somni *n.m.* dream, reverie
somnolent *adj.* drowsy
somriure *v./n.m.* smile
sonar *n.m.* sound
sonda *n.f.* probe
sopa *n.f.* soup
sopar *v.* dine | *n.m.* dinner, supper
sorbet *n.m.* sorbet, sherbet
sord *adj.* deaf
sorgir *v.* arise
sorgo *n.m.* sorghum
soroll *n.m.* noise, loudness
sorollós *adj.* loud; **més ~** louder
sorollosament *adv.* loudly
sorprendre *v.* surprise, astonish, amaze
sorprenent *adj.* surprising, amazing

sorprenentment *adv.* surprisingly
sorprès *adj.* surprised, amazed
sorpresa *n.f.* astonishment, surprise
sorra *n.f.* sand
sorrenc *adj.* sandy
sort *n.f.* luck
sortida *n.f.* exit, departure; outlet; output | *adj.* **de ~** outgoing *(clerical)*
sortida del sol *n.f.* sunrise
sortir *v.* depart
sospita *n.f.* suspicion
sospitar *v.* suspect
sospitós *adj.* suspicious | *n.* suspect
sostenible *adj.* sustainable
sostenidors *n.m.* brassiere, bra
sostenir *v.* sustain
sostre *n.m.* ceiling
sot *n.m.* pothole
sota *prep./adv.* below, beneath, under, underneath
soterrani *n.m.* basement
sotragueig *n.m.* rattle
sou *n.m.* salary
sovint *adv.* often, oftentimes
spork *n.m.* spork
Sr. *abbr.* Mr.
Sra. *abbr.* Mrs.
stir-fry *n.* stir-fry
strudel *n.m.* strudel
suar *v.* sweat
suau *adj.* soft
suaument *adv.* smoothly, softly, gently
suavitzant *n.m.* hair conditioner
subhasta *n.f.* auction
subjacent *adj.* underlying
subjectar *v.* fasten
submarí *adj.* underwater

submergir *v.* plunge, dip
subministrament *n.m.* supply
subministraments *n.m.* supplies
subministrar *v.* supply
subornar *v.* bribe
subratllar *v.* underline
subscripció *n.f.* subscription
subscriure *v.* subscribe
subsegüent *adj.* subsequent
subsegüentment *adv.* subsequently
substància *n.f.* substance
substancial *adj.* substantial
substancialment *adv.* substantially
substantiu *n.m.* noun
substituir *v.* substitute, replace
substitut *n.* replacement *(person)*
subterrani *adj.* underground
subtil *adj.* subtle
subtilesa *n.f.* quibble
subtilitzar *v.* quibble
subtítols *n.m.* subtitles
suburbi *n.m.* suburb
suc *n.m.* juice
suc de raïm *n.m.* grape juice
suc de taronja *n.m.* orange juice
succeir *v.* happen
sucós *adj.* juicy
sucre *n.m.* sugar
sud *n.m.* south | *adj.* **del ~**
   southern
Sud-Àfrica *n.f.* South Africa
Suècia *n.f.* Sweden
suèter *n.m.* sweater
suficient *adj.* sufficient
suficientment *adv.* sufficiently
sufix *n.m.* suffix

suflé *n.m.* soufflé
sufocar *v.* quell
suggeriment *n.m.* suggestion
suggerir *v.* suggest
suís *adj.* Swiss
Suïssa *n.f.* Switzerland
suite *n.f.* suite
suma *n.f.* sum
sundae *n.m.* sundae
suor *n.f.* sweat
súper *n.* super
superar *v.* overcome
superfície *n.f.* surface
superior *adj.* superior; upper
superlatiu *adj./n.m.* superlative
supermercat *n.m.* supermarket
superposar *v.* overlap
supervisar *v.* supervise
supervisió *n.f.* supervision
supervivència *n.f.* survival
suplement *n.m.* supplement
suplent *adj./n.* substitute, alternate
suport *n.m.* support
suportar *v.* support, bear
suposadament *adv.* purportedly
suposar *v.* suppose, assume
suposició *n.f.* assumption
supositori *n.m.* suppository
suprem *adj.* supreme, paramount
suprimir *v.* suppress
surf *n.m.* surfing | *v.* **fer ~ surf**
surfista *n.* surfer
Surinam *n.m.* Suriname
suro *n.m.* cork
sushi *n.m.* sushi

T

tabac *n.m.* tobacco
tabú *adj.* taboo
taca *n.f.* stain, spot *(mark)*
tacar *v.* stain
tafaner *adj.* nosy
tal *pron.* such
talent *n.m.* talent
talentós *adj.* talented
tall d'energia *n.m.* power outage
tallar *v.* cut, chop, incise
tallat *adj.* chopped
taller *n.m.* workshop
taló *n.m.* heel
talonari *n.m.* checkbook
talp *n.m.* mole
també *adv.* also, too
tambor *n.m.* drum
tamboret *n.m.* stool
tamís *n.m.* sieve
tampó *n.m.* tampon
tan *adv.* so
tanc de combustible *n.m.* fuel
  tank, gas tank
tanca *n.f.* fence
tancar *v.* close, shut; lock
tancar a fora *v.* lock out
tancar la cremallera *v.* zip
tancat *adj.* closed, shut
tap *n.m.* stopper
tapa *n.f.* lid
tapa de l'objectiu *n.f.* lens cap
tapaboques *n.m.* hubcap
tàpera *n.f.* caper
tapioca *n.f.* tapioca
tapís *n.m.* tapestry

taquilla *n.f.* box office
tard *adj.* late; **més** ~ later
tarda *n.f.* afternoon | *adv.* **a la** ~
  adv. p.m. *(early)*
tardor *n.f.* autumn, fall
targeta *n.f.* card
targeta de crèdit *n.f.* credit card
targeta postal *n.f.* postcard
targeta telefònica *n.f.* phone card
tarifa *n.f.* fare
tarongina *n.f.* orange blossom
taronja *n.f.* orange
taronja sanguina *n.f.* blood orange
tasca *n.f.* task
tassa *n.f.* cup, mug, coffee mug
taula *n.f.* table
taula de surf *n.f.* surfboard
taulell *n.m.* counter
taulell d'anuncis *n.m.* bulletin
  board
taulell d'informació *n.m.*
  information desk
tauler d'escacs *n.m.* chessboard
tauleta *n.f.* tablet
tauló *n.m.* plank
Taure *n.m.* Taurus
tauró *n.m.* shark
tavella de pèsol *n.f.* peapod
taxa *n.f.* rate
taxa de canvi *n.f.* exchange rate
taxi *n.m.* taxi, cab
te *n.m.* tea
te calent *n.m.* hot tea
te d'herbes *n.m.* herbal tea
te verd *n.m.* green tea

teatre *n.m.* theater
teatre d'òpera *n.m.* opera house
tebi *adj.* lukewarm
tecla d'esborrar *n.f.* backspace key
teclat *n.m.* keyboard
teclejar *v.* type
tècnic *adj.* technical
tècnica *n.f.* technique
tecnologia *n.f.* technology
teixir *v.* knit
teixit *n.m.* fabric; tissue *(biology)*
tela *n.f.* cloth
telecomunicacions *n.f.* telecommunications
telefèric *n.m.* cable car
telèfon *n.m.* telephone, phone
telèfon públic *n.m.* pay phone
telegrama *n.m.* telegram
telescopi *n.m.* telescope
televisió *n.f.* television
televisió per cable *n.f.* cable TV
tema *n.m.* theme, subject, topic
temperatura *n.f.* temperature
temperatura ambient *n.f.* room temperature
tempesta *n.f.* storm
tempestuós *adj.* stormy
templa *n.f.* temple *(head)*
temple *n.m.* temple *(religious)*
temporal *adj.* temporary
temporalment *adv.* temporarily
temporitzador *n.m.* timer
temps *n.m.* time; tense; weather
temps lliure *n.m.* free time
temps parcial *adj.* part-time
temptador *adj.* enticing
tenda *n.f.* tent
tendència *n.f.* tendency, trend
tendir *v.* tend

tendó *n.m.* tendon
tendre *adj.* tender
tenir *v.* have
tenir confiança en *v.* trust
tenir èxit *v.* succeed
tenir por *adj./v.* afraid (to be ~), scared (to be ~)
tenir por de *v.* fear
Tennessee *n.* Tennessee
tennis *n.m.* tennis
tensió *n.f.* tension, strain
tenyir *v.* dye
teoria *n.f.* theory
teòric *adj.* theoretical
teranyina *n.f.* spider web
terapèutic *adj.* therapeutic
teràpia *n.f.* therapy
teràpia física *n.f.* physical therapy
tercer *adj.* third
terminal *n.f.* terminal
terminal d'autobusos *n.f.* bus terminal
terminar *v.* end
termini *n.m.* term; deadline
termòmetre *n.m.* thermometer
termos *n.m.* thermos
terra *n.f.* ground, land, earth; Earth
terracota *n.f.* terra-cotta
terraplè *n.m.* rampart
terrassa *n.f.* terrace, deck *(of a building)*
terratrèmol *n.m.* earthquake, quake
terres baixes *n.f.* lowland
terrible *adj.* terrible, awful
terriblement *adv.* terribly, awfully
terrissa *n.f.* pottery, earthenware pot

terrissaire *n.* potter
territori *n.m.* territory
terrorisme *n.m.* terrorism
terrorista *n.* terrorist
testicle *n.m.* testicle
testimoni *n.m.* testimony; *n.*
  witness
tètanus *n.m.* tetanus
teu *pos. adj. sing.* your | *pron.*
  sing. yours
teula *n.f.* tile
teulada *n.f.* roof
teus *pos. adj. sing.* your | *pron.*
  sing. yours
teva *pos. adj. sing.* your | *pron.*
  sing. yours
teves *pos. adj. sing.* your | *pron.*
  sing. yours
texans *n.m.* jeans
Texas *n.* Texas
text *n.m.* text
tèxtil *n.m.* textile
textura *n.f.* texture
tia *n.f.* aunt
tija *n.f.* stem
tilàpia *n.f.* tilapia
til·ler *n.m.* linden tree
tímid *adj.* shy
tinent *n.* lieutenant
tint *n.m.* dye
tinta *n.f.* ink
tintoreria *n.f.* dry cleaner
tinya *n.f.* ringworm
típic *adj.* typical
típicament *adv.* typically
tipus *n.m.* type, kind; fellow
tipus de lletra *n.m.* font
tira *n.f.* strip
tirar *v.* throw, cast
tireta *n.f.* band-aid

tisores *n.f.* scissors
tisoreta *n.f.* earwig
titella *n.m.* puppet
títol *n.m.* title
titular *n.m.* headline; holder; *n.*
  incumbent
to *n.m.* tone
toc *n.m.* touch
toc de queda *n.m.* curfew
tocar *v.* touch
tòfona *n.f.* truffle
tofu *n.m.* tofu
tomàquet *n.m.* tomato
tomba *n.f.* grave
tona *n.f.* ton
tonyina *n.f.* tuna
torb *n.m.* blizzard
torçada *n.f.* twist, sprain
torçar *v.* sprain
torçar-se *v.* twist
torçat *adj.* sprained
tornada *n.f.* return
tornar *v.* return, come back; repay
tornavís *n.m.* screwdriver
toro *n.m.* bull
torrada *n.f.* toast
torradora *n.f.* toaster
torrar *v.* toast
torre *n.f.* tower
torrent *n.m.* torrent
torreta *n.f.* turret
torró *n.m.* nougat
tortuga *n.f.* tortoise, turtle
tortura *n.f.* torture
torturar *v.* torture
tos *n.m.* cough
tossir *v.* cough
tossut *adj.* stubborn
tot *adj.* whole | *pron.* everything
  | *adv.* **a ~ arreu** everywhere

total *adj.* total
totalment *adv.* totally
tothom *pron.* everyone, everybody
tots *pron.* all
tots dos *adj.* both
tovalló *n.m.* napkin
tovallola *n.f.* towel
tovalloleta de bebè *n.m.* baby
wipe
tòxic *adj.* toxic
toxiinfecció alimentària *n.f.*
food poisoning
toxina *n.f.* toxin
traçar *v.* trace
tracció a les quatre rodes *n.f.*
four-wheel drive
tractament *n.m.* treatment
tractament alternatiu *n.m.*
alternative treatment
tractar *v.* treat
tractat *n.m.* treaty
tradició *n.f.* tradition
tradicional *adj.* traditional
tradicionalment *adv.* traditionally
traducció *n.f.* translation
traductor *n.* translator
traduir *v.* translate
traficant de drogues *n.* drug
dealer
tragèdia *n.f.* tragedy
tràiler *n.m.* trailer
trama *n.f.* plot *(story)*
trampa *n.f.* trap, pitfall
trampolí *n.m.* diving board
tramvia *n.m.* streetcar, tramway
tranquil *adj.* calm, quiet, mild;
més ~ quieter
tranquil·lament *adv.* calmly
tranquil·litzar *v.* reassure

transacció *n.f.* transaction
transaccions *n.f.* dealings
transbordador *n.m.* shuttle, ferry
transcendental *adj.* momentous
transcripció *n.f.* transcript
transferència *n.f.* transfer
transferir *v.* transfer
transformació *n.f.* transformation
transformar *v.* transform
transfusió *n.f.* transfusion
transició *n.f.* transition
transigir *v.* compromise
trànsit *n.m.* transit; traffic
transmetre *v.* transmit
transmissió *n.f.* transmission
transmissió automàtica *n.f.*
automatic transmission
transmissió manual *n.f.* manual
transmission
transparent *adj.* transparent
transpiració *n.f.* perspiration
transpirar *v.* perspire
transport *n.m.* transportation,
transport
transport públic *n.m.* public
transportation
transportar *v.* transport
trasbalsar *v.* upset
trasplantament *n.m.* transplant
trasplantar *v.* transplant
trastorn d'horari *n.m.* jet lag
través: a ~ *prep.* across
treball *n.m.* work, labor, job
treballador *n.* worker
treballar *v.* work
treballs preparatoris *n.m.*
groundwork
tremend *adj.* tremendous
tremolar *v.* shiver, quiver, quake
tremolor *n.m.* shiver

tren *n.m.* train
tren local *n.m.* local train
tren ràpid *n.m.* express train
trencar *v.* break, smash
trencat *adj.* broken
trenta *num.* thirty
trentè *adj.* thirtieth
tres *num.* three
tresor *n.m.* treasure
tresoreria *n.f.* treasury
tret *n.m.* gunshot, shot
tretzè *adj.* thirteenth
tretze *num.* thirteen
trèvol *n.m.* clover
triangle *n.m.* triangle
triar *v.* pick *(choose)*
tribu *n.m.* tribe
tribunal *n.m.* court
tribut *n.m.* tribute
trimestre *n.m.* quarter *(time)*
triomf *n.m.* triumph
trípode *n.m.* tripod
tripulació *n.f.* crew
trist *adj.* sad, mournful, rueful
tristesa *n.f.* sadness
tro *n.m.* thunder
trobada *n.f.* meeting
trobar *v.* meet; find
trombosi *n.f.* thrombosis
tronc *n.m.* trunk *(tree)*

tropical *adj.* tropical
tros *n.m.* piece, bit
truc *n.m.* trick
trucada *n.f.* phone call; **fer una ~**
  v. make a phone call
trucada de llarga distància *n.f.*
  long-distance call
trucada internacional *n.f.*
  international call
trucada telefònica *n.f.* phone call
trucar *v.* call
truita *n.f.* trout; omelet
tu *pron. sing. fam.* you
tub *n.m.* tube, pipe
tub d'escapament *n.m.* exhaust
  pipe
tumor *n.m.* tumor
túnel *n.m.* tunnel
túnica *n.f.* robe
turbot *n.m.* turbot
turisme *n.m.* sightseeing
turista *n.* tourist
turmell *n.m.* ankle
turó *n.m.* hill
Turquia *n.f.* Turkey
tutela *n.f.* guardianship
tutor *n.* tutor; guardian
tutorial *n.m.* tutorial
TV *n.f.* TV

U

Ucraïna *n.f.* Ukraine
UE (Unió Europea) *abbr.* EU (European Union)
úlcera *n.f.* ulcer
ull *n.m.* eye
ulleres *n.f.* eyeglasses, glasses, spectacles; goggles
ulleres de sol *n.f.* sunglasses
ullet *n.m.* eyelet
últim *adj.* last, ultimate, latter
ultrasò *n.m.* ultrasound
ultramar: a ~ *adv.* overseas
un *indef. art.* a, an | *num.* one
un altre *adj.* another
una *indef. art.* a, an
una mica *adv.* somewhat | *n.f.* little (a ~)
una vegada *adv.* once, one time
unça *n.f.* ounce
ungla *n.f.* fingernail, nail *(hand or foot)*
ungla del peu *n.f.* toenail
ungüent *n.m.* ointment

únic *adj.* unique
uniforme *n.m.* uniform
unió *n.f.* union, junction
unir *v.* join, unite
unit *adj.* united
unitat *n.f.* unit
unitat de cures intensives *n.f.* intensive care unit
univers *n.m.* universe
universitat *n.f.* university
urbà *adj.* urban
urgent *adj.* urgent
URL *n.m.* URL
Uruguai *n.m.* Uruguay
ús *n.m.* use, usage
usar *v.* use
usat *adj.* used
usuari *n.* user
usura *n.f.* usury
Utah *n.* Utah
útil *adj.* useful, helpful
utilitat *n.f.* utility

V

vaca *n.f.* cow
vacances *n.f.* vacation, holiday
vacant *adj.* vacant | *n.m.* vacancy
vacil·lar *v.* hesitate
vacuna *n.f.* vaccine
vacunació *n.f.* vaccination
vacunar *v.* vaccinate
vaga *(protest) n.f.* strike | *v.* **fer ~** strike
vagabund *n.* rover
vagar *v.* roam, wander
vagina *n.f.* vagina
vagó llit *n.m.* sleeping car
vainilla *n.f.* vanilla
vaixell *n.m.* ship, boat
vaixell de vapor *n.m.* steamer *(ship)*
vaixella *n.f.* tableware
valent *adj.* brave
vàlid *adj.* valid
validació *n.f.* validation
validar *v.* validate
vall *n.f.* valley
valor *adj.* worth | *n.m.* value, worth
valoració *n.f.* valuation
valuós *adj.* valuable
vapor *n.m.* vapor, steam
vara *n.f.* rod
variable *adj.* variable
variació *n.f.* variation
variar *v.* vary
variat *adj.* varied
varietat *n.f.* variety
vast *adj.* vast

vector *n.m.* vector
vedella *n.f.* veal; heifer
vegà *adj./n.* vegan
vegades: de ~ *adv.* sometimes
vegetació *n.f.* vegetation
vegetarià *adj./n.* vegetarian
vehicle *n.m.* vehicle
veí *adj.* neighboring | *n.* neighbor
vel *n.m.* veil
vela *n.f.* sail
vell *adj.* old, aged
vellesa *n.f.* old age
vellut *n.m.* velvet
velocímetre *n.m.* speedometer
velocitat *n.f.* velocity, speed
vena *n.f.* vein
venda *n.f.* sale
venda al detall *n.f.* retail, retailing
vendaval *n.m.* gale
vendes *n.f.* sales
vendre *v.* sell
Veneçuela *n.f.* Venezuela
venedor *n.* vendor, seller
veneri *adj.* venereal
venir *v.* come
venjança *n.f.* revenge
vent *n.m.* wind
ventilador *n.m.* ventilator; fan
ventós *adj.* windy
ventre *n.m.* belly
venut *adj.* sold
verat *n.m.* mackerel
verb *n.m.* verb
verb amb partícules *n.m.* phrasal verb

verd *adj.* green
verdulaire *n.* greengrocer
verdura *n.f.* vegetable
verdures *n.f.* greens
veredicte *n.m.* verdict
verema *n.f.* vintage
verge *n.f.* virgin; Virgo
vergonya *n.f.* embarrassment, shame
vergonyós *adj.* embarrassing
verí *n.m.* venom, poison
verinós *adj.* poisonous
veritable *adj.* true
veritablement *adv.* truly
veritat *n.f.* truth
vermell *adj.* red
Vermont *n.* Vermont
vers *n.m.* verse
versió *n.f.* version
versió original *n.f.* original version
vertical *adj.* vertical
vespa *n.f.* wasp
vespre *n.m.* evening | *adv.* al ~ p.m. *(later)*
vessament *n.m.* spill
vessar *v.* spill, pour
vestíbul *n.m.* foyer, lobby, hallway
vestidor *n.m.* changing room
vestit *adj.* dressed | *n.m.* dress; suit; costume
vestit humit *n.m.* wetsuit
veu *n.f.* voice | *adv.* en ~ alta aloud
veure *v.* see
vi *n.m.* wine
vi calent *n.m.* mulled wine
via *prep.* via
vianant *n.* pedestrian
viatge *n.m.* trip, journey, voyage, tour, ride, travel

viatger *n.* traveler
viatjar *v.* travel
viatjar al lloc de treball *v.* commute
vibració *n.f.* vibration
vibrar *v.* vibrate; **fer** ~ rattle
víctima *n.* victim
victòria *n.f.* victory
victoriós *adj.* victorious
vida *n.f.* life
vida nocturna *n.f.* nightlife
vídeo *n.m.* video
vidre *n.m.* glass, pane
vidu *n.m.* widower
vídua *n.f.* widow
vieira *n.f.* scallops
vigilància *n.f.* surveillance
VIH *n.m.* HIV
VIH positiu *adj.* HIV-positive
vinagre *n.m.* vinegar
vinagreta *n.f.* vinaigrette
vinateria *n.f.* winery
vincle *n.m.* bond
vint *num.* twenty
vintè *adj.* twentieth
vinya *n.f.* vine; vineyard
viola *n.f.* viola
violació *n.f.* violation; rape; trespassing
violat *adj.* raped
violar *v.* violate; rape
violar la propietat *v.* trespass
violència *n.f.* violence
violent *adj.* violent
violentament *adv.* violently
violí *n.m.* violin
violinista *n.* violinist
violoncel *n.m.* cello
Virgínia *n.* Virginia
Virgínia de l'Oest *n.* West Virginia

virtual *adj.* virtual
virtualment *adv.* virtually
virtut *n.f.* virtue
virus *n.m.* virus
visat *n.m.* visa
visera *n.f.* visor
visible *adj.* visible
visió *n.f.* vision
visita *n.f.* visit
visita de pàgina *n.f.* pageview
visita guiada *n.f.* guided tour
visita turística *n.f.* sightseeing tour
visitant *n.* visitor
visitar *v.* visit
vista *n.f.* view, sight
visual *adj.* visual
vital *adj.* vital
vitamina *n.f.* vitamin
vitrall *n.m.* stained glass
viu *adj.* alive, living
viure *v.* live
vocabulari *n.m.* vocabulary
vocal *adj.* vocal | *n.f.* vowel
vodka *n.m.* vodka
vol *n.m.* flight
vol xàrter *n.m.* charter flight
voladís *adj.* overhanging
volant *adj.* flying | *n.m.* steering wheel; ruffle
volants *adj.* ruffled
volar *v.* fly
volcà *n.m.* volcano

voleibol *n.m.* volleyball
voler *v.* want
volta *n.f.* vault
voltant: al ~ *adv.* around | *adj.* surrounding
voltants *n.m.* surroundings
voltatge *n.m.* voltage
volum *n.m.* volume
voluntari *adj.* voluntary | *n.* volunteer
voluntàriament *adv.* voluntarily
voluntat *n.f.* will
vòmit *n.m.* vomit
vomitar *v.* vomit
vora *n.f.* edge, rim
vorera *n.f.* sidewalk
vosaltres *pron. pl. fam.* you
vostè *pron. sing. form.* you
vostès *pron. pl. form.* you
vostra *pos. adj. pl.* your | *pron. pl.* yours
vostre *pos. adj. pl.* your | *pron. pl.* yours
vostres *pos. adj. pl.* your | *pron. pl.* yours
vot *n.m.* vote; vow
votant *n.* voter
votar *v.* vote
vuit *num.* eight
vuitanta *num.* eighty
vuitantè *adj.* eightieth
vuitè *adj.* eighth

W

Washington *n.* Washington
Washington DC *n.m.* Washington, DC
web *n.m.* web
whisky *n.m.* whiskey; scotch
windsurf *n.m.* windsurfing
Wisconsin *n.* Wisconsin
Wyoming *n.* Wyoming

X-Z

xai *n.m.* lamb
xalet *n.m.* chalet
xampany *n.m.* champagne
xampú *n.m.* shampoo
xancletes *n.f.* flip-flops
xantatge a algú: fer ~ *v.* black-mail
xarampió *n.m.* measles
xarcuteria *n.f.* charcuterie; delicatessen, deli
xarop *n.m.* syrup
xarop d'auró *n.m.* maple syrup
xarop de xocolata *n.m.* chocolate syrup
xàrter *n.m.* charter
xarxa *n.f.* net, network
xarxa de pesca *n.f.* fishing net
xec reclamatiu *n.m.* claim check
xef *n.m.* chef
xemeneia *n.f.* chimney
xerès *n.m.* sherry
xèrif *n.m.* sheriff
xeringa *n.f.* syringe
xerrar *v.* chat, prattle
xiclet *n.m.* chewing gum, gum
xicoira *n.f.* chicory
xicot *n.m.* boyfriend
xicota *n.f.* girlfriend
Xile *n.m.* Chile
xili *n.m.* chili
xili de Jalapa *n.m.* jalapeño

ximple *adj.* silly
Xina *n.f.* China
xinès *adj.* Chinese
xinxa *n.f.* bug
xip *n.m.* chip
Xipre *n.m.* Cyprus
xirivia *n.f.* parsnip
xiular *v.* whistle
xiulet *n.m.* whistle
xoc *n.m.* shock; crash
xocar *v.* shock
xocolata *n.f.* chocolate
xocolata desfeta *n.f.* hot chocolate
xofer *n.* chauffeur
xoriço *n.m.* chorizo
xuclar *v.* suck
xumet *n.m.* pacifier

zebra *n.f.* zebra
zero *num.* zero
zinc *n.m.* zinc
zodíac *n.m.* Zodiac
zombi *n.* zombie
zona *n.f.* zone
zona comercial *n.f.* commercial zone
zonificació *n.f.* zoning
zoo *n.m.* zoo

ENGLISH-CATALAN
DICTIONARY

A

a *indef. art.* un, una
a.m. *adv. (morning)* del matí, *(early morning)* de la matinada
abandon *v.* abandonar
abandoned *adj.* abandonat
abbey *n.f.* abadia
abbreviation *n.f.* abreviatura
abdomen *n.m.* abdomen
abduction *n.m.* segrest
ability *n.f.* capacitat
able *adj.* capaç
aboard *adv.* a bord
aboriginal *adj.* aborigen
abort *v.* avortar
abortion *n.m.* avortament
about *adv.* sobre
above *adv.* damunt
abroad *adv.* a l'estranger
abrupt *adj.* abrupte
abscess *n.m.* abscés
abscond *v.* escapolir
absence *n.f.* absència
absent *adj.* absent
absinthe *n.f.* absenta
absolute *adj.* absolut
absolutely *adv.* absolutament
absorb *v.* absorbir
abstract *adj.* abstracte
absurd *adj.* absurd
abuse *n.m.* abús
academic *adj.* acadèmic
academy *n.f.* acadèmia
accelerator *n.m.* accelerador
accent *n.m.* accent
accept *v.* acceptar

acceptable *adj.* acceptable
access *n.m.* accés
accident *n.m.* accident
accidental *adj.* accidental
accidentally *adv.* accidentalment
accommodation *n.m.* allotjament
accompany *v.* acompanyar
accomplish *v.* acomplir
accomplished *adj.* complet
accomplishment *n.m.* assoliment
accordance *n.m.* acord
account *n.m.* compte
accountant *n.* comptable
accumulation *n.f.* acumulació
accumulate *v.* acumular
accurate *adj.* exacte
accurately *adv.* exactament
accuse *v.* acusar
ache *n.m.* dolor
achieve *v.* aconseguir
achievement *n.m.* assoliment
acid *n.m.* àcid
acidify *v.* acidificar
acknowledge *v.* reconèixer
acne *n.f.* acne
acorn *n.f.* gla
acquaintance *n.* conegut
acquire *v.* adquirir
acquisition *n.f.* adquisició
acquit *v.* absoldre
acquittal *n.f.* absolució
acre *n.m.* acre
across *prep.* a través
acrylic *adj.* acrílic
act *n.m.* acte

action *n.f.* acció
activate *v.* activar
active *adj.* actiu
actively *adv.* activament
activist *n.f.* activista
activity *n.f.* activitat
actor *n.m.* actor
actress *n.f.* actriu
actual *adj.* real
actually *adv.* de fet
acupuncture *n.f.* acupuntura
acute *adj.* agut
adapt *v.* adaptar
adapter *n.m.* adaptador
add *v.* afegir
addicted *adj.* addicte
addiction *n.f.* addicció
addition *n.f.* addició
additional *adj.* addicional
address *n.f.* adreça
addressee *n.m.* destinatari
adept *adj.* adepte
adequate *adj.* adequat
adequately *adv.* adequadament
adhere *v.* adherir
adherence *n.f.* adhesió
adhesion *n.f.* adhesió
adhesive *adj.* adhesiu
adjacent *adj.* adjacent
adjective *n.m.* adjectiu
adjoining *adj.* contigu
adjust *v.* ajustar
adjustment *n.m.* ajust
administration *n.f.* administració
administrative *adj.* administratiu
admiration *n.f.* admiració
admire *v.* admirar
admission *n.f.* admissió
admit *v.* admetre
admittance *n.f.* admissió

adopt *v.* adoptar
adorable *adj.* adorable
adore *v.* adorar
adulation *n.f.* adulació
adult *n.* adult
advance *v.* avançar
advanced *adj.* avançat
advantage *n.m.* avantatge
adventure *n.f.* aventura
adverb *n.m.* adverbi
adversary *n.* adversari
adversity *n.f.* adversitat
advertise *v.* anunciar
advertisement *n.m.* anunci
advertising *n.f.* publicitat
advice *n.m.* consell
advise *v.* aconsellar
advisor *n.* conseller
advocacy *n.f.* defensa
advocate *v.* defensar
aerial *adj.* aeri
aerobic *n.m.* aeròbic
aesthetic *adj.* estètic
affair *n.m.* assumpte
affect *v.* afectar
affectation *n.f.* afectació
affection *n.m.* afecte
affidavit *n.f.* declaració jurada
affiliation *n.f.* afiliació
affinity *n.f.* afinitat
affirm *v.* afirmar
affirmation *n.f.* afirmació
afflict *v.* afligir
affliction *n.f.* aflicció
affluence *n.f.* afluència
afford *v.* permetre
afraid (to be ~) *adj.* tenir por
Africa *n.f.* Àfrica
African *adj.* africà
after *prep.* després de | *adv.* després

afternoon *n.f.* tarda
aftershave *n.f.* loció postafaitat
afterwards *adv.* després
again *adv.* de nou
against *prep.* contra
agave *n.f.* atzavara
age *n.f.* edat
aged *adj.* vell
agency *n.f.* agència
agenda *n.m.* ordre del dia
agent *n.* agent
aggravate *v.* agreujar
aggravation *n.* agreujament
aggression *n.f.* agressió
aggressive *adj.* agressiu
agile *adj.* àgil
aging *adj.* envelliment
agitate *v.* agitar
agitation *n.f.* agitació
ago *adv.* **five years ago** fa cinc
anys (*Lit:* five years have oc-
curred)
agonize *v.* angoixar
agony *(physical) n.m.* dolor agut;
(mental) n.f. angoixa
agrarian *adj.* agrari
agree *v.* assentir
agreement *n.m.* acord
agricultural *adj.* agrícola
agriculture *n.f.* agricultura
agronomy *n.f.* agronomia
ahead *adv.* davant
aid *n.f.* ajuda
AIDS *n.f.* SIDA
ailing *adj.* malalt
ailment *n.f.* malaltia
aim *v. (point)* apuntar; *(aspire)*
aspirar | *n.m.* objectiu
air *n.m.* aire
air conditioning *n.m.* aire condi-

cionat
air-conditioned *adj.* amb aire
condicionat
aircraft *n.m.* avió
airline *n.f.* aerolínia
airmail *n.m.* correu aeri
airplane *n.m.* avió
airport *n.m.* aeroport
aisle *n.m.* passadís
Alabama *n.* Alabama
alarm *n.f.* alarma
alarmed *adj.* alarmat
alarming *adj.* alarmant
Alaska *n.* Alaska
Albania *n.f.* Albània
albeit *conj.* encara que
album *n.m.* àlbum
alchemy *n.f.* alquímia
alcohol *n.m.* alcohol
alcoholic *adj./n.* alcohòlic
alcove *n.m.* nínxol
ale *n.f.* cervesa
alfalfa sprouts *n.m.* brots d'alfals
algebra *n.f.* àlgebra
alias *n.m.* àlies
alibi *n.f.* coartada
alien *adj.* estrany | *n.* estranger
align *v.* alinear
alignment *n.f.* alineació
alimony *n.f.* pensió alimentària
alive *adj.* viu
all *pron.* tots
all right *adj.* satisfactori
allegation *n.f.* al·legació
allegiance *n.f.* lleialtat
allergen *n.m.* al·lergen
allergic *adj.* al·lèrgic
allergy *n.f.* al·lèrgia
alleviation *n.m.* alleujament
alley *n.m.* carreró

allied *adj.* aliat
allocate *v.* assignar
allocation *n.f.* assignació
allow *v.* permetre
allowance *n.f.* pensió
allowed *adj.* permès
alluring *adj.* seductor
allusion *n.f.* al·lusió
ally *n.* aliat
almond *n.f.* ametlla
almost *adv.* quasi
alms *n.f.* almoina
aloe *n.m.* àloe
alone *adj.* sol
along *prep.* al llarg de
alongside *prep.* al costat de
aloud *adv.* en veu alta
alphabet *n.m.* alfabet
alphabetical *adj.* alfabètic
alphabetically *adv.* alfabèticament
already *adv.* ja
also *adv.* també
altar *n.m.* altar
alter *v.* alterar
alteration *n.f.* alteració
alternate *adj.* suplent
alternative *adj.* alternatiu | *n.f.*
  alternativa
alternative treatment *n.m.*
  tractament alternatiu
alternatively *adv.* alternativament
alternator *n.m.* alternador
although *conj.* encara que
altimeter *n.m.* altímetre
altitude *n.f.* altitud
altogether *adv.* en conjunt
aluminum *n.m.* alumini
always *adv.* sempre
amaranth *n.m.* amarant
amateur *n.* aficionat

amaze *v.* sorprendre
amazed *adj.* sorprès
amazing *adj.* sorprenent
ambassador *n.m.* ambaixador
ambiguity *n.f.* ambigüitat
ambiguous *adj.* ambigu
ambition *n.f.* ambició
amble *v.* amblar
ambrosia *n.f.* ambrosia
ambulance *n.f.* ambulància
ambush *v.* emboscar
amenable *adj.* dòcil
amenity *n.f.* servei
American *adj.* americà
amiable *adj.* amable
amicable *adj.* amistós
amino acid *n.m.* aminoàcid
amity *n.* amistat
amnesia *n.f.* amnèsia
amnesty *n.f.* amnistia
among *prep.* entre
amount *n.f.* quantitat
ampere *n.m.* ampere
ample *adj.* ampli
amplification *n.f.* amplificació
amplifier *n.m.* amplificador
amplify *v.* amplificar
ampule *n.f.* ampolla
amulet *n.m.* amulet
amuse *v.* divertir
amused *adj.* divertit
amusement *n.f.* diversió
amusing *adj.* divertit
an *indef. art.* un, una
analogy *n.f.* analogia
analysis *n.f.* anàlisi
analyst *n.* analista
analyze *v.* analitzar
anarchist *n.* anarquista
anatomy *n.f.* anatomia

ancestor *n.* avantpassat
anchor *n.f.* àncora
anchorage *n.m.* ancoratge
anchovy *n.f.* anxova
ancient *adj.* antic
and *conj.* i
Andorra *n.f.* Andorra
anemia *n.f.* anèmia
anemic *adj.* anèmic
anesthesia *n.f.* anestèsia
anesthetic *adj.* anestèsic
angel *n.m.* àngel
anger *n.f.* ira
angina *n.f.* angina
angle *n.m.* angle
angler fish *n.m.* rap
angry *adj.* enfadat
angular *adj.* angular
animal *n.m.* animal
animated *adj.* animat
animation *n.f.* animació
animosity *n.f.* animositat
anise *n.m.* anís
ankle *n.m.* turmell
annihilate *v.* anihilar
annihilation *n.f.* anihilació
anniversary *n.m.* aniversari
announce *v.* anunciar
announcement *n.m.* anunci
announcer *n.* locutor
annoy *v.* molestar
annoyed *adj.* irritat
annoying *adj.* molest
annual *adj.* anual
annually *adv.* anualment
anonymity *n.m.* anonimat
anonymous *adj.* anònim
anorak *n.m.* anorac
another *adj.* un altre
answer *n.f.* resposta

ant *n.f.* formiga
Antarctica *n.f.* Antàrtida
antelope *n.m.* antílop
antenna *n.f.* antena
anthem *n.m.* himne
anthology *n.f.* antologia
anti- *prefix* anti
anti-government *adj.* anti-govern
antibiotic *n.m.* antibiòtic
antibody *n.m.* anticòs
anticipate *v.* anticipar
antidote *n.m.* antídot
antifreeze *n.m.* anticongelant
antinuclear *adj.* antinuclear
antipathy *n.f.* antipatia
antique *n.* antiguitat
antiseptic *adj./n.m.* antisèptic
antler *n.f.* banya
anxiety *n.f.* ansietat
anxious *adj.* ansiós
anxiously *adv.* ansiosament
any *adj.* qualsevol
anybody *pron.* algú
anyone *pron.* qualsevol
anything *pron.* qualsevol cosa
anyway *adv.* de totes maneres
anywhere *adv.* a qualsevol lloc
apart *adv.* a part
apart from *prep.* a part de
apartment *n.m.* apartament
aperitif *n.m.* aperitiu
apiary *n.m.* abellar
apologize *v.* disculpar
apology *n.f.* apologia
apostrophe *n.m.* apòstrof
apparent *adj.* aparent
apparently *adv.* aparentment
appeal *n.f.* apel·lació
appear *v.* aparèixer
appearance *n.f.* aparença

appendicitis *n.f.* apendicitis
appendix *n.m. (anat.)* apèndix
appetite *n.f.* gana
appetizer *n.m.* aperitiu
appetizing *adj.* apetitós
apple *n.f.* poma
application *n.f.* sol·licitud
apply *v.* aplicar
appoint *v.* nomenar
appointment *n.f.* cita
appraisal *n.f.* avaluació
appraise *v.* avaluar
appreciate *v.* apreciar
apprentice *n.* aprenent
approach *v.* apropar
appropriate *adj.* apropiat
approval *n.f.* aprovació
approve (of) *v.* aprovar
approximate *adj.* aproximat
approximately *adv.* aproximadament
apricot *n.* albercoc
April *n.m.* abril
apron *n.m.* davantal
apse *n.f.* absis
aquarium *n.m.* aquàrium
Aquarius *n.* aquari
aqueduct *n.m.* aqüeducte
Arab *adj.* àrab
Arabic *n.m.* àrab
arable *adj.* cultivable
arbitration *n.m.* arbitratge
arcade game *n.m.* joc d'arcade
arch *n.m.* arc
archbishop *n.m.* arquebisbe
archeological *adj.* arqueològic
archeology *n.f.* arqueologia
architect *n.* arquitecte
architectural *adj.* arquitectònic
architecture *n.f.* arquitectura

archive *n.m.* arxiu
Arctic *n.* àrtic
area *n.f.* àrea
Argentina *n.f.* Argentina
argue *v.* discutir
argument *n.m.* argument
Aries *n.* àries
arise *v.* sorgir
aristocracy *n.f.* aristocràcia
aristocrat *n.* aristòcrata
Arizona *n.* Arizona
ark *n.f.* arca
Arkansas *n.* Arkansas
arm *n.m.* braç
armed *adj.* armat
Armenia *n.f.* Armènia
armor *n.f.* armadura
armory *n.f.* armeria
arms *n.f. (weapons)* armes
army *n.m.* exèrcit
aroma *n.f.* aroma
around *adv.* al voltant
arrange *v.* organitzar, arranjar
arrangement *n.m.* arranjament
array *n.f.* formació
arrest *v.* arrestar
arrival *n.f.* arribada
arrive *v.* arribar
arrow *n.f.* fletxa
arsenal *n.m.* arsenal
arsenic *n.m.* arsènic
arson *n.m.* incendi provocat
art *n.m.* art
artery *n.f.* artèria
arthritis *n.f.* artritis
artichoke *n.f.* carxofa
article *n.m.* article
artificial *adj.* artificial
artificially *adv.* artificialment
artillery *n.f.* artilleria

artisan *n.* artesà
artist *n.* artista
artistic *adj.* artístic
artwork *n.f.* obra d'art
arugula *n.f.* ruca
as *prep./conj./adv.* com
ascetic *n.* asceta
ash *n.f.* cendra
ashamed *adj.* avergonyit
ashtray *n.m.* cendrer
Asia *n.f.* Àsia
Asian *adj.* asiàtic
aside *adv.* a part
ask *v.* preguntar
asleep *adj.* adormit
asparagus *n.m.* espàrrec
aspartame *n.m.* aspartam
aspect *n.m.* aspecte
aspic *n.m.* àspic
aspirin *n.f.* aspirina
assassin *n.* assassí
assassinate *v.* assassinar
assassination *n.m.* assassinat
assault *n.m.* assalt
assaulted *adj.* assaltat
assess *v.* avaluar
assessment *n.f.* avaluació
asset *n.m.* haver
assist *v.* assistir
assistance *n.f.* assistència
assistant *n.* ajudant
associate *v.* associar
association *n.f.* associació
assorted *adj.* assortit
assume *v.* suposar
assumption *n.f.* suposició
assure *v.* assegurar
asterisk *n.m.* asterisc
asteroid *n.m.* asteroide
asthma *n.f.* asma

asthmatic *adj.* asmàtic
astonish *v.* sorprendre
astonishment *n.f.* sorpresa
astray *adv.* per mal camí
astrology *n.f.* astrologia
astronaut *n.* astronauta
astronomer *n.* astrònom
astronomy *n.f.* astronomia
asylum *n.m.* asil
at *prep.* a
atheist *n.* ateu
athletics *n.m.* atletisme
ATM *n.m.* caixer automàtic
atmosphere *n.f.* atmosfera
atom *n.m.* àtom
atomic *adj.* atòmic
atonement *n.f.* expiació
attach *v.* adjuntar
attached *adj.* adjunt
attack *n.m.* atac
attempt *n.m.* atemptat, intent
attempted *adj.* atemptat
attend *v.* assistir
attention *n.f.* atenció
attitude *n.f.* actitud
attorney *n.* advocat
attract *v.* atreure
attraction *n.f.* atracció
attractive *adj.* atractiu
attribute *n.m.* atribut
auction *n.f.* subhasta
audience *n.f.* audiència
audio-guide *n.f.* audioguia
audit *v.* auditar; intervenir | *n.f.*
  auditoria; intervenció
auditor *n.* auditor; interventor
auditorium *n.m.* auditori
auditory *adj.* auditiu
August *n.m.* agost
aunt *n.f.* tia

aurora *n.f.* Aurora
auspice *n.m.* auspici
auspicious *adj.* propici
austere *adj.* auster
austerity *n.f.* austeritat
Australia *n.f.* Austràlia
Australian *adj.* australià
Austria *n.f.* Àustria
authentic *adj.* autèntic
authenticity *n.f.* autenticitat
author *n.* autor
authority *n.f.* autoritat
authorize *v.* autoritzar
authorized *adj.* autoritzat
autocracy *n.f.* autocràcia
autocrat *n.* autòcrata
automatic *adj.* automàtic
automatic transmission *n.f.*
  transmissió automàtica
automatically *adv.* automàticament
automobile *n.m.* automòbil
autumn *n.f.* tardor
auxiliary *n.* auxiliar

availability *n.f.* disponibilitat
available *adj.* disponible
avalanche *n.f.* allau
avant-garde *n.f.* avantguarda
avenue *n.f.* avinguda
average *adj.* mitjana
aviation *n.f.* aviació
avocado *n.m.* alvocat
avoid *v.* evitar
awake *adj.* despert
award *n.m.* premi
aware *adj.* conscient
awareness *n.f.* consciència
away *adv.* lluny
awe *n.f.* reverència
awful *adj.* terrible
awfully *adv.* terriblement
awkward *adj.* incòmode
awkwardly *adv.* maldestrament
axe *n.f.* destral
axis *n.m.* eix
axle *n.m.* arbre
Azerbaijan *n.m.* Azerbaidjan

B

babble *v.* balbotejar
baby *n.m.* bebè
baby wipe *n.m.* tovalloleta de bebè
babysitter *n.* cangur
bachelor *n.m.* solter
bachelorette *n.f.* soltera
back *n.f.* esquena | *adv.* endarrere
background *n.m.* fons
backhand *n.m.* revés
backpack *n.f.* motxilla
backspace key *n.f.* tecla d'esborrar
backward *adj.* endarrerit
bacon *n.f.* cansalada
bacteria *n.m.* bacteris
bacterial *adj.* bacterià
bad *adj.* mal, dolent
bad-tempered *adj.* malhumorat
badly *adv.* malament
badminton *n.m.* bàdminton
bag *n.f.* bossa
baggage *n.m.* equipatge
bail *n.f.* fiança
bail bond *n.f.* fiança
bailiff *n.m.* agutzil
bake *v.* fornejar
baked *adj.* fornejat
baker *n.* forner
bakery *n.f.* fleca
baking pan *n.f.* cassola de forn
baking powder *n.m.* llevat
baking sheet *n.f.* safata de forn
baking soda *n.m.* bicarbonat de
  sodi
balance *n.m.* equilibri
balcony *n.m.* balcó

balding *adj.* de calvície incipient
ball *n.f.* pilota
ballet *n.m.* ballet
balloon *n.m.* globus
ballot *n.f.* papereta
balm *n.m.* bàlsam
bamboo *n.m.* bambú
ban *v.* prohibir
banana *n.m.* plàtan
band *n.m.* grup
band-aid *n.f.* tireta
bandage *n.f.* bena
bandit *n.m.* bandit
bank *n.m.* banc
bank account *n.m.* compte bancari
banker *n.* banquer
banknote *n.m.* bitllet
bankrupt *adj.* insolvent
bankruptcy *n.f.* fallida
baptism *n.m.* baptisme
bar *(tavern)* *n.m.* bar
barber *n.m.* barber
bargain *n.f.* ganga
bark *n.f.* escorça
barley *n.m.* ordi
barometer *n.m.* baròmetre
barrel *n.m.* barril
barrier *n.f.* barrera
bartender *n.m.* cambrer
base *n.f.* base
basement *n.m.* soterrani
basic *adj.* bàsic
basically *adv.* bàsicament
basil *n.f.* alfàbrega
basin *n.f.* gibrella

basis *n.f.* base
basket *n.f.* cistella
basketball *n.m.* bàsquet
bass *n.m.* baix
bastard *n.m.* malparit
baste *v. (culinary)* regar
bat *(zool.) n.m.* rat-penat
bath *n.m.* bany
bathe *v.* banyar
bathing suit *n.m.* banyador
bathroom *n.f.* cambra de bany
batter *(food) v.* arrebossar | *n.m.*
 arrebossat
battery *n.f.* pila
battle *n.f.* batalla
battlement *n.m.* merlet
bay *n.f.* badia
bay leaf *n.f.* fulla de llorer
be *v.* ser, ésser, estar
beach *n.f.* platja
beacon *n.f.* balisa
beak *n.m.* bec
beam *n.m.* raig
bean *n.f.* mongeta
bear *v. (carry)* suportar | *n.m.*
 (animal) os
beard *n.f.* barba
beat *v.* pegar
beautiful *adj.* bonic
beautifully *adv.* bellament
beauty *n.f.* bellesa
because *conj.* perquè
become *v.* esdevenir
bed *n.m.* llit
bedding *n.f.* roba de llit
bedroom *n.m.* dormitori
bee *n.f.* abella
beef *n.f.* carn de vaca
beehive *n.m.* rusc
beer *n.f.* cervesa

beet *n.f.* remolatxa
beetle *n.m.* escarabat
beetroot *n.f.* remolatxa
before *prep.* abans de
beforehand *adv.* abans
beggar *n.m.* captaire
begin *v.* començar
beginner *n.* principiant
beginning *n.m.* principi
behalf *n.m.* benefici
behave *v.* comportar-se
behavior *n.m.* comportament
behind *prep.* darrere
beige *adj.* beix
being *n.m.* ésser
Belarus *n.f.* Bielorússia
Belgium *n.f.* Bèlgica
belief *n.f.* creença
believe *v.* creure
Belize *n.m.* Belize
bell *n.f.* campana
bell pepper *n.m.* pebrot
belly *n.m.* ventre
belong *v.* pertànyer
below *prep./adv.* sota
belt *n.m.* cinturó
bench *n.f.* banqueta, banc
bench warrant *n.m.* ordre de
 detenció
bend *v.* doblegar
beneath *prep.* sota
benefit *n.m.* benefici
benevolence *n.f.* benevolència
benevolent *adj.* benèvol
benign *adj.* benigne
bent *adj.* doblegat
berry *n.f.* baia
berth *n.f.* llitera
beside *prep.* al costat de
best *adj.* millor

bet v. apostar
better adj. millor
between prep. entre
beverage n.f. beguda
beware v. anar amb compte
beyond adv. més enllà
bias n.m. prejudici
bib n.m. pitet
Bible n.f. Bíblia
bicycle n.f. bicicleta
bicyclist n. ciclista
bid v. oferir
bidet n.m. bidet
big adj. gran
bigger adj. més gran
bikini n.m. biquini
bilingual adj. bilingüe
bill n.f. factura
billiards n.m. billar
billion n.m. mil milions
bin n.f. paperera
binary adj. binari
bind v. lligar
binoculars n.m. binocles
biodegradable adj. biodegradable
biodiversity n.f. biodiversitat
biography n.f. biografia
biological adj. biològic
biology n.f. biologia
biopsy n.f. biòpsia
biotechnology n.f. biotecnologia
bird n.m. ocell
birth n.m. naixement
birthday n.m. aniversari
birthday party n.f. festa
   d'aniversari
biscuit n.f. galeta
bishop n.m. bisbe
bison n.m. bisó
bit n.m. tros

bite v. mossegar
bitter adj. amarg
bitterly adv. amb amargura
bizarre adj. estrany
black adj. negre
black currant n.f. grosella negra
blackberry n.f. mora
blackmail v. fer xantatge a algú
bladder n.f. bufeta
blade n.f. fulla
blame v. culpar
bland adj. insípid
blank adj. en blanc
blanket n.f. manta
blankly adv. amb la mirada perduda
blaze n.m. incendi
bleach n.m. lleixiu
bleed v. sagnar
blend v. barrejar
blender n.f. liquadora
bless v. beneir
blind adj. cec
blink v. parpellejar
blister n.f. butllofa
blizzard n.m. torb
bloated adj. inflat
block n.m. bloc
blockage n.f. obstrucció
blocked adj. obstruït
blonde adj. ros
blood n.f. sang
blood orange n.f. taronja sanguina
blood type n.m. grup sanguini
blouse n.f. brusa
blow v. bufar
blow-dry v. assecar amb assecador
blow-dryer n.m. assecador de
   cabells
blue adj. blau
blueberry n.m. nabiu

bluff *v.* enganyar
blurred *adj.* borrós
blush *n.m.* coloret
board *n.m.* post
boarding *n.m.* embarcament
boat *n.m.* vaixell
body *n.m.* cos
boil *v.* bullir
boiled *adj.* bullida
boiler *n.f.* caldera
Bolivia *n.f.* Bolívia
bomb *n.f.* bomba
bombard *v.* bombardejar
bombardment *n.m.* bombardeig
bon appetit! *phr.* bon profit!
bon voyage! *phr.* bon viatge!
bond *n.m.* vincle
bone *n.m.* os
boneless *adj.* sense ossos
bonus *n.f.* prima
book *n.m.* llibre
booking *n.f.* reserva
booklet *n.m.* fullet
bookmark *n.m.* punt de llibre
bookstore *n.f.* llibreria
boom *n.m.* boom
boost *n.f.* empenta
boot *n.f.* bota
border *n.f.* frontera
bore *v.* avorrir
bored *adj.* avorrit
boring *adj.* avorrit
born *adj.* nascut
borrow *v.* manllevar
borrower *n.* prestatari
Bosnia and Herzegovina *n.f.*
Bòsnia i Hercegovina
bosom *n.m.* pit
boss *n.* cap
botanical *adj.* botànic

botanical garden *n.m.* jardí botànic
both *adj.* tots dos
bother *v.* molestar
bottle *n.f.* ampolla
bottled *adj.* embotellat
bottom *n.m.* fons
bouillon *n.m.* caldo
bound *adj.* lligat
boundary *n.m.* límit
bourgeois *adj.* burgès
bowel *n.m.* intestí
bowl *n.m.* bol
bowling *n.f.* bitlles
bowling ball *n.f.* bola de bitlles
box *n.f.* caixa
box office *n.f.* taquilla
boxing *n.f.* boxa
boy *n.m.* noi
boycott *v.* boicotejar | *n.m.* boicot
boyfriend *n.m.* xicot
boysenberry *n.m.* boysenberry
bra *n.m.* sostenidors
bracelet *n.m.* braçalet
braces *n.m.* ferros
bracket *n.m.* parèntesi
braille *n.m.* braille
brain *n.m.* cervell
braise *v.* coure a foc lent
braised *adj.* cuit a foc lent
brake *n.m.* fre
bran *n.m.* segó
branch *n.f.* branca
brand *n.f.* marca
brass *n.m.* llautó
brassiere *n.m.* sostenidors
brave *adj.* valent
Brazil *n.m.* Brasil
Brazil nut *n.f.* nou del Brasil
breach *v.* infringir
bread *n.m.* pa; **loaf of ~** *n.f.* barra
de pa

breadcrumbs *n.m.* pa ratllat
breaded *adj.* arrebossat
breading *n.m.* arrebossament
break *v.* trencar
breakdown *n.f.* avaria
breakfast *n.m.* esmorzar
breast *n.m.* pit
breastfeed *v.* alletar
breastfeeding *n.f.* lactància
  materna
breath *n.m.* alè
breathe *v.* respirar
breathing *n.f.* respiració
breed *v.* reproduir-se
breeze *n.f.* brisa
brewery *n.f.* cerveseria
bribe *v.* subornar
brick *n.m.* maó
bridal *adj.* nupcial
bride *n.f.* núvia
bridegroom *n.m.* nuvi
bridesmaid *n.f.* dama d'honor
bridge *n.m.* pont
brief *adj.* breu
briefly *adv.* breument
briefs *n.m.* calçotets
bright *adj.* brillant
brightly *adv.* brillantment
brilliant *adj.* brillant
brine *n.f.* salmorra
bring *v.* portar
brisket *n.f.* carn del pit
Britain *n.f.* Gran Bretanya
British *adj.* britànic
broad *adj.* ample
broadband *n.f.* banda ampla
broadcast *n.f.* emissió
broadly *adv.* en general
broccoli *n.m.* bròquil
brochure *n.m.* fullet

broil *v.* rostir
broken *adj.* trencat
broker *n.* corredor
bronchitis *n.f.* bronquitis
bronze *n.m.* bronze
brooch *n.m.* fermall
broth *n.m.* brou
brother *n.m.* germà
brotherhood *n.m.* germandat
brown *adj.* marró
browned *adj.* daurat
brownie *n.m.* brownie
browse *v.* navegar
browser *n.m.* navegador
bruise *v.* fer un blau | *n.m.* blau
brunch *n.m.* brunch
brunette *adj.* morena
brush *v. (~ one's hair)* pentinar-se;
  (~ one's teeth) raspallar-se
Brussels sprouts *n.m.* cols de
  Brussel·les
bubble *n.f.* bombolla
bucket *n.m.* cubell
buckwheat *n.m.* fajol
budget *n.m.* pressupost
bug *n.f.* xinxa
build *v.* construir
builder *n.* constructor
building *n.m.* edifici
built *adj.* construït
Bulgaria *n.f.* Bulgària
bull *n.m.* toro
bullet *n.f.* bala
bullet-proof *adj.* antibales
bulletin board *n.m.* taulell
  d'anuncis
bumper *n.m.* para-xocs
bun *n.m.* panet
bunch *n.m.* manat
bungalow *n.m.* bungalou

bungee-jumping *n.m.* salt de pont
burden *n.f.* càrrega
burden of proof *n.f.* càrrega de la prova
bureaucracy *n.f.* burocràcia
bureaucrat *n.* buròcrata
burger *n.f.* hamburguesa
burn *v.* cremar
burned *adj.* cremat
burnt *adj.* cremat
burrito *n.m.* burrito
burst *v.* rebentar
bury *v.* enterrar
bus *n.m.* autobús
bus terminal *n.f.* terminal d'autobusos
bush *n.m.* arbust
business *n.m.* negoci
businessperson *n.f.* persona de negocis

busy *adj.* ocupat
but *conj.* però
butane gas *n.m.* butà
butcher *n.* carnisser
butter *n.f.* mantega
buttered *adj.* amb mantega
butterfly *n.f.* papallona
buttermilk *n.f.* llet de mantega
butterscotch *n.m.* butterscotch
button *n.m.* botó
buttress *n.m.* contrafort
buy *v.* comprar
buyer *n.m.* comprador
by *prep.* per
by-product *n.m.* rebuig
bye! *interj.* adeu!
bypass *n.f.* desviació

C

cab *n.m.* taxi
cabaret *n.m.* cabaret
cabbage *n.m.* col
cabin *n.f.* cabina
cabinet *n.m.* gabinet
cable *n.m.* cable
cable car *n.m.* telefèric
cable TV *n.f.* televisió per cable
cactus *n.m.* cactus
Caesar salad *n.f.* amanida Cèsar
café *n.f.* cafeteria
cafeteria *n.f.* cafeteria
caffeine *n.f.* cafeïna
caffeine-free *adj.* sense cafeïna
cage *n.f.* gàbia
cajole *v.* entabanar
cake *n.m.* pastís
calamity *n.f.* calamitat
calcium *n.m.* calci
calculate *v.* calcular
calculating *adj.* calculador
calculation *n.m.* càlcul
calculator *n.f.* calculadora
calendar *n.m.* calendari
California *n.* Califòrnia
call *v.* trucar
calligraphy *n.f.* cal·ligrafia
calm *adj.* tranquil
calmly *adv.* tranquil·lament
calorie *n.f.* caloria
camera *n.f.* càmera
camomile *n.f.* camamilla
camp *n.m.* campament
campaign *n.f.* campanya
camper *n.* acampador

campground *n.m.* càmping
can *v. (be able)* poder | *n.f.*
  (container) llauna
Canada *n.m.* Canadà
Canadian *adj.* canadenc
canal *n.m.* canal
Canary Islands *n.f.* Illes Canàries
cancel *v.* cancel·lar
canceled *adj.* cancel·lat
cancer *n.m.* càncer
cancerous *adj.* cancerós
candidate *n.m.* candidat
candied *adj.* ensucrat
candle *n.f.* espelma
candlestick *n.m.* candeler
candy *n.m.* dolços
canned *adj.* enllaunat
canoe *n.f.* canoa
cantaloupe *n.m.* cantalup
canvas *n.f.* lona
cap *n.f.* gorra
capability *n.f.* capacitat
capable (of) *adj.* capaç (de)
capacity *n.f.* capacitat
caper *(food) n.f.* tàpera
capital *n.f.* capital
capricious *adj.* capritxós
Capricorn *n.m.* Capricorn
caps lock *n.f.* bloq maj
capsicum *n.m.* pebrot
capsule *n.f.* càpsula
captain *n.m.* capità
captive *n.* captiu
captivity *n.f.* captivitat
capture *v.* capturar

car *n.m.* cotxe
carafe *n.f.* gerra
caramel *n.m.* caramel
caramelized *adj.* caramel·litzat
caraway *n.m.* comí
carbohydrate *n.m.* carbohidrat
carbon *n.m.* carboni
carbonated *adj.* carbonatat
carburetor *n.m.* carburador
carcinogenic *adj.* cancerigen
card *n.f.* targeta
cardboard *n.m.* cartó
care *n.f.* cura
career *n.f.* carrera
careful *adj.* cautelós
carefully *adv.* amb cura
careless *adj.* negligent
carelessly *adv.* negligentment
caricature *n.f.* caricatura
caring *adj.* amb cura
carnival *n.m.* carnaval
carp *n.f.* carpa
carpet *n.f.* catifa
carrier *n.m.* portador
carrot *n.f.* pastanaga
carry *v.* portar
carry-on *n.m.* equipatge de mà
cart *n.m.* carro
cartilage *n.m.* cartílag
carton *n.f.* caixa de cartró
cartoon *n.m.* dibuixos animats
carve *v.* esculpir
carving *n.* entalladura
case *n.m.* cas
case law *n.f.* jurisprudència
cash *n.m.* diners
cash register *n.f.* caixa enregistradora
cashew *n.m.* anacard
cashier *n.* caixer

casing *n.f.* coberta
casino *n.m.* casino
casserole *n.f.* cassola
cassette *n.f.* casset
cast *v.* tirar
cast iron *n.m.* ferro colat
castle *n.m.* castell
casual *adj.* informal
cat *n.m.* gat
Catalan *adj./n.* català
catalog *n.m.* catàleg
Catalonia *n.f.* Catalunya
catch *v.* atrapar, agafar
category *n.f.* categoria
cater *v.* fornir
catering *n.m.* servei d'àpats
cathedral *n.f.* catedral
Catholic *adj./n.* catòlic
cattle *n.m.* bestiar boví
cauliflower *n.f.* coliflor
cause *n.f.* causa
caution *n.f.* cautela
cavalry *n.f.* cavalleria
cave *n.f.* cova
caviar *n.m.* caviar
cavity *n.f.* cavitat
cayenne pepper *n.m.* pebre de caiena
CD *n.m.* CD
CD-player *n.m.* lector de CD
cease *v.* cessar
ceiling *n.m.* sostre
celebrate *v.* celebrar
celebration *n.f.* celebració
celery *n.m.* api
cell *n.f.* cèl·lula
cello *n.m.* violoncel
cellphone *n.m.* mòbil
cellulose *n.f.* cel·lulosa
Celsius *n.m.* grau Celsius

cement *n.m.* ciment
cemetery *n.m.* cementiri
censorship *n.f.* censura
census *n.m.* cens
cent *n.m.* cèntim
centenary *n.m.* centenari
center *n.m.* centre
center of town *n.m.* centre de la
  ciutat
centigrade *n.m.* centígrad
centimeter *n.m.* centímetre
centipede *n.m.* centpeus
central *adj.* central
central heating *n.f.* calefacció
  central
century *n.m.* segle
ceramic *adj.* ceràmic
ceramics *n.f.* ceràmica
cereal *n.m.* cereal
ceremony *n.f.* cerimònia
certain *adj.* cert
certainly *adv.* certament
certificate *n.m.* certificat
chain *n.f.* cadena
chain guard *n.f.* caixa de la cadena
chair *n.f.* cadira
chairman *n.m.* president
chairperson *n.* president
chairwoman *n.f.* presidenta
chalet *n.m.* xalet
challenge *n.m.* desafiament
chamber *n.f.* cambra
champagne *n.m.* xampany; *n.f.*
  cava
championship *n.m.* campionat
chance *n.f.* oportunitat
chancellor *n.* canceller
change *v.* canviar
changing room *n.m.* vestidor
channel *n.m.* canal

chapel *n.f.* capella
chapter *n.m.* capítol
char *v.* socarrar
char-broiled *adj.* char-rostit
character *n.m.* personatge
characteristic *adj.* característic |
  n.f. característica
charcoal *n.m.* carbó vegetal
charcoal-grilled *adj.* a la graella
charcuterie *n.f.* xarcuteria
chard *n.f.* bleda
charge *v.* cobrar
charity *n.f.* caritat
charm *v.* encantar
charming *adj.* encantador
chart *n.f.* gràfica
charter *n.m.* xàrter
charter flight *n.m.* vol xàrter
chase *v.* perseguir
chat *v.* xerrar
chauffeur *n.* xofer
cheap *adj.* barat
cheaper *adj.* més barat
cheaply *adv.* barata
cheat *v.* estafar
check *v.* comprovar
checkbook *n.m.* talonari
checkers *n.f.* dames
checkpoint *n.m.* punt de control
cheek *n.f.* galta
cheer *v.* aplaudir
cheerful *adj.* alegre
cheerfully *adv.* alegrement
cheers! *interj.* salut!
cheese *n.m.* formatge
chef *n.* cuiner en cap, xef
chemical *adj.* químic
chemist *n.* químic
chemistry *n.f.* química
cherry *n.f.* cirera

chess *n.m.* escacs
chess set *n.m.* joc d'escacs
chessboard *n.m.* tauler d'escacs
chest *n.m.* pit
chestnut *n.f.* castanya
chew *v.* mastegar
chewable *adj.* masticable
chewing gum *n.m.* xiclet
chicken *n.m.* pollastre
chickpea *n.m.* cigró
chicory *n.f.* xicoira
chief *n.m.* cap
child *n.* nen
childcare *n.f.* cura dels nens
childhood *n.f.* infància
children *n.m.* nens
Chile *n.m.* Xile
chili *n.m.* xili
chill *v.* refredar
chilled *adj.* refredat
chills *n.f.* calfreds
chilly *adj.* fred
chimney *n.f.* xemeneia
chin *n.f.* barbeta
China *n.f.* Xina
Chinese *adj.* xinès
chip *n.m.* xip
chips *n.f.* patates xips
chiropractor *n.* quiropràctic
chives *n.m.* cibulet
chlorine *n.m.* clor
chocolate *n.f.* xocolata
chocolate bar *n.f.* barra de
  xocolata
chocolate syrup *n.m.* xarop de
  xocolata
choice *n.f.* selecció
choir *n.m.* cor
choke *v.* ennuegar-se
choose *v.* elegir

chop *v.* tallar
chopped *adj.* tallat
chopsticks *n.m.* bastonets
chord *n.m.* acord
choreographer *n.* coreògraf
choreography *n.f.* coreografia
chorizo *n.m.* xoriço
chorus *n.m.* cor
Christian *adj./n.* cristià
Christmas *n.m.* Nadal; Merry ~
  phr. Bon Nadal
Christmas Day *n.m.* dia de
  Nadal
Christmas Eve *n.f.* nit de Nadal
chromosome *n.f.* cromosoma
chronic *adj.* crònic
chubby *adj.* grassó
chuck steak *n.m.* filet de llonzes
chunky *adj.* fornit
church *n.f.* església
chutney *n.m.* chutney
cider *n.f.* sidra
cigar *n.m.* cigar
cigarette *n.m.* cigarret
cilantro *n.m.* coriandre
cinema *n.m.* cinema
cinnamon *n.f.* canyella
circle *n.m.* cercle
circuit *n.m.* circuit
circulation *n.f.* circulació
circulatory system *n.m.* sistema
  circulatori
circumstance *n.f.* circumstància
circumstantial *adj.* circumstancial
citizen *n.m.* ciutadà
citizenship *n.f.* ciutadania
citron *n.m.* poncem
citrus *n.m.* cítric
city *n.f.* ciutat
civil *adj.* civil

civil rights *n.m.* drets civils
civilian *n.m.* civil
claim *v.* reclamar | *n.f.* reclamació
claim check *n.m.* xec reclamatiu
clairvoyant *adj.* clarivident
clam *n.f.* cloïssa
clamor *n.m.* clamor
clap *v.* aplaudir
clarified *adj.* clarificat
clarify *v.* aclarir
class *n.f.* classe
classic *adj.* clàssic
classical *adj.* clàssic
classical music *n.f.* música clàssica
Classicism *n.m.* classicisme
classics *n.m.* clàssics
classification *n.f.* classificació
classify *v.* classificar
classroom *n.f.* aula
classy *adj.* amb classe
clause *n.f.* clàusula
clay *n.f.* argila
clean *v.* netejar
cleaning *n.f.* neteja
clear *adj.* clar | *v.* netejar
clearly *adv.* clarament
clementine *n.f.* clementina
clerk *n.* oficinista
clever *adj.* llest
click *v.* clicar
client *n.* client
cliff *n.f.* penya-segat
climate *n.m.* clima
climax *n.m.* clímax
climb *v.* pujar
climbing *n.f.* escalada
clinic *n.f.* clínica
clinical *adj.* clínic
cloakroom *n.f.* guarda-roba
clock *n.m.* rellotge

clog *n.m.* esclop
clone *v.* clonar | *n.m.* clon
cloning *n.f.* clonació
close *v.* tancar
close to *prep.* a prop de
closed *adj.* tancat
closely *adv.* de prop
closet *n.m.* guarda-roba
clot *n.m.* coàgul
cloth *n.f.* tela
clothes *n.f.* roba
clothing *n.f.* roba
clotted *adj.* coagulada
cloud *n.m.* núvol
cloudy *adj.* ennuvolat
clove *n.m.* clavell
clover *n.m.* trèvol
clown *n.m.* pallasso
club *(social)* *n.m.* club
cluster *n.m.* clúster
clutch *(mech.)* *n.m.* embragatge
| *v.* agafar
coach *n.m.* autocar
coal *n.m.* carbó
coarse *adj.* aspre
coast *n.f.* costa
coat *n.m.* abric
coated *adj.* recobert
coating *n.f.* capa
cocaine *n.f.* cocaïna
cockroach *n.f.* panerola
cocktail *n.m.* còctel
cocoa *n.m.* cacau
coconut *n.m.* coco
cod *n.m.* bacallà
code *n.m.* codi
coffee *n.m.* cafè
coffee mug *n.f.* tassa
coin *n.f.* moneda
coincide *v.* coincidir

cold *adj. (temp.)* fred | *n.m. (illness)* constipat
cold cuts *n.f.* carn freda
cold pack *n.f.* compresa freda
coldly *adv.* fredament
coleslaw *n.f.* coleslaw
collapse *v.* esfondrar-se
collarbone *n.f.* clavícula
collard greens *n.f.* col de cabdell
colleague *n.* col·lega
collect *v.* recollir
collection *n.f.* col·lecció
collector *n.* col·leccionista
college *n.m.* col·legi
Colombia *n.f.* Colòmbia
colon *n.m. (anat.)* còlon
color *n.m.* color
Colorado *n.* Colorado
colored *adj.* de colors
colorfast *adj.* indeleble
coloring *n.m.* colorant
column *n.f.* columna
columnist *n.* articulista
coma *n.f.* coma
comb *n.f.* pinta
combination *n.* combinació
combine *v.* combinar
come *v.* venir
come back *v.* tornar
comedy *n.f.* comèdia
comfort *n.m.* confort
comfortable *adj.* còmode
comfortably *adv.* còmodament
comic *adj.* còmic
comics *n.f.* historietes; *n.m.* còmic
comma *n.f.* coma
command *v.* ordenar
commemoration *n.f.* commemoració
commence *v.* començar

comment *n.m.* comentari
commentary *n.m.* comentari
commercial *adj.* comercial
commercial zone *n.f.* zona comercial
commission *n.f.* comissió
commit *v.* cometre
commitment *n.m.* compromís
committee *n.m.* comitè
commodity *n.f.* mercaderia
common *adj.* comú
commonly *adv.* comunament
communicate *v.* comunicar
communication *n.f.* comunicació
communion *n.f.* comunió
communism *n.m.* comunisme
communist *n.* comunista
community *n.f.* comunitat
commute *v.* viatjar al lloc de treball
compact *adj.* compacte
compact disc *n.m.* CD
companion *n.* company
company *n.f.* companyia
comparative *adj.* comparatiu
compare *v.* comparar
comparison *n.f.* comparació
compass *n.f.* brúixola
compensation *n.f.* compensació
compete *v.* competir
competition *n.f.* competició
competitive *adj.* competitiu
competitor *n.* competidor
complain *v.* queixar-se
complainant *n.* querellant
complaint *n.f.* queixa
complete *adj.* complet
completely *adv.* completament
completion *n.m.* acabament
complex *adj.* complicat

complexion *n.m.* cutis
complexity *n.f.* complexitat
complicate *v.* complicar
complicated *adj.* complicat
comply *v.* complir
component *n.m.* component
compose *v.* compondre
composed *adj.* compost
composer *n.* compositor
composition *n.f.* composició
compost *n.m.* compost
composure *n.f.* calma
compote *n.f.* compota
compound *n.m.* compost
comprise *v.* comprendre
compromise *v.* transigir
compute *v.* calcular
computer *n.m.* ordinador
computing *n.f.* informàtica
conceal *v.* ocultar
conceive *v.* concebre
concentrate *v.* concentrar
concentration *n.f.* concentració
concept *n.f.* concepte
conception *n.f.* concepció
conceptual *adj.* conceptual
concern *n.f.* preocupació
concerned *adj.* preocupat
concerning *prep.* referent a
concert *n.m.* concert
concerto *n.m.* concert
concession *n.f.* concessió
conclude *v.* concloure
conclusion *n.f.* conclusió
concrete *adj.* concret
concussion *n.f.* commoció
condense *v.* condensar
condensed *adj.* condensat
condiment *n.m.* condiment
condition *n.f.* condició

conditional *adj.* condicional
conditioner *n.m.* condicionador
condolence *n.m.* condol
condom *n.m.* condó
conduct *v.* dirigir
conductor *n.m.* conductor
confection *n.f.* llaminadura
conference *n.f.* conferència
confess *v.* confessar
confession *n.f.* confessió
confidence *n.f.* confiança
confident *adj.* confiat
confidential *adj.* confidencial
confidently *adv.* amb confiança
confine *v.* confinar
confined *adj.* confinat
confirm *v.* confirmar
conflict *n.m.* conflicte
confront *v.* confrontar
confuse *v.* confondre
confused *adj.* confós
confusing *adj.* confús
confusion *n.f.* confusió
congealed *adj.* coagulat
Congolese *adj.* congolès
congratulate *v.* felicitar
congratulation *n.f.* felicitació
congratulations! *interj.* felicitats!
congress *n.m.* congrés
conjunction *n.f.* conjunció
connect *v.* connectar
connected *adj.* connectat
Connecticut *n.* Connecticut
connection *n.f.* connexió
conscious *adj.* conscient
consciousness *n.m.* coneixement; consciència
consequence *n.f.* conseqüència
consequently *adv.* conseqüentment
conservation *n.f.* conservació

conservation area *n.f.* àrea de conservació
conservative *adj.* conservador
conserve *v.* conservar
consider *v.* considerar
considerable *adj.* considerable
considerably *adv.* considerablement
consideration *n.f.* consideració
consist *v.* consistir
consistent *adj.* consistent
consistently *adv.* conseqüentment
consommé *n.m.* consomé
consonant *n.f.* consonant
constant *adj.* constant
constantly *adv.* constantment
constellation *n.f.* constel·lació
constipated *adj.* restret
constipation *n.m.* restrenyiment
constitute *v.* constituir
constitution *n.f.* constitució
constitutional *adj.* constitucional
constraint *n.f.* restricció
construct *v.* construir
construction *n.f.* construcció
consulate *n.m.* consolat
consult *v.* consultar
consultant *n.* consultor
consultation *n.f.* consulta
consumer *n.* consumidor
consumption *n.m.* consum
contact *v.* contactar | *n.m.* contacte
contact lens *n.f.* lent de contacte
contagious *adj.* contagiós
contain *v.* contenir
container *n.m.* recipient
contemporary *adj.* contemporani
content *n.m.* contingut
contest *n.m.* concurs
context *n.m.* context

continent *n.m.* continent
continental *adj.* continental
continuance *n.m.* ajornament
continue *v.* continuar
continuous *adj.* continu
continuously *adv.* contínuament
contraception *n.f.* anticoncepció
contraceptive *adj./n.m.* anticonceptiu
contract *n.m.* contracte
contraction *n.f.* contracció
contractor *n.* contractista
contrast *v.* contrastar | *n.m.* contrast
contrasting *adj.* en contrast
contribute *v.* contribuir
contribution *n.f.* contribució
control *v.* controlar | *n.m.* control
controlled *adj.* controlada
contusion *n.f.* contusió
convenience store *n.f.* botiga de conveniència
convenient *adj.* convenient
convent *n.m.* convent
convention *n.f.* convenció
conventional *adj.* convencional
conversation *n.f.* conversa
convert *v.* convertir
convey *v.* comunicar
convince *v.* convèncer
cook *v.* cuinar
cookbook *n.m.* llibre de cuina
cooker *n.f.* cuina
cookie *n.f.* galeta
cooking *n.f.* cuina
cool *adj.* fresc
cooperation *n.f.* cooperació
cooperative *adj.* cooperatiu
coordinate *v.* coordinar
cope (~ with) *v.* enfrontar-se a

copper *n.m.* coure
copy *v.* copiar | *n.f.* còpia
copyright *n.m.* drets d'autor
cord *n.m.* cordó
core *n.m.* cor
coriander *n.m.* coriandre
cork *n.m.* suro
corkscrew *n.m.* llevataps
corn *n.m.* blat de moro
cornbread *n.m.* pa de blat de moro
corner *n.m.* racó
cornerstone *n.f.* pedra angular
cornmeal *n.f.* farina de blat de moro
cornstarch *n.m.* midó de blat de moro
corporate *adj.* corporatiu
corporation *n.f.* corporació
correct *adj.* correcte
correctly *adv.* correctament
correlation *n.f.* correlació
correspond *v.* correspondre
corresponding *adj.* corresponent
corrupt *v.* corrompre | *adj.* corrupte
corrupted *adj.* corromput
corruption *n.f.* corrupció
cosmetic *n.m.* cosmètic
cosmos *n.m.* cosmos
cost *v.* costar | *n.m.* cost
Costa Rica *n.f.* Costa Rica
costume *n.m.* vestit
cot *n.m.* catre
cottage *n.f.* cabanya
cottage cheese *n.m.* formatge fresc
cotton *n.m.* cotó
cough *v.* tossir | *n.m.* tos
council *n.m.* consell
counsel *n.m.* cònsell

counselor *n.* conseller
count *v.* comptar
countable *adj.* comptable
counter *n.m.* taulell
country *n.m.* país
country code *n.m.* codi del país
countryside *n.m.* camp
county *n.m.* comtat
couple *n.f.* parella
coupon *n.m.* cupó
courage *n.m.* coratge
course *n.m.* curs
court *n.m.* tribunal
courtesy *n.f.* cortesia
courthouse *n.m.* palau de justícia
courtyard *n.m.* pati
couscous *n.m.* cuscús
cousin *n.m.* cosí; *n.f.* cosina
cover *v.* cobrir | *n.f.* coberta
covered *adj.* cobert
covering *n.m.* cobriment
cow *n.f.* vaca
coward *n.m.* covard
CPU *n.f.* CPU
crab *n.m.* cranc
crack *n.f.* esquerda
cracked *adj.* esquerdat
cracker *n.f.* galeta
craft *n.m.* ofici
crafts *n.f.* artesanies
cramp *n.f.* rampa
cranberry *n.f.* nabiu de grua
crash *v.* estavellar-se | *n.m.* xoc
crayfish *n.m.* cranc de riu
crazy *adj.* boig
cream *n.f.* nata
cream puff *n.m.* profiterol
create *v.* crear
creation *n.f.* creació
creative *adj.* creatiu

creativity *n.f.* creativitat
creature *n.f.* criatura
credit *n.m.* crèdit
credit card *n.f.* targeta de crèdit
creditor *n.* creditor
creep *v.* arrossegar-se
crepe *n.m.* crep
crew *n.f.* tripulació
crib *n.m.* bressol
crime *n.m.* crim
criminal *adj./n.* criminal
crimp *v.* arrissar
crisis *n.f.* crisi
crisp *adj.* cruixent
criteria *n.m.* criteri
critic *n.* crític
critical *adj.* crític
criticism *n.f.* crítica
criticize *v.* criticar
critique *n.f.* crítica
Croatia *n.f.* Croàcia
crop *n.f.* collita
croquette *n.f.* croqueta
cross *v.* creuar; creu
cross-country *n.m.* camp a través
crossing *n.m.* encreuament
crouton *n.m.* crostó
crowd *n.f.* multitud
crowded *adj.* apinyat
crown *n.f.* corona
crucial *adj.* crucial
cruel *adj.* cruel
cruelty *n.f.* crueltat
cruise *n.m.* creuer
crumb *n.f.* engruna
crumble *v.* esmicolar
crunch *v.* cruixir
crush *v.* aixafar
crushed *adj.* aixafat
crust *n.f.* crosta

crustacean *n.m.* crustaci
crusted *adj.* crostat
crutch *n.f.* crossa
cry *v.* plorar
crypt *n.f.* cripta
crystal *n.m.* cristall
crystallized *adj.* cristal·litzat
Cuba *n.f.* Cuba
cube *n.m.* cub
cubed *adj.* cubicat
cucumber *n.m.* cogombre
cuisine *n.f.* cuina
culinary *adj.* culinari
cultivate *v.* cultivar
cultivated *adj.* cultivat
cultural *adj.* cultural
culture *n.f.* cultura
cumin *n.m.* comí
cunning *adj.* astut
cup *n.f.* tassa
cupboard *n.m.* armari
cupcake *n.m.* cupcake
curator *n.* conservador
curb *v.* refrenar
curd *n.f.* quallada
curdle *v.* quallar
cure *v.* curar | *n.m.* remei
cured *adj.* curat
cured meat *n.f.* carn curada
curfew *n.m.* toc de queda
curiosity *n.f.* curiositat
curious *adj.* curiós
curiously *adv.* curiosament
curl *v.* arrissar | *n.m.* ris
curly *adj.* arrissat
currant *n.f.* grosella
currency *n.f.* moneda
currency exchange *n.m.* canvi de divises
current *adj.* actual

current affairs *n.f.* actualitats
currently *adv.* actualment
curry *n.m.* curri
cursor *n.m.* cursor
curtain *n.f.* cortina
curve *n.f.* corba
curved *adj.* corb
custard *n.f.* natilles; *n.m. (flan)* flam
custody *n.f.* custòdia
custom *n.m.* costum
customer *n.m.* client
customize *v.* personalitzar
customs *n.f.* duana

customs declaration *n.f.* declaració duanera
cut *v.* tallar
cutlery *n.m.* coberts
cutlet *n.f.* costella
cycle *n.m.* cicle
cycling *n.m.* ciclisme
cylindrical *adj.* cilíndric
Cyprus *n.m.* Xipre
cyst *n.m.* quist
cystitis *n.f.* cistitis
Czech Republic *n.f.* República Txeca

D

dad *n.m.* papa
daily *adj.* diari
dairy *n.m.* lactis
damage *v.* danyar | *n.m.* dany
damaged *adj.* espatllat
damp *adj.* humit
dance *v.* ballar | *n.f.* dansa
dancer *n.* ballador
dandelion *n.f.* dent de lleó
danger *n.m.* perill
dangerous *adj.* perillós
dare *v.* desafiar
dark *adj.* fosc
darker *adj.* més fosc
dash *n.m.* guió
data *n.f.* dades
database *n.f.* base de dades
date *n.f.* data
daughter *n.f.* filla
daughter-in-law *n.f.* nora
dawn *n.f.* alba
day *n.m.* dia
daycare *n.f.* llar d'infants
daytime *n.m.* dia
dead *adj.* mort
dead end *n.m.* carreró sense
  sortida
deadline *n.m.* termini
deaf *adj.* sord
deal *n.m.* pacte
dealer *n.* comerciant
dealings *n.f.* transaccions
dear *adj.* estimat
death *n.f.* mort
debate *n.m.* debat

debt *n.m.* deute
debtor *n.* deutor
debut *n.m.* debut
decade *n.f.* dècada
decaffeinated *adj.* descafeïnat
decant *v.* decantar
decanter *n.m.* decantador
decay *n.f.* descomposició
December *n.m.* desembre
decide *v.* decidir
decision *n.f.* decisió
deck *n.f.* (~ *of a ship*) coberta;
  (~ *of a building*) terrassa
deck of cards *n.f.* baralla de cartes
declare *v.* declarar
decline *v.* declinar
decorate *v.* decorar
decoration *n.f.* decoració
decorative *adj.* decoratiu
decrease *v.* disminuir
decree *n.m.* decret
dedicate *v.* dedicar
dedicated *adj.* dedicat
dedication *n.f.* dedicació
deduct *v.* deduir
deep *adj.* profund
deeply *adv.* profundament
deer *n.m.* cérvol
defeat *v.* derrotar | *n.f.* derrota
defend *v.* defensar
defendant *n.* acusat
defense *n.f.* defensa
deficiency *n.f.* deficiència
deficit *n.m.* dèficit
define *v.* definir

definite *adj*. definit
definitely *adv*. definitivament
definition *n.f.* definició
deforestation *n.f.* desforestació
defrost *v*. descongelar
degrease *v*. desengreixar
degree *n.m.* grau
deity *n.f.* deïtat
Delaware *n*. Delaware
delay *n.m.* retard
delayed *adj*. retardat
delegate *n*. delegat
delete *v*. esborrar
deli *n.f.* xarcuteria
deliberate *adj*. deliberat
deliberately *adv*. deliberadament
delicacy *n.f.* delicadesa
delicate *adj*. delicat
delicatessen *n.f.* xarcuteria
delicious *adj*. deliciós
delight *n.m.* delit
delighted *adj*. encantat
delightful *adj*. encantador
delirious *adj*. delirant
deliver *v*. lliurar
delivery *n.m.* lliurament
delusion *n.m.* engany
demand *v*. exigir | *n.f.* demanda
democracy *n.f.* democràcia
demonstrate *v*. demostrar
demonstration *n.f.* demostració
denim *n.m.* denim
Denmark *n.f.* Dinamarca
density *n.f.* densitat
dental *adj*. dental
dental floss *n.m.* fil dental
dentist *n*. dentista
dentures *n.f.* dentadura postissa
deny *v*. negar
deodorant *n.m.* desodorant

depart *v*. sortir
department *n.m.* departament
department store *n.m.* gran
  magatzem
departure *n.f.* sortida
depend *v*. dependre
dependence *n.f.* dependència
dependent *adj*. dependent
depending on *prep*. segons
depict *v*. representar
deposit *v*. ingressar | *n.m.* ingrés
deposition *n.f.* deposició
depot *n.m.* magatzem
depreciation *n.f.* depreciació
depress *v*. deprimir
depressed *adj*. deprimit
depressing *adj*. depriment
depression *n.f.* depressió
depth *n.f.* profunditat
derivative *adj*. derivat
derive *v*. derivar
describe *v*. descriure
description *n.f.* descripció
desert *v*. abandonar | *n.m.* desert
deserted *adj*. abandonat
deserve *v*. merèixer
design *v*. dissenyar | *n.m.* disseny
designed *adj*. dissenyat
designer *n*. dissenyador
desire *v*. desitjar | *n.m.* desig
desk *n.m.* escriptori
desperate *adj*. desesperat
desperately *adv*. desesperadament
despicable *adj*. menyspreable
despite *prep*. malgrat
dessert *n.f.* postres
destination *n.f.* destinació
destroy *v*. destruir
destroyed *adj*. destruït
destruction *n.f.* destrucció

detach *v.* separar
detail *n.m.* detall
detailed *adj.* detallat
detect *v.* descobrir
detective *n.* detectiu
detergent *n.m.* detergent
determination *n.f.* determinació
determine *v.* determinar
determined *adj.* determinat
detour *n.f.* desviació
develop *v.* desenvolupar
development *n.m.* desenvolupament
device *n.m.* dispositiu
devil *n.m.* diable
devote *v.* dedicar
devoted *adj.* dedicat
devour *v.* devorar
diabetes *n.f.* diabetis
diabetic *adj.* diabètic
diagnose *v.* diagnosticar
diagnosis *n.f.* diagnosi
diagram *n.m.* diagrama
dial *v.* marcar
dialect *n.m.* dialecte
dialogue *n.m.* diàleg
diameter *n.m.* diàmetre
diamond *n.m.* diamant
diaper *n.m.* bolquer
diaphragm *n.m.* diafragma
diarrhea *n.f.* diarrea
diary *n.m.* diari
dice *n.m.* daus
dictate *v.* dictar
dictation *n.m.* dictat
dictionary *n.m.* diccionari
die *v.* morir
diesel *n.m.* dièsel
diesel engine *n.m.* motor dièsel
diet *n.f.* dieta

dietary *adj.* dietètic
differ *v.* diferir
difference *n.f.* diferència
different *adj.* diferent
differently *adv.* diferentment
difficult *adj.* difícil
difficulty *n.f.* dificultat
dig *v.* cavar
digest *v.* digerir
digestive system *n.m.* aparell
digestiu
digital *adj.* digital
dill *n.m.* anet
dilute *v.* diluir
dimension *n.f.* dimensió
dine *v.* sopar
diner *n.* comensal
dining room *n.m.* menjador
dinner *n.m.* sopar
dip *v.* submergir
diplomacy *n.f.* diplomàcia
diplomat *n.* diplomàtic
direct *adj.* directe
direction *n.f.* direcció
directive *n.f.* directiva
directly *adv.* directament
director *n.* director
directory *n.m.* directori
dirt *n.f.* brutícia
dirty *adj.* brut
disability *n.f.* discapacitat
disable *v.* desactivar
disabled *adj.* invàlid
disadvantage *n.m.* desavantatge
disagree *v.* discrepar
disagreement *n.m.* desacord
disappear *v.* desaparèixer
disappearance *n.f.* desaparició
disappoint *v.* decebre
disappointed *adj.* decebut

disappointing *adj*. decebedor
disappointment *n.f.* decepció
disapprove *v*. desaprovar
disapproving *adj*. desaprovació
disaster *n.m.* desastre
disc *n.m.* disc
discharge *v*. descarregar | *n.f.* descàrrega
discharged *adj*. descarregat
discipline *n.f.* disciplina
disclose *v*. revelar
disclosure *n.f.* revelació
discotheque *n.f.* discoteca
discount *n.m.* descompte
discourse *n.m.* discurs
discover *v*. descobrir
discovered *adj*. descobert
discovery *n.m.* descobriment
discriminate *v*. discriminar
discrimination *n.f.* discriminació
discuss *v*. discutir
discussion *n.f.* discussió
disease *n.f.* malaltia
disgust *n.m.* fàstic
disgusting *adj*. fastigós
dish *n.m.* plat
dish cloth *n.m.* drap de cuina
dishonest *adj*. deshonest
dishonestly *adv*. deshonestament
dishwasher *n.m.* rentaplats
disinfect *v*. desinfectar
disk *n.m.* disc
dislike *n.f.* aversió
dislocated *adj*. dislocat
dismiss *v*. acomiadar
dismissal *n.m.* acomiadament
disorder *n.m.* desordre
display *v*. exhibir
disposable *adj*. d'un sol ús
disposal *n.f.* disposició

dispute *n.f.* disputa
dissolve *v*. dissoldre
distance *n.f.* distància
distant *adj*. distant
distill *v*. destil·lar
distilled *adj*. destil·lat
distinct *adj*. distint
distinction *n.f.* distinció
distinctive *adj*. distintiu
distinguish *v*. distingir
distribute *v*. distribuir
distribution *n.f.* distribució
distributor *n*. distribuïdor
district *n.m.* districte
disturb *v*. molestar
disturbing *adj*. pertorbador
diuretic *n.m.* diürètic
dive *v*. capbussar-se
divide *v*. dividir
dividend *n.m.* dividend
diving *n.m.* busseig
diving board *n.m.* trampolí
division *n.f.* divisió
divorce *n.m.* divorci
divorced *adj*. divorciat
dizzy *adj*. marejat
DNA *n.m.* ADN
do *v*. fer
do-it-yourself *n.m.* fes-ho tu mateix
dock *n.m.* moll
doctor *n*. metge
document *n.m.* document
documentary *n.m.* documental
dog *n.m.* gos
doll *n.f.* nina
dollar *n.m.* dòlar
domain *n.m.* domini
dome *n.f.* cúpula
domestic *adj*. domèstic

dominant *adj.* dominant
dominate *v.* dominar
Dominican Republic *n.f.*
República Dominicana
dominoes *n.m.* dòmino
donate *v.* donar
donation *n.f.* donació
donkey *n.m.* ruc
donor *n.* donant
door *n.f.* porta
doorway *n.f.* porta, portal
dormitory *n.m.* dormitori
dosage *n.f.* dosi
dose *n.f.* dosi
dot *n.m.* punt
dotcom *n.f.* puntcom
double *adj.* doble
doubt *v.* dubtar | *n.m.* dubte
dough *n.f.* pasta
doughnut *n.m.* dònut
dove *n.m.* colom
down *adj.* baix
downhill skiing *n.m.* esquí alpí
download *v.* descarregar
downloadable *adj.* descarregable
downstairs *adv.* a baix
downtown *n.m.* centre de la ciutat
downward *adv.* cap avall
dowry *n.m.* dot
doze *v.* dormisquejar
dozen *n.f.* dotzena
Dr. *abbr.* Dr.
draft *n.m.* esborrany
drag *v.* arrossegar
drain *v.* escórrer
drama *n.m.* drama
dramatic *adj.* dramàtic
dramatically *adv.* dramàticament
draw *v.* dibuixar
drawbridge *n.m.* pont llevadís

drawer *n.m.* calaix
drawing *n.m.* dibuix
dream *v.* somiar | *n.m.* somni
dredge *v.* dragar
dress *n.m.* vestit
dressed *adj.* vestit
dressing (salad ~) *n.m.* amaniment
dried *adj.* sec
drink *v.* beure | *n.f.* beguda
drinkable water *n.f.* aigua potable
drip *v.* gotejar | *n.f.* gota
drive *v.* conduir
driver *n.* conductor
driver's license *n.m.* carnet de
conduir
driving *n.f.* conducció
drizzle *v.* plovisquejar | *n.m.*
plugim
drop *v.* deixar caure | *n.f.* gota
drought *n.f.* sequera
drown *v.* ofegar-se
drowsy *adj.* somnolent
drug *n.f.* droga
drug dealer *n.* traficant de drogues
drugstore *n.f.* farmàcia
drum *n.m.* tambor
drunk *adj.* borratxo
dry *adj.* sec
dry cleaner *n.f.* tintoreria
dryer *n.f.* assecadora
dub *v.* doblar
dubbed *adj.* doblat
dubbing *n.m.* doblatge
duck *n.m.* ànec
duckling *n.m.* aneguet
due *adj.* degut
due process *n.m.* degut procés
dull *adj.* avorrit
dumb *adj.* estúpid
dump *v.* abocar

dumpling *n.m.* dumpling
durian *n.m.* durian
during *prep.* durant
dust *n.f.* pols
duty *n.m.* deure; **on ~** *phr.* de
  servei
duty-free *adj.* lliure d'impostos
duvet *n.m.* edredó

DVD *n.m.* DVD
dye *v.* tenyir | *n.m.* tint
dying *adj.* moribund
dynamic *adj.* dinàmic
dynamite *n.f.* dinamita
dynasty *n.f.* dinastia

E

e.g. (for example) *abbr.* p.ex. (per exemple)
each *pron.* cada
ear *n.f.* orella
earache *n.m.* mal d'orella
earlier *adj.* més d'hora
early *adv.* d'hora
earn *v.* guanyar
earnings *n.m.* guanys
earring *n.f.* arracada
Earth *n.f.* Terra
earth *n.f.* terra
earthenware pot *n.f.* terrissa
earthquake *n.m.* terratrèmol
earthworm *n.m.* cuc
earwig *n.f.* tisoreta
ease *n.f.* facilitat
easily *adv.* fàcilment
east *n.m.* est
Easter *n.f.* Pasqua
eastern *adj.* oriental
easy *adj.* fàcil
eat *v.* menjar
eatery *n.m.* restaurant
echo *n.m.* eco
éclair *n.* eclair
eclipse *v.* eclipsar | *n.m.* eclipsi
economic *adj.* econòmic
economics *n.f.* economia
economist *n.* economista
economy *n.f.* economia
ecosystem *n.m.* ecosistema
Ecuador *n.m.* Equador
edamame *n.* edamame
edge *n.f.* vora

edible *adj.* comestible
edit *v.* editar
edition *n.f.* edició
editor *n.* redactor
educate *v.* educar
educated *adj.* educat
education *n.f.* educació
eel *n.f.* anguila
effect *n.m.* efecte
effective *adj.* eficaç
effectively *adv.* eficaçment
effectiveness *n.f.* eficàcia
efficiency *n.f.* eficiència
efficient *adj.* eficient
efficiently *adv.* eficientment
effort *n.m.* esforç
egg *n.m.* ou
egg shell *n.f.* closca d'ou
eggplant *n.f.* albergínia
ego *n.m.* ego
egotism *n.m.* egotisme
eight *num.* vuit
eighteen *num.* divuit
eighteenth *adj.* divuitè
eighth *adj.* vuitè
eightieth *adj.* vuitantè
eighty *num.* vuitanta
either *pron.* qualsevol
El Salvador *n.f.* El Salvador
elaborate *v.* elaborar | *adj.* complicat
elastic *adj.* elàstic
elbow *n.m.* colze
elderly *adj.* ancià
elect *v.* elegir

election *n.f.* elecció
elective *adj.* electiu
electorate *n.m.* electorat
electric *adj.* elèctric
electrical *adj.* elèctric
electrical outlet *n.f.* presa de corrent elèctric
electricity *n.f.* electricitat
electrolyte *n.m.* electròlit
electron *n.m.* electró
electronic *adj.* electrònic
electronics *n.f.* electrònica
elegance *n.f.* elegància
elegant *adj.* elegant
element *n.m.* element
elevator *n.m.* ascensor
eleven *num.* onze
eleventh *adj.* onzè
elf *n.m.* elf
eliminate *v.* eliminar
elimination *n.f.* eliminació
elixir *n.m.* elixir
elk *n.m.* ant
eloquence *n.f.* eloqüència
eloquent *adj.* eloqüent
else *adv.* més
elsewhere *adv.* en altre lloc
e-mail *n.m.* correu electrònic
emancipate *v.* emancipar
emancipation *n.f.* emancipació
embarrass *v.* avergonyir
embarrassed *adj.* avergonyit
embarrassing *adj.* vergonyós
embarrassment *n.f.* vergonya
embassy *n.f.* ambaixada
embedded *adj.* incrustat
embrace *v.* abraçar
embroidery *n.m.* brodat
embryo *n.m.* embrió
emerald *n.f.* maragda

emerge *v.* emergir
emergency *n.f.* emergència
emergency room *n.f.* sala d'urgències
emergent *adj.* emergent
emigrate *v.* emigrar
emigration *n.f.* emigració
emissary *n.* emissari
emission *n.f.* emissió
emotion *n.f.* emoció
emotional *adj.* emocional
emotionally *adv.* emocionalment
emphasis *n.m.* èmfasi
emphasize *v.* emfatitzar
empire *n.m.* imperi
employ *v.* donar feina
employee *n.* empleat
employer *n.* patró
employment *n.f.* ocupació
empress *n.f.* emperadriu
empty *adj.* buit
emulsion *n.f.* emulsió
enable *v.* habilitar
enamel *n.m.* esmalt
encase *v.* encaixonar
encased *adj.* encaixonat
encounter *v.* encontrar | *n.m.* encontre
encourage *v.* encoratjar
encouragement *n.m.* encoratjament
encrusted *adj.* incrustat
end *v.* terminar | *n.f.* fi
endangered species *n.f.* espècie amenaçada
ending *n.f.* fi
endive *n.f.* endívia
enemy *n.m.* enemic; *n.f.* enemiga
energy *n.f.* energia
engage *v.* contractar
engaged *adj.* ocupat

engagement *n.m.* compromís
engine *n.m.* motor
engineer *n.* enginyer
engineering *n.f.* enginyeria
England *n.f.* Anglaterra
English *adj./n.m.* anglès
English-speaking *adj.* que parla
  anglès
engraving *n.m.* gravat
engross *v.* absorbir
engulf *v.* engolir
enhance *v.* millorar
enhanced *adj.* millorat
enjoy *v.* gaudir de; ~ **your meal!**
  interj. bon profit!
enjoyable *adj.* agradable
enjoyment *n.m.* plaer
enlarge *v.* engrandir
enmity *n.f.* enemistat
enormous *adj.* enorme
enough *adj.* prou
ensure *v.* assegurar
enter *v.* entrar
enterprise *n.f.* empresa
entertain *v.* entretenir
entertainer *n.* artista
entertaining *adj.* divertit
entertainment *n.m.* entreteniment
enthusiasm *n.m.* entusiasme
enthusiastic *adj.* entusiasta
enticing *adj.* temptador
entire *adj.* enter
entirely *adv.* enterament
entitle *v.* autoritzar
entomology *n.f.* entomologia
entrance *n.f.* entrada
entrapment *n.m.* atrapament
entree *n.m.* entrant
entry *n.f.* entrada
envelope *n.m.* sobre

environment *n.m.* medi ambient
environmental *adj.* ambiental
environs *n.m.* entorns
enzyme *n.m.* enzim
epicurean *adj.* epicuri
epidemic *n.f.* epidèmia
epileptic *adj.* epilèptic
episode *n.m.* episodi
epoch *n.f.* època
equal *adj.* igual
equal rights *n.m.* drets iguals
equality *n.f.* igualtat
equally *adv.* igualment
equation *n.f.* equació
equilibrium *n.m.* equilibri
equipment *n.m.* equipament
equity *n.f.* equitat
equivalent *adj.* equivalent
era *n.f.* era
eradicate *v.* erradicar
erect *v.* erigir
erected *adj.* erigit
erotic *adj.* eròtic
error *n.m.* error
escalate *v.* escalar
escalator *n.f.* escala mecànica
escape *v.* fugir
escrow *n.m.* dipòsit
especially *adv.* especialment
espresso *n.m.* cafè exprés
essay *n.m.* assaig
essence *n.f.* essència
essential *adj.* essencial
essentially *adv.* essencialment
establish *v.* establir
establishment *n.m.* establiment;
  classe dirigent
estate *n.f.* finca
estimate *v.* estimar | *n.f.* estimació
Estonia *n.f.* Estònia

et cetera *(abbr.* **etc.)** *n.* etcètera
etching *n.m.* aiguafort
ethical *adj.* ètic
ethics *n.f.* ètica
ethnic *adj.* ètnic
etiquette *n.f.* etiqueta
EU (European Union) *abbr.* UE
  (Unió Europea)
eunuch *n.m.* eunuc
euro *n.m.* euro
Europe *n.f.* Europa
European *adj.* europeu
European Union (EU) *n.* Unió
  Europea (UE)
evacuate *v.* evacuar
evacuation *n.f.* evacuació
evaluate *v.* avaluar
evaluation *n.f.* avaluació
evaporated *adj.* evaporat
even *adv.* fins i tot
evening *n.m.* vespre
event *n.m.* esdeveniment
eventual *adj.* final
eventually *adv.* finalment
ever *adv.* sempre
evergreen *n.m.* arbre de fulla
  perenne
everlasting *adj.* etern
every *adj.* cada
everybody *pron.* tothom
everyday *adj.* diari
everyone *pron.* tothom
everything *pron.* tot
everywhere *adv.* a tot arreu
evict *v.* desnonar
eviction *n.m.* desnonament
evidence *n.f.* evidència
evident *adj.* evident
evil *adj.* malvat
evolution *n.f.* evolució

evolutionary *adj.* evolutiu
evolve *v.* evolucionar
ex- *prefix* ex-
exact *adj.* exacte
exactly *adv.* exactament
exaggerate *v.* exagerar
exaggerated *adj.* exagerat
exaggeration *n.f.* exageració
exam *n.m.* examen
examination *n.m.* examen
examine *v.* examinar
example *n.m.* exemple; **for ~**
  phr. per exemple
exceed *v.* excedir
excellent *adj.* excel·lent
except *prep.* excepte
exception *n.f.* excepció
excess *n.f.* excés
excessive *adj.* excessiu
exchange *v.* intercanviar | *n.m.*
  intercanvi
exchange office *n.f.* oficina de
  canvi
exchange rate *n.f.* taxa de canvi
excite *v.* emocionar
excited *adj.* emocionat
excitement *n.f.* emoció
exciting *adj.* emocionant
exclamation *n.f.* exclamació
exclamation point *n.m.* signe
  d'exclamació
exclude *v.* excloure
excluding *prep.* excepte
exclusion *n.f.* exclusió
exclusive *adj.* exclusiu
exclusively *adv.* exclusivament
excursion *n.f.* excursió
excuse *v.* excusar | *n.f.* excusa
excuse me *phr. (for pardon)*
  disculpi, *(for attention)* perdoni

execution *n.f.* execució
executive *n.* executiu
exempt *adj.* exempt
exemption *n.f.* exempció
exercise *v.* exercir | *n.m.* exercici
exhaust *v.* fatigar
exhaust pipe *n.m.* tub d'escapament
exhausted *adj.* esgotat
exhibit *v.* exposar
exhibition *n.f.* exhibició, exposició
exist *v.* existir
existence *n.f.* existència
exit *n.f.* sortida
exonerate *v.* exonerar
exotic *adj.* exòtic
expand *v.* expandir
expansion *n.f.* expansió
expect *v.* esperar
expectation *n.f.* expectació
expected *adj.* esperat
expenditure *n.f.* despesa
expense *n.f.* despesa
expensive *adj.* car
experience *v.* experimentar | *n.f.* experiència
experienced *adj.* experimentat
experiment *v.* experimentar | *n.m.* experiment
experimental *adj.* experimental
expert *adj./n.* expert
expertise *n.f.* perícia
expiration *n.f.* expiració
expiration date *n.f.* data de caducitat
expire *v.* caducar

explain *v.* explicar
explanation *n.f.* explicació
explode *v.* explotar
exploit *v.* explotar
exploitation *n.f.* explotació
exploration *n.f.* exploració
explore *v.* explorar
explosion *n.f.* explosió
export *v.* exportar | *n.f.* exportació
expose *v.* exposar
exposure *n.f.* exposició
express *v.* expressar
express train *n.m.* tren ràpid
expression *n.f.* expressió
expunge *v.* esborrar
extend *v.* estendre
extension *n.f.* extensió
extensive *adj.* extens
extent *n.m.* grau
external *adj.* extern
extra *adj.* extra
extract *v.* extreure | *n.m.* extracte
extraordinary *adj.* extraordinari
extreme *adj.* extrem
extremely *adv.* extremadament
eye *n.m.* ull
eyeball *n.m.* globus ocular
eyebrow *n.f.* cella
eyeglasses *n.f.* ulleres
eyelash *n.f.* pestanya
eyelet *n.m.* ullet
eyelid *n.f.* parpella
eyewash station *(med.)* *n.m.* rentaülls

F

fabric *n.m.* teixit
fabricate *v.* inventar
fabrication *n.f.* invenció
face *n.f.* cara
facial *adj.* facial
facility *n.f.* instal·lació
fact *n.m.* fet
factor *n.m.* factor
factory *n.f.* fàbrica
Fahrenheit *adj.* fahrenheit
fail *v.* fracassar
failure *n.m.* fracàs
faint *v.* desmaiar-se
faith *n.f.* fe
faithful *adj.* fidel
faithfully *adv.* fidelment
falafel *n.m.* falàfel
falcon *n.m.* falcó
fall *v.* caure | *n.f.* caiguda; *(season)* tardor
fallacy *n.f.* fal·làcia
false *adj.* fals
fame *n.f.* fama
familiar *adj.* familiar
family *n.f.* família
family tree *n.m.* arbre genealògic
famous *adj.* famós
fan *n.m. (mech.)* ventilador; *n. (person)* aficionat
fan belt *n.f.* corretja del ventilador
fancy *v.* agradar
fantastic *adj.* fantàstic
fantasy *n.f.* fantasia
far *adv.* lluny
far-sightedness *n.f.* hipermetropia

fare *n.f.* tarifa
farm *n.f.* granja
farmer *n.* granger
farming *n.f.* agricultura
farther *adv.* més lluny
farthest *adj.* més llunyà
fascinate *v.* fascinar
fascinated *adj.* fascinat
fascinating *adj.* fascinant
fascination *n.f.* fascinació
fashion *n.f.* moda
fashionable *adj.* de moda
fast *adj.* ràpid
fasten *v.* subjectar
fat *adj.* gras | *n.m.* greix
fat-free *adj.* desnatada
fate *n.m.* destí
father *n.m.* pare
father-in-law *n.m.* sogre
fattening *adj.* que engreixa
fatty *adj.* gras
faucet *n.f.* aixeta
fault *n.f. (blame)* culpa; *n.m. (defect)* defecte
faulty *adj.* defectuós
favor *n.m.* favor
favorite *adj.* favorit
fax *v.* enviar un fax | *n.m.* fax
fax machine *n.f.* màquina de fax
fear *v.* tenir por de | *n.f.* por
feasible *adj.* factible
feast *n.m.* festí
feather *n.f.* ploma
feature *n.f.* característica
February *n.m.* febrer

federal *adj.* federal
fee *n.m.* honoraris
feed *v.* alimentar
feeding bottle *n.m.* biberó
feel *v.* sentir
feeling *n.m. (emotional)* sentiment;
  n.f. (physical) sensació
fellow *n.m.* tipus
felony *n.m.* delicte
female *adj.* femení | *n.f.* femella
feminine *adj.* femení
feminism *n.m.* feminisme
feminist *adj./n.* feminista
fence *n.f.* tanca
fencing *(sport) n.f.* esgrima
fender *n.m.* parafang
fennel *n.m.* fonoll
ferment *v.* fermentar
ferry *n.m.* transbordador, ferri
fervent *adj.* fervent
fervor *n.m.* fervor
festival *n.m.* festival
fetch *v.* portar
feud *n.f.* enemistat
feudal *adj.* feudal
fever *n.f.* febre
few *adj.* pocs
fiancé *n.m.* promès
fiancée *n.f.* promesa
fiasco *n.m.* fiasco
fiber *n.f.* fibra
fiction *n.f.* ficció
fictional *adj.* fictici
fiduciary *n.m.* fiduciari
field *n.m.* camp
fierce *adj.* ferotge
fiery *adj.* fogós
fifteen *num.* quinze
fifteenth *adj.* quinzè
fifth *adj.* cinquè

fiftieth *adj.* cinquantè
fifty *num.* cinquanta
fig *n.f.* figa
fight *v.* lluitar | *n.f.* lluita
fighter *n.* lluitador
fighting *n.f.* lluita
figment *n.f.* ficció
figurative *adj.* figuratiu
figure *n.f.* figura
figurine *n.f.* estatueta
file *v. (records)* arxivar; *(with
  a tool)* llimar | *n.m. (records)*
  arxiu, fitxer; *n.f. (tool)* llima
fill *v.* omplir
fillet *n.m.* filet
filling *n.m.* farcit
film *n.f.* pel·lícula
filter *v.* filtrar | *n.m.* filtre
filtered *adj.* filtrat
filth *n.f.* immundícia
filthy *adj.* immund
final *adj.* final
finally *adv.* finalment
finance *v.* finançar | *n.f.* finances
financial *adj.* financer
find *v.* trobar
finding *n.m.* descobriment
fine *adj.* fi | *n.f.* multa
finely *adv.* finament
finger *n.m.* dit
fingernail *n.f.* ungla
fingertip *n.f.* punta del dit
finish *v.* acabar
finished *adj.* acabat
Finland *n.f.* Finlàndia
fir *n.m.* avet
fire *n.m.* foc
fire alarm *n.f.* alarma d'incendis
fire department *n.m.* bombers
fire extinguisher *n.m.* extintor

firecracker *n.m.* foc artificial
firefighter *n.* bomber
fireplace *n.f.* llar de foc
firewood *n.f.* llenya
fireworks *n.m.* focs artificials
firm *adj.* ferm
firmly *adv.* amb fermesa
first *adj.* primer
first aid *n.m.* primers auxilis
first class *adj.* primera classe
first lady *n.f.* primera dama
first place *n.m.* primer lloc
fiscal *adj.* fiscal
fish *n.m.* peix
fisherman *n.* pescador
fishhook *n.m.* ham
fishing *n.f.* pesca
fishing license *n.f.* llicència de pesca
fishing net *n.f.* xarxa de pesca
fishing rod *n.f.* canya de pescar
fishmonger *n.* peixater
fist *n.m.* puny
fit *v.* encaixar
fitness *n.f.* salut
fitting *adj.* propi
five *num.* cinc
fix *v.* arreglar
fixed *adj.* fix
fixed price *n.m.* preu fix
flag *n.f.* bandera
flake *n.m.* floc
flaky *adj.* escamós
flambé *n.f.* flambé
flame *n.f.* flama
flan *n.m.* flam
flank *n.m.* flanc
flare *n.f.* flamarada
flash *n.m.* flaix
flash photography *n.f.* fotografia amb flaix

flashlight *n.f.* llanterna
flat *adj.* pla
flat tire *n.f.* punxada
flatter *v.* afalagar
flattery *n.f.* adulació
flavor *n.m.* gust
flavored *adj.* aromatitzat
flavoring *n.f.* aromatització
flax *n.m.* lli
flea *n.f.* puça
flea market *n.m.* encants
flesh *n.f.* carn
flexibility *n.f.* flexibilitat
flexible *adj.* flexible
flicker *v.* parpellejar
flight *n.m.* vol
flimsy *adj.* feble
flip *v.* llençar
flip-flops *n.f.* xancletes
float *v.* flotar
flood *n.f.* inundació
floor *n.f.* planta
Florida *n.* Florida
florist *n.* florista
flounder *n.f.* palaia
flour *n.f.* farina
floured *adj.* enfarinada
flourish *v.* florir
flow *v.* fluir | *n.m.* corrent
flower *n.f.* flor
flu *n.f.* grip
fluency *n.f.* fluïdesa
fluent *adj.* fluid
fluid *n.m.* fluid
flush *v.* expel·lir
flute *n.f.* flauta
fly *v.* volar
flying *adj.* volant
focus *v.* enfocar
fog *n.f.* boira

fog light *n.f.* llum antiboira
foggy *adj.* boirós
foie gras *n.m.* foie-gras
fold *v.* plegar
foliage *n.m.* fullatge
folk *n.f.* gent
folk art *n.* art tradicional
folk music *n.f.* música tradicional
follow *v.* seguir
following *adj.* següent
font *n.f.* tipus de lletra
food *n.m.* menjar
food additive *n.m.* additiu
alimentari
food coloring *n.m.* colorant
alimentari
food poisoning *n.f.* toxiinfecció
alimentària
food preservative *n.m.* conservant
food pyramid *n.f.* piràmide dels
aliments
fool *n.* idiota
foot *n.m.* peu; **on ~** *phr.* a peu
football *n.m.* futbol
footer *n.m.* peu de pàgina
footpath *n.* sender
for *prep.* per
for example *phr.* per exemple
for instance *phr.* per exemple
forbidden *adj.* prohibit
force *n.f.* força
forceful *adj.* enèrgic
forearm *n.m.* avantbraç
forecast *v.* pronosticar | *n.m.*
pronòstic
forefinger *n.m.* dit índex
forehead *n.m.* front
foreign *adj.* estranger
foreign currency *n.f.* moneda
estrangera

foreign language *n.f.* llengua
estrangera
foreigner *n.* estranger
foreleg *n.f.* pota davantera
foreman *n.m.* encarregat
foremost *adj.* primer
forerunner *n.* precursor
foresight *n.f.* previsió
forest *n.m.* bosc
forestry *n.f.* silvicultura
forever *adv.* per sempre
forge *v.* falsificar
forgery *n.f.* falsificació
forget *v.* oblidar
forgetful *adj.* oblidadís
forgive *v.* perdonar
fork *n.f.* forquilla
form *n.m.* formulari
formal *adj.* formal
formally *adv.* formalment
format *v.* formatar | *n.m.* format
formation *n.f.* formació
former *adj.* anterior
formerly *adv.* anteriorment
formula *n.f.* fórmula
formulate *v.* formular
forsake *v.* abandonar
fortieth *adj.* quarantè
fortified *adj.* fortificat
fortnight *n.f.* quinzena
fortress *n.f.* fortalesa
fortunately *adv.* afortunadament
fortune *n.f.* fortuna
fortune teller *n.* endevinador
forty *num.* quaranta
forum *n.m.* fòrum
forward *adj.* endavant
fossil *n.m.* fòssil
foster *v.* fomentar
foul *n.f.* falta

found *v.* fundar
foundation *n.f.* fundació
fountain *n.f.* font
four *num.* quatre
four-wheel drive *n.f.* tracció a les quatre rodes
fourteen *num.* catorze
fourteenth *adj.* catorzè
fourth *adj.* quart
fowl *n.m.* ocell de corral
foyer *n.m.* vestíbul
fraction *n.f.* fracció
fracture *n.f.* fractura
fragment *n.m.* fragment
fragrance *n.f.* fragància
fragrant *adj.* fragant
frame *n.m.* marc
framework *n.m.* marc
France *n.f.* França
franchise *n.f.* franquícia
frantic *adj.* frenètic
fraud *n.m.* frau
fraudulent *adj.* fraudulent
free *adj.* gratis
free of charge *adj.* gratis
free time *n.m.* temps lliure
freedom *n.f.* llibertat
freely *adv.* lliurement
freeze *v.* congelar
freeze-dried *adj.* liofilitzat
freezer *n.m.* congelador
freezing *adj.* fred
French *adj./n.* francès
french fries *n.f.* patates fregides
french toast *n.f.* rostes de Santa Teresa
frequency *n.f.* freqüència
frequent *adj.* freqüent
frequently *adv.* freqüentment
fresco *n.m.* fresc

fresh *adj.* fresc
fresh water *n.f.* aigua dolça
freshly *adv.* recentment
Friday *n.m.* divendres
fridge *n.f.* nevera
fried *adj.* fregit
friend *n.* amic
friendly *adj.* amistós
friendship *n.f.* amistat
fries *n.f.* patates fregides
frighten *v.* espantar
frightened *adj.* espantat
frightening *adj.* espantós
fritter *n.m.* bunyol
frog *n.f.* granota
front *n.m.* front
front desk *n.f.* recepció
front door *n.f.* porta d'entrada
front page *n.f.* portada
front seat *n.m.* seient davanter
frost *n.m.* gebre
frosted *adj.* gebrat
frosting *n.m.* glacejat
frozen *adj.* congelat
fructose *n.f.* fructosa
frugal *adj.* frugal
fruit *n.f.* fruita
fry *v.* fregir
frying pan *n.f.* paella
fudge *n.m.* fudge
fuel *n.m.* combustible
fuel gauge *n.m.* indicador de combustible
fuel tank *n.m.* tanc de combustible
full *adj.* ple
fully *adv.* plenament
fumble *n.f.* pèrdua de pilota
fume *n.m.* fum
fun *n.f.* diversió
function *n.f.* funció

functional *adj.* funcional
functionality *n.f.* funcionalitat
fund *n.m.* fons
fundamental *adj.* fonamental
funding *n.m.* fons
fundraiser *n.f.* recaptació de fons
funeral *n.m.* funeral
fungus *n.m.* fongs
funny *adj.* divertit
fur *n.f.* pell
fur coat *n.m.* abric de pell
furnace *n.m.* forn

furnish *v.* moblar
furnished *adj.* moblat
furniture *n.m.* mobles
further *adj.* més lluny
furthermore *adv.* a més
furthest *adj.* més llunyà
fuse *n.m.* fusible
fuse box *n.m.* quadre de distribució
fuselage *n.m.* fuselatge
fusion *n.f.* fusió
future *n.m.* futur

G

gain *v.* guanyar
galaxy *n.f.* galàxia
gale *n.m.* vendaval
Galicia *n.* Galícia
Galician *adj./n.* gallec
gallery *n.f.* galeria
gallon *n.m.* galó
gambit *n.m.* gambit
gamble *v.* jugar
gambler *n.* jugador
gambling *n.m.* joc
game *n.m.* joc
game show *n.m.* concurs de TV
gap *n.f.* bretxa
garage *n.m.* garatge
garbage *n.f.* escombraries
garbage bag *n.f.* bossa
  d'escombraries
garbage can *n.f.* paperera
garbage truck *n.m.* camió
  d'escombraries
garden *n.m.* jardí
gardening *n.f.* jardineria
gargoyle *n.f.* gàrgola
garlic *n.m.* all
garnet *n.m.* granat
garnish *v.* adornar
gas *n.f.* gasolina
gas gauge *n.m.* indicador de
  combustible
gas station *n.f.* gasolinera
gas tank *n.m.* tanc de combustible
gasoline *n.f.* gasolina
gastritis *n.f.* gastritis
gastroenteritis *n.f.* gastroenteritis

gastronomy *n.f.* gastronomia
gastropod *n.m.* gasteròpode
gate *n.f.* porta
gate keeper *n.* porter
gather *v.* reunir-se
gathering place *n.m.* lloc de
  reunió
gauge *n.m.* indicador
gauze *n.f.* gasa
gay *adj.* gai
gay club *n.m.* club gai
GDP (Gross Domestic Product)
  n.m. PIB (producte interior brut)
gear *n.f.* marxa
gearbox *n.f.* caixa de canvis
gearshift lever *n.f.* palanca de
  canvis
gel *n.m.* gel
gelatin *n.f.* gelatina
gem *n.f.* gemma
Gemini *n.m.* Bessons
gemstone *n.f.* gemma
gender *n.m.* gènere
gene *n.m.* gen
general *adj.* general
general election *n.f.* eleccions
  generals
generally *adv.* generalment
generate *v.* generar
generation *n.f.* generació
generator *n.m.* generador
generosity *n.f.* generositat
generous *adj.* generós
generously *adv.* generosament
genetic *adj.* genètic

genetically *adv.* genèticament
genetically modified food *n.m.*
  aliment modificat genèticament
genetics *n.f.* genètica
genitals *n.m.* genitals
genius *n.* geni
genre *n.m.* gènere
gentle *adj.* amable
gentleman *n.m.* senyor
gently *adv.* suaument
genuine *adj.* genuí
genuinely *adv.* sincerament
geography *n.f.* geografia
geological *adj.* geològic
geologist *n.* geòleg
geology *n.f.* geologia
Georgia *n.f.* Geòrgia
germ *n.m.* germen
German *adj./n.* alemany
Germany *n.f.* Alemanya
germicide *n.m.* germicida
gerund *n.m.* gerundi
gesture *n.m.* gest
get *v.* obtenir
get rid of *v.* desfer-se de
giant *n.* gegant
giblets *n.m.* menuts
gift *n.m.* regal
gift shop *n.f.* botiga de regals
gift store *n.f.* botiga de regals
gig *n.f.* actuació
gilded *adj.* daurat
gin *n.f.* ginebra
gin and tonic *n.m.* gintònic
ginger *n.m.* gingebre
ginkgo *n.m.* ginkgo
giraffe *n.f.* girafa
girl *n.f.* noia
girlfriend *n.f.* xicota
give *v.* donar

give (something) away *v.* regalar
give birth (to) *v.* donar a llum
give (something) up *v.* deixar de
gizzard *n.m.* pedrer
glacier *n.f.* glacera
glad *adj.* content
gladly *adv.* amb molt de gust
glamorous *adj.* encantador
gland *n.f.* glàndula
glass *n.m.* vidre
glasses *n.f.* ulleres
glassware *n.f.* cristalleria
glaze *n.m.* llustre
glider *n.m.* planador
glimpse *v.* entreveure
global *adj.* global
globalization *n.f.* globalització
glory *n.f.* glòria
gloss *n.m.* llustre
glossary *n.m.* glossari
glove *n.m.* guant
glucose *n.f.* glucosa
glue *n.f.* cola
gluten *n.m.* gluten
glycerin *n.f.* glicerina
go *v.* anar
goal *n.m.* gol
goalkeeper *n.* porter
goat *n.f.* cabra
goblet *n.f.* copa
God *n.* Déu
god *n.m.* déu
goggles *n.f.* ulleres
gold *n.m.* or
gold plate *n.m.* bany d'or
golden *adj.* daurat
golf *n.m.* golf
golf ball *n.f.* pilota de golf
golf club *n.m.* pal de golf
golf course *n.m.* camp de golf

gondola *n.f.* góndola
gone *adj.* passat
good *adj.* bo
goodbye *phr.* adéu
goods *n.m.* béns
goose *n.f.* oca
gospel *n.m.* evangeli
Gothic style *n.m.* estil gòtic
gourd *n.f.* carbassa
govern *v.* governar
government *n.m.* govern
governor *n.* governador
grab *v.* agafar
grade *n.m.* grau
gradient *n.m.* gradient
gradual *adj.* gradual
gradually *adv.* gradualment
graduate *n.* graduat
grain *n.m.* gra
gram *n.m.* gram
grammar *n.f.* gramàtica
grand *adj.* gran
grandchild *n.* net
granddaughter *n.f.* neta
grandfather *n.m.* avi
grandmother *n.f.* àvia
grandparent *n.* avi
grandson *n.m.* net
granola *n.f.* granola
grant *v.* concedir
granulated *adj.* granulat
granule *n.m.* grànul
grape *n.m.* raïm
grape juice *n.m.* suc de raïm
grapefruit *n.f.* aranja
grapeseed oil *n.m.* oli de llavors
  de raïm
graph *n.m.* gràfic
graphic *adj.* gràfic
graphic arts *n.m.* arts gràfiques

graphics *n.m.* gràfics
grass *n.f.* herba
grate *v.* ratllar
grated *adj.* ratllat
grateful *adj.* agraït
grater *n.m.* ratllador
gratuity *n.f.* propina
grave *n.f.* tomba
gravestone *n.f.* làpida sepulcral
gravitational *adj.* gravitacional
gravity *n.f.* gravetat
gravy *n.f.* salsa
gray *adj.* gris
gray-haired *adj.* canós
graze *v.* pasturar
grease *n.m.* greix
great *adj.* gran, fantàstic | *phr.* ~!
  Fantàstic!
Great Britain *n.f.* Gran Bretanya
greatly *adv.* molt
Greece *n.f.* Grècia
green *adj.* verd
green beans *n.f.* mongetes verdes
green pepper *n.m.* pebrot de
  morro de bou
green tea *n.m.* te verd
greengrocer *n.* verdulaire
greens *n.f.* verdures
greet *v.* saludar
greeting *n.f.* salutació
grey *adj.* gris
grief *n.m.* dolor
grievance *n.m.* greuge
grill *n.f.* graella
grilled *adj.* a la graella
grind *v.* moldre
grits *n.f.* sèmola
grocer *n.* botiguer
grocery *n.f.* botiga de comestibles
grocery store *n.f.* botiga de
  comestibles

gross *adj.* brut
Gross Domestic Product (GDP) *n.m.* producte interior brut (PIB)
ground *n.f.* terra
ground floor *n.f.* planta baixa
groundwork *n.m.* treballs preparatoris
group *n.m.* grup
grouse *n.f.* queixa
grow *v.* créixer
grow up *v.* fer-se adult
growth *n.m.* creixement
gruel *n.f.* farinetes
guarantee *v.* garantir | *n.f.* garantia
guard *n.f.* guàrdia
guardian *n.* tutor
guardianship *n.f.* tutela
Guatemala *n.f.* Guatemala
guava *n.f.* guaiaba
guess *v.* endevinar | *n.f.* conjectura
guest *n.* convidat
guesthouse *n.m.* hostal
guidance *n.f.* guia

guide *v.* guiar | *n.f.* guia
guidebook *n.f.* guia
guided tour *n.f.* visita guiada
guidedog *n.m.* gos pigall
guideline *n.f.* directriu
guilt *n.f.* culpa
guilty *adj.* culpable
guinea fowl *n.f.* gallina de Guinea
guinea pig *n.m.* conillet d'Índies
guitar *n.f.* guitarra
guitarist *n.* guitarrista
gum *n.m.* xiclet
gumdrop *n.f.* gominola
gun *n.f.* arma de foc
gunshot *n.m.* tret
guy *n.m.* home
Guyana *n.f.* Guaiana
gym *n.m.* gimnàs
gymnasium *n.m.* gimnàs
gymnast *n.* gimnasta
gymnastics *n.f.* gimnàstica
gynecologist *n.* ginecòleg

H

habit *n.m.* hàbit
habitat *n.m.* hàbitat
haddock *n.m.* eglefí
hair *n.m.* cabell
hair conditioner *n.m.* suavitzant
hair dryer *n.m.* assecador de cabells
hair mousse *n.f.* escuma de cabells
hair salon *n.f.* perruqueria
hairbrush *n.m.* raspall de cabells
haircut *n.m.* pentinat
hairdo *n.m.* pentinat
hairdresser *n.* perruquer
hairspray *n.m.* laca
Haiti *n.f.* Haití
hake *n.m.* lluç
half *adj.* mig | *n.f.* meitat
halibut *n.m.* halibut
hall *n.f. (events)* sala; *(residence)* residència
hallway *n.m.* vestíbul
ham *n.m.* pernil
hamburger *n.f.* hamburguesa
hammer *n.m.* martell
hammock *n.f.* hamaca
hamster *n.m.* hàmster
hand *n.f.* mà
hand baggage *n.m.* equipatge de mà
handbag *n.f.* bossa de mà
handbrake *n.m.* fre de mà
handcuff *v.* emmanillar
handcuffs *n.f.* manilles
handicap *n.m. (golf)* handicap; *(physical)* discapacitat

handicapped *adj.* minusvàlid
handkerchief *n.m.* mocador
handle *n.f.* nansa
handlebar *n.m.* manillar
handmade *adj.* fet a mà
handsome *adj.* atractiu
hang *v.* penjar
hang glider *n.f.* ala delta
hanger *n.m.* penja-robes
hangover *n.f.* ressaca
happen *v.* succeir
happily *adv.* feliçment
happiness *n.f.* felicitat
happy *adj.* feliç
harass *v.* assetjar
harassment *n.m.* assetjament
harbor *n.m.* port
hard *adj.* dur
hard liquor *n.f.* beguda destil·lada
hard-boiled egg *n.m.* ou dur
hardly *adv.* a penes
hardware *n.m.* maquinari
hare *n.m.* llebre
harm *v.* danyar
harmful *adj.* perjudicial
harmless *adj.* inofensiu
harmony *n.f.* harmonia
harness *n.m.* arnès
harp *n.f.* arpa
harvest *n.f.* collita
hash *n.f.* picada
hashish *n.m.* haixix
hat *n.m.* barret
hate *v.* odiar | *n.m.* odi
hatred *n.m.* odi

have *v.* tenir
Hawaii *n.* Hawaii
hay *n.m.* fenc
hay fever *n.f.* rinitis al·lèrgica
hazard *n.m.* perill
hazelnut *n.f.* avellana
he *pron.* ell
head *n.m.* cap
headache *n.m.* mal de cap
header *n.f.* capçalera
heading *n.f.* capçalera
headlight *n.m.* far
headline *n.m.* titular
headstrong *adj.* obstinat
heal *v.* curar
health *n.f.* salut
health center *n.m.* centre de salut
health insurance *n.f.* assegurança
healthy *adj.* saludable
hear *v.* sentir
hearing *n.f.* oïda
hearing aid *n.m.* audífon
hearsay *n.m.* rumor
heart *n.m.* cor
heart attack *n.m.* atac de cor
heart condition *n.f.* afecció
  cardíaca
heart of palm *n.m.* margalló
heartbeat *n.m.* batec
heat *n.m.* calor
heater *n.m.* escalfador
heating *n.f.* calefacció
heaven *n.m.* cel
heavily *adv.* pesadament
heavy *adj.* pesat
heel *n.m.* taló
heifer *n.f.* vedella
height *n.f.* alçada, altura; ~ **above
  sea level** altura sobre el nivell
  del mar

helicopter *n.m.* helicòpter
hell *n.m.* infern
hello *interj* hola
helmet *n.m.* casc
help *v.* ajudar
helpful *adj.* útil
hemorrhoids *n.f.* hemorroides
hen *n.f.* gallina
hence *adv.* per això
her *pron.* la, li, l' *(see page 8)*
her(s) *pos. adj./pron.* el seu, la
  seva, els seus, les seves
herb *n.f.* herba
herbal tea *n.m.* te d'herbes
herbivore *n.m.* herbívor
here *adv.* aquí
heritage *n.m.* patrimoni
hernia *n.f.* hèrnia
hero *n.m.* heroi
heroin *n.f.* heroïna
heroine *n.f.* heroïna
herring *n.m.* areng
herself *pron.* ella mateixa
hesitate *v.* vacil·lar
heterosexual *adj.* heterosexual
hey *interj.* ep
heyday *n.m.* apogeu
hi *interj.* hola
hibernate *v.* hibernar
hibernation *n.f.* hibernació
hiccup *n.m.* singlot
hide *v.* amagar
high *adj.* alt
high quality *adj.* alta qualitat
high school *n.f.* escola secundària
high-tech *adj.* alta tecnologia
highlight *v.* destacar
highly *adv.* molt
highway *n.f.* carretera
hike *v.* fer senderisme | *n.f.* excursió

hilarious *adj.* divertit
hill *n.m.* turó
hilly *adj.* muntanyós
him *pron.* el, li, l', -lo *(see page 8)*
himself *pron.* ell mateix
hint *n.f.* pista
hip *n.m.* maluc
hire *v.* contractar
his *pos. adj, pron.* el seu, la seva,
  els seus, les seves
historian *n.* historiador
historic *adj.* històric
historic building *n.m.* edifici
  històric
historic site *n.m.* lloc històric
historical *adj.* històric
history *n.f.* història
hit *v.* pegar | *n.m.* cop
hitchhike *v.* fer autoestop
hither *adv.* aquí
HIV *n.m.* VIH
HIV-positive *adj.* VIH positiu
hobby *n.m.* entreteniment
hockey *n.m.* hoquei
hold *v.* agafar
holder *n.m.* titular
holding *n.f.* possessió
hole *n.m.* forat
holiday *n.f.* vacances
hollow *adj.* buit
holocaust *n.m.* holocaust
holy *adj.* sagrat
home *n.f.* casa, llar
home-style cooking *n.f.* cuina
  casolana
homeland *n.f.* pàtria
homeless *adj.* sense llar
homeless person *n.f.* persona
  sense llar
homemade *adj.* fet a casa

homeopathy *n.f.* homeopatia
homepage *n.f.* pàgina inicial
homework *n.m.* deures
homicide *n.m.* homicidi
homogenized *adj.* homogeneïtzat
homosexual *adj.* homosexual
Honduras *n.f.* Hondures
honest *adj.* honest
honestly *adv.* honestament
honey *n.m.* mel
honeycomb *n.f.* bresca
honeydew *n.m.* meló
honeymoon *n.f.* lluna de mel
honor *n.m.* honor
hood *n.f.* caputxa
hook *n.m.* ganxo
hookah *n.m.* narguil
hooray *interj* hurra
hope *v.* esperar | *n.f.* esperança
hopeful *adj.* esperançat
hops *n.m.* llúpol
horizontal *adj.* horitzontal
horn *n.f.* botzina
horrible *adj.* horrible
horror *n.m.* horror
horror film *n.m.* cinema de terror
horse *n.m.* cavall
horse racing *n.f.* cursa de cavalls
horseback riding *n.* hípica
horseradish *n.m.* rave picant
horseshoe crab *n.m.* limúlid
hospital *n.m.* hospital
hospitality *n.f.* hospitalitat
host *n.* amfitrió
hostage *n.* ostatge
hostel *n.m.* alberg
hostile *adj.* hostil
hot *adj.* calent
hot chocolate *n.f.* xocolata desfeta
hot dog *n.m.* frankfurt

hot sauce *n.f.* salsa picant
hot spring *n.f.* font termal
hot tea *n.m.* te calent
hot water *n.f.* aigua calenta
hotel *n.m.* hotel
hour *n.f.* hora
house *n.f.* casa
household *n.f.* casa
housekeeper *n.f.* majordoma
housewife *n.f.* mestressa de casa
housework *n.f.* feina de casa
housing *n.m.* habitatge
how *adv.* com
how many? *phr.* quants?
how much? *phr.* quant?
however *adv.* però
hubcap *n.m.* tapaboques
hug *v.* abraçar | *n.f.* abraçada
huge *adj.* gegant
human *adj.* humà
human rights *n.m.* drets humans
humble *adj.* humil
humidity *n.f.* humitat
humiliate *v.* humiliar
humiliation *n.f.* humiliació
humility *n.f.* humilitat
hummus *n.m.* humus

humor *n.m.* humor
humorous *adj.* humorístic
hundred *num.* cent
hundredth *adj.* centèsim
Hungary *n.f.* Hongria
hunger *n.m.* fam
hungry *adj.* afamat
hunt *v.* caçar
hunter *n.* caçador
hunting *n.f.* caça
hurry *v.* apressar
hurt *v.* ferir
husband *n.m.* marit
husk *n.f.* closca
hut *n.f.* cabana
hybrid *adj./n.m.* híbrid
hydrogen *n.m.* hidrogen
hygienist *n.* higienista
hyphen *n.m.* guió
hypnotism *n.m.* hipnotisme
hypnotize *v.* hipnotitzar
hypodermic needle *n.f.* agulla
  hipodèrmica
hypothesis *n.m.* hipòtesi
hysteria *n.f.* histèria
hysterical *adj.* histèric

I

I *pron.* jo
ice *n.m.* gel
ice cream *n.m.* gelat
ice cream cone *n.m.* gelat de neula
ice cream parlor *n.f.* geladeria
ice hockey *n.m.* hoquei sobre gel
ice skate *v.* patinar sobre gel
iceberg *n.m.* iceberg
iceberg lettuce *n.m.* enciam
  iceberg
iced *adj.* glacejat
Iceland *n.f.* Islàndia
icing *n.m.* glacejat
icy *adj.* gelat
ID card *n.m.* carnet d'identitat
Idaho *n.* Idaho
idea *n.f.* idea
ideal *adj.* ideal
idealism *n.m.* idealisme
idealist *n.* idealista
idealistic *adj.* idealista
ideally *adv.* idealment
identical *adj.* idèntic
identification *n.f.* identificació
identify *v.* identificar
identity card *n.m.* carnet
  d'identitat
identity document *n.m.* document
  d'identitat
ideological *adj.* ideològic
idiom *n.m.* idioma
idle *adj.* ociós
if *conj.* si
ignite *v.* encendre
ignition *n.f.* ignició

ignition key *n.f.* clau de contacte
ignorance *n.f.* ignorància
ignorant *adj.* ignorant
ignore *v.* no fer cas
ill *adj.* malalt
illegal *adj.* il·legal
illegal entry *n.f.* entrada il·legal
illegally *adv.* il·legalment
illegibility *n.f.* il·legibilitat
illegible *adj.* il·legible
illegitimate *adj.* il·legítim
Illinois *n.* Illinois
illiteracy *n.m.* analfabetisme
illiterate *adj.* analfabet
illness *n.f.* malaltia
illuminate *v.* il·luminar
illumination *n.f.* il·luminació
illustrate *v.* il·lustrar
illustration *n.f.* il·lustració
image *n.f.* imatge
imagery *n.f.* imatges
imaginary *adj.* imaginari
imagination *n.f.* imaginació
imaginative *adj.* imaginatiu
imagine *v.* imaginar
imitate *v.* imitar
imitation *n.f.* imitació
immediate *adj.* immediat
immediately *adv.* immediatament
immigrant *n.* immigrant
immigration *n.f.* immigració
immoral *adj.* immoral
immune *adj.* immune
immune system *n.m.* sistema
  immunitari

immunity *n.f.* immunitat
immunization *n.f.* immunització
impact *n.m.* impacte
impatience *n.f.* impaciència
impatient *adj.* impacient
impatiently *adv.* impacientment
imperative *adj.* imperatiu
impersonate *v.* imitar
implement *v.* implementar
implementation *n.f.* implementació
implication *n.f.* implicació
imply *v.* implicar
impolite *adj.* descortès
import *n.f.* importació
importance *n.f.* importància
important *adj.* important
importantly *adv.* important
impose *v.* imposar
impossible *adj.* impossible
impostor *n.* impostor
imposture *n.f.* impostura
impress *v.* impressionar
impressed *adj.* impressionat
impression *n.f.* impressió
impressive *adj.* impressionant
improve *v.* millorar
improved *n.* millorat
improvement *n.f.* millora
in *prep.* a
inability *n.f.* incapacitat
inaccessible *adj.* inaccessible
incarcerate *v.* empresonar
incarceration *n.m.* empresonament
incentive *n.m.* incentiu
inch *n.f.* polzada
incidence *n.f.* incidència
incident *n.m.* incident
incise *v.* tallar
incline *n.m.* pendent

include *v.* incloure
included *adj.* inclòs
including *prep.* incloent
inclusive *adj.* inclusiu
income *n.m.* ingressos
income tax *n.m.* impost sobre
la renda
incompetent *adj.* incompetent
incorporate *v.* incorporar
incorporated *adj.* incorporat
incorrect *adj.* incorrecte
incorrectly *adv.* incorrectament
increase *v.* augmentar
increasingly *adv.* cada vegada més
incredible *adj.* increïble
incriminate *v.* incriminar
incubate *v.* incubar
incumbent *n.* titular
incur *v.* incórrer en
indeed *adv.* en efecte
independence *n.f.* independència
independent *adj.* independent
independently *adv.* independentment
index *n.m.* índex
India *n.f.* Índia
Indian *adj.* indi
Indiana *n.* Indiana
indicate *v.* indicar
indication *n.f.* indicació
indict *v.* processar
indictment *n.m.* processament
indigestion *n.f.* indigestió
indirect *adj.* indirecte
indirectly *adv.* indirectament
individual *adj.* individual
indoor *adj.* interior
indoor pool *n.f.* piscina coberta
indoors *adv.* a casa
induce *v.* induir

induction *n.f.* inducció
industrial *adj.* industrial
industry *n.f.* indústria
inequality *n.f.* desigualtat
inevitable *adj.* inevitable
inevitably *adv.* inevitablement
inexpensive *adj.* barat
infant *n.m.* infant
infant formula *n.f.* llet maternitzada
infantry *n.f.* infanteria
infect *v.* infectar
infected *adj.* infectat
infection *n.f.* infecció
infectious *adj.* infecciós
infectious mononucleosis *n.f.*
mononucleosi infecciosa
infinitive *n.m.* infinitiu
infirmary *n.f.* infermeria
inflammation *n.f.* inflamació
inflammatory *adj.* inflamatori
inflation *n.f.* inflació
influence *v.* influir | *n.f.* influència
influenza *n.f.* grip
inform *v.* informar
informal *adj.* informal
information *n.f.* informació
information desk *n.m.* taulell
d'informació
information office *n.f.* oficina
d'informació
infraction *n.f.* infracció
infrared *adj.* infraroig
infrastructure *n.f.* infraestructura
infusion *n.f.* infusió
ingredient *n.m.* ingredient
initial *adj.* inicial
initially *adv.* inicialment
initiative *n.f.* iniciativa
inject *v.* injectar

injection *n.f.* injecció
injunction *n.f.* injunció
injure *v.* lesionar
injured *adj.* lesionat
injury *n.f.* ferida
ink *n.f.* tinta
inn *n.f.* fonda
innate *adj.* innat
inner *adj.* interior
inner tube *n.f.* cambra d'aire
innocent *adj.* innocent
innovate *v.* innovar
innovation *n.f.* innovació
inoculation *n.f.* inoculació
input *n.f.* entrada
inquiry *n.f.* investigació
insect *n.m.* insecte
insect bite *n.f.* picada
insect repellant *n.m.* repel·lent
d'insectes
insert *v.* inserir
inside *prep.* dins
insight *n.f.* perspicàcia
insist *v.* insistir
insistence *n.f.* insistència
insomnia *n.m.* insomni
inspect *v.* inspeccionar
inspection *n.f.* inspecció
inspiration *n.f.* inspiració
inspire *v.* inspirar
install *v.* instal·lar
installation *n.f.* instal·lació
instance *n.f.* instància; **for ~** *phr.*
per exemple
instant *adj.* instantani
instead *adv.* en comptes
instead of *prep.* en lloc de
instigate *v.* instigar
instigation *n.f.* instigació
instinct *n.m.* instint

institute *n.m.* institut
institution *n.f.* institució
institutional *adj.* institucional
instruction *n.f.* instrucció
instructional *adj.* instructiu
instructor *n.* instructor
instrument *n.m.* instrument
instrumental *adj.* instrumental
insufficient *adj.* insuficient
insulin *n.f.* insulina
insult *v.* insultar | *n.m.* insult
insulting *adj.* insultant
insurance *n.f.* assegurança
insurance card *n.m.* carnet
  d'assegurança
insurance company *n.f.*
  companyia d'assegurances
insurance policy *n.f.* pòlissa
  d'assegurança
integrate *v.* integrar
integrated *adj.* integrat
integration *n.f.* integració
intellectual *adj.* intel·lectual
intellectual property *n.f.*
  propietat intel·lectual
intelligence *n.f.* intel·ligència
intelligent *adj.* intel·ligent
intend *v.* intentar
intense *adj.* intens
intensity *n.f.* intensitat
intensive *adj.* intensiu
intensive care unit (ICU) *n.f.*
  unitat de cures intensives
intention *n.f.* intenció
interact *v.* interaccionar
interaction *n.f.* interacció
interactive *adj.* interactiu
interest *n.m.* interès
interested *adj.* interessat
interesting *adj.* interessant

interference *n.f.* interferència
interim *adj.* provisional
interior *adj.* interior
intermediate *adj.* intermedi
intermission *n.m.* entreacte
internal *adj.* intern
international *adj.* internacional
international call *n.f.* trucada
  internacional
Internet *n.* Internet
Internet café *n.m.* cibercafè
interpret *v.* interpretar
interpretation *n.f.* interpretació
interpreter *n.* intèrpret
interrupt *v.* interrompre
interruption *n.f.* interrupció
intersection *n.f.* intersecció
interval *n.m.* interval
intervene *v.* intervenir
intervention *n.f.* intervenció
interview *v.* entrevistar | *n.f.*
  entrevista
intimacy *n.f.* intimitat
intimate *adj.* íntim
into *prep.* a
intrinsic *adj.* intrínsec
introduce *v.* introduir
introduce oneself *v.* presentar-se
introduction *n.f.* introducció
introspection *n.f.* introspecció
intrude *v.* imposar
intruder *n.* intrús
intrusion *n.f.* intrusió
invade *v.* envair
invent *v.* inventar
invention *n.f.* invenció
invest *v.* invertir
investigate *v.* investigar
investigation *n.f.* investigació
investment *n.f.* inversió

investor *n.* inversor
invitation *n.f.* invitació
invite *v.* invitar
invoice *n.f.* factura
involve *v.* involucrar
involvement *n.f.* participació
inwards *adv.* cap a dins
iodine *n.m.* iode
ion *n.m.* ió
Iowa *n.* Iowa
Iran *n.m.* Iran
Iranian *adj./n.* iranià
Iraq *n.m.* Iraq
Iraqi *adj./n.* iraquià
Ireland *n.f.* Irlanda
Ireland, Northern *n.f.* Irlanda
  del Nord
Irish *adj./n.* irlandès
iron *v.* planxar | *n.f. (appliance)*
  planxa; *n.m. (metal)* ferro
ironic *adj.* irònic
irony *n.f.* ironia
irregular *adj.* irregular
irrigation *n.m.* regatge

irritate *v.* irritar
irritated *adj.* irritat
irritating *adj.* irritant
Islam *n.m.* islam
Islamic *adj.* islàmic
island *n.f.* illa
isolate *v.* aïllar
isolated *adj.* aïllat
isolation *n.m.* aïllament
Israel *n.m.* Israel
Israeli *adj./n.* israelià
issue *n.m.* assumpte
it *pron.* ho, -ho *(see page 8)*
Italy *n.f.* Itàlia
itch *v.* fer picor | *n.f.* picor
item *n.m.* article
itemize *v.* detallar
itemized *adj.* detallat
itemized bill *n.f.* factura detallada
itinerary *n.m.* itinerari
its *pos. adj./pron.* el seu, la seva,
  els seus, les seves
itself *pron.* si mateix

J

jacket *n.f.* jaqueta
jail *n.m.* presó
jalapeño *n.m.* jalapeño, xili de
  Jalapa
jam *n.f.* melmelada
January *n.m.* gener
Japan *n.m.* Japó
Japanese *adj./n.* japonès
jar *n.m.* pot
jasmine *n.m.* gessamí
jaundice *n.f.* icterícia
jaw *n.f.* mandíbula
jazz *n.m.* jazz
jealous *adj.* gelós
jeans *n.m.* texans
jeep *n.m.* jeep
jello *n.f.* gelatina
jelly *n.f.* gelea
jellyfish *n.f.* medusa
jerk *v.* sacsejar
Jerusalem *n.m.* Jerusalem
jet *n.m.* jet
jet lag *n.m.* trastorn d'horari
jet-ski *n.f.* moto d'aigua
jetty *n.m.* desembarcador
Jew *n.* jueu
jewel *n.f.* joia
jeweler *n.* joier
jewelry *n.f.* joies
Jewish *adj.* jueu
job *n.m.* treball
job description *n.f.* descripció
  de treball
jockey *n.m.* joquei
jogging *n.m.* jogging

join *v.* unir
joint *n.f.* junta
jointly *adv.* conjuntament
joke *v.* fer broma | *n.f.* broma
Jordan *n.f.* Jordània
Jordanian *adj./n.* jordà
journal *n.f.* revista
journalism *n.m.* periodisme
journalist *n.* periodista
journey *n.m.* viatge
joy *n.f.* alegria
judge *n.* jutge
judgement *n.m.* judici
judiciary *n.* judicial
jug *n.f.* gerra
juice *n.m.* suc
juicy *adj.* sucós
July *n.m.* juliol
jump *v.* saltar
jumper *n.* saltador
junction *n.f.* unió
June *n.m.* juny
jungle *n.f.* jungla
junior *adj.* menor
junior high school *n.m.* institut
  d'educació secundària
juniper *n.m.* ginebre
jurisdiction *n.f.* jurisdicció
jurisprudence *n.f.* jurisprudència
jury *n.m.* jurat
just *adj., adv.* just
justice *n.f.* justícia
justified *adj.* justificat
justify *v.* justificar

K

kale *n.f.* col verda
kangaroo *n.m.* cangur
Kansas *n.* Kansas
karaoke *n.m.* karaoke
karate *n.m.* karate
Kazakhstan *n.m.* Kazakhstan
kebab *n.m.* kebab
keen *adj.* agut
keen on *adj.* aficionat
keep *v.* guardar
keep out *v.* no entrar
kennel *n.f.* gossada
Kentucky *n.* Kentucky
kernel *n.m.* nucli
kerosene *n.m.* querosè
kerosene lamp *n.m.* llum de querosè
kerosene stove *n.f.* estufa de querosè
ketchup *n.m.* quètxup
kettle *n.m.* bullidor
key *n.f.* clau
key chain *n.m.* clauer
key ring *n.m.* clauer
keyboard *n.m.* teclat
keyword *n.f.* paraula clau
kick *v.* donar un cop de peu
kick-off *n.m.* servei inicial
kid *n.m.* nen; *n.f.* nena
kidnap *v.* segrestar
kidnapper *n.* segrestador
kidney *n.m.* ronyó
kidney bean *n.f.* mongeta
kidney stone *n.m.* càlcul renal

kill *v.* matar
killing *n.f.* matança
kilobyte *n.m.* kilobyte
kilogram *n.m.* quilogram
kilometer *n.m.* quilòmetre
kind *adj.* amable | *n.m.* tipus
kindergarten *n.m.* parvulari
kindergartener *n.* pàrvul
kindly *adv.* amablement
kindness *n.f.* bondat
king *n.m.* rei
kinship *n.m.* parentiu
kiss *v.* besar | *n.m.* petó
kit *n.m.* equip
kitchen *n.f.* cuina
kitten *n.m.* gatet
kiwi *n.m.* kiwi
knapsack *n.f.* motxilla
knead *v.* pastar
knee *n.m.* genoll
knife *n.m.* ganivet
knit *v.* teixir
knock *v.* picar
knot *n.m.* nus
know *v.* *(relationships)* conèixer; *(knowledge)* saber
knowledge *n.m.* coneixement
knuckle *n.m.* artell
Korea *n.* Corea; **North** ~ Corea del Nord; **South** ~ Corea del Sud
Korean *adj./n.* coreà
kosher *adj.* caixer

L

label *n.f.* etiqueta
labor *n.m.* treball
laboratory *n.m.* laboratori
lace *n.f. (material)* punta; *n.m.*
 (string) cordó
lack *v.* mancar
lacquer *n.f.* laca
lactose *n.f.* lactosa
lad *n.m.* noi
ladder *n.f.* escala
ladies restroom *n.m.* lavabos
 femenins
ladle *n.m.* cullerot
lady *n.f.* senyora
lag *v.* disminuir
lake *n.m.* llac
lamb *n.m.* xai
lame *adj.* coix
lament *v.* lamentar
lamentable *adj.* lamentable
lamentation *n.f.* lamentació
lamp *n.f.* llum
lance *n.f.* llança
land *n.m.* terra
landlord *n.m.* propietari
landmark *n.f.* fita
landscape *n.m.* paisatge
lane *n.m.* camí
language *n.m.* idioma
language course *n.m.* curs
 d'idioma
languish *v.* llanguir
lapse *n.m.* lapse
laptop *n.m.* portàtil
larceny *n.m.* furt

lard *n.m.* llard
large *adj.* gran
largely *adv.* en gran part
lark *n.f.* alosa
laryngitis *n.f.* laringitis
lasagna *n.f.* lasanya
laser *n.m.* làser
last *adj.* últim
last name *n.m.* cognom
last night *n.f.* anit
late *adj.* tard
later *adv.* més tard
latest *adj.* més recent
latitude *n.f.* latitud
latter *adj.* últim
Latvia *n.f.* Letònia
laudable *adj.* lloable
laugh *v, n.m.* riure
laughter *n.m.* riure
launch *v.* llançar
launderette *n.f.* bugaderia
laundromat *n.f.* bugaderia
laundry *n.f.* bugada
laundry facilities *n.f.* bugaderia
laundry service *n.m.* servei de
 bugaderia
laurel *n.m.* llorer
lava *n.f.* lava
lavatory *n.m.* lavabo
lavender *n.f.* lavanda
law *n.f.* llei
lawsuit *n.m.* plet
lawyer *n.* advocat
laxative *n.m.* laxant
lay *v.* posar

lay person *n.* laic
layer *n.f.* capa
layout *n.m.* format
lazy *adj.* mandrós
lead *v.* dirigir
lead-free *adj.* sense plom
leaded *adj.* amb plom
leaded gasoline *n.f.* gasolina amb plom
leader *n.* líder
leadership *n.m.* lideratge
leading *adj.* principal
leaf *n.f.* fulla
league *n.f.* lliga
leak *n.f.* fuga
lean *adj.* magre
leap *v.* saltar
learn *v.* aprendre
lease *n.m.* arrendament
least *pron.* menys
leather *n.m.* cuir
leave *v.* deixar
leave out *v.* ometre
leaven *n.m.* llevat
lecture *n.f.* conferència
lecturer *n.* conferenciant
ledge *n.f.* lleixa
leech *n.f.* sangonera
leek *n.m.* porro
left *n.f.* esquerra
left-wing *adj.* esquerra, esquerrà
leftover *adj.* sobrant
leg *n.f.* cama
legal *adj.* legal
legalization *n.f.* legalització
legalize *v.* legalitzar
legally *adv.* legalment
legend *n.f.* llegenda
leggings *n.f.* malles
legislation *n.f.* legislació

legislator *n.* legislador
legislature *n.m.* legislatura
legume *n.m.* llegum
leisure *n.m.* oci
lemon *n.f.* llimona
lemonade *n.f.* llimonada
lemongrass *n.f.* citronel·la
lend *v.* prestar
lender *n.* prestador
length *n.f.* llargada
leniency *n.f.* indulgència
lenient *adj.* indulgent
lens *n.f.* lent
lens cap *n.f.* tapa de l'objectiu
Lent *n.f.* Quaresma
lentil *n.f.* llentia
Leo *n.m.* lleó
leopard *n.m.* lleopard
lesbian *n.f.* lesbiana
less *adv.* menys
lesson *n.f.* lliçó
let *v.* deixar
lethargy *n.f.* letargia
letter *n.f. (postal)* carta; *(alphabet)* lletra
letter box *n.f.* bústia
lettuce *n.m.* enciam
level *n.m.* nivell
level crossing *n.m.* pas a nivell
levy *v.* recaptar | *n.f.* recaptació
liability *n.f.* responsabilitat
liable *adj.* responsable
liar *n.* mentider
libel *n.f.* difamació
liberal arts *n.m.* arts liberals
Libra *n.f.* Balança
librarian *n.* bibliotecari
library *n.f.* biblioteca
lice *n.m.* polls
license *n.f.* llicència

license plate *n.f.* matrícula
license plate number *n.f.* matrícula
licorice *n.f.* regalèssia
lid *n.f.* tapa
lie *v.* mentir | *n.f.* mentida
lie down *v.* jeure
Liechtenstein *n.m.* Liechtenstein
lien *n.m.* dret de retenció
lieutenant *n.* tinent
life *n.f.* vida
life belt *n.m.* cinturó salvavides
life jacket *n.f.* armilla salvavides
life preserver *n.f.* armilla salvavides
lifeboat *n.m.* bot salvavides
lifeguard *n.* socorrista
lift *v.* aixecar
light *adj.* clar | *v.* encendre | *n.f.* llum
light meter *n.m.* fotòmetre
lightbulb *n.f.* bombeta
lightening *n.m.* llamp
lighter *n.m.* encenedor
lighting *n.f.* il·luminació
lightly *adv.* lleugerament
like *conj./prep.* com | *v.* agradar
likely *adj.* probable
lilac *n.m.* lilà
lily *n.m.* lliri
lima beans *n.m.* garrofó
limber *adj.* àgil
lime *n.f.* llima
limit *v.* limitar | *n.m.* límit
limitation *n.f.* limitació
limited *adj.* limitat
limousine *n.f.* limusina
linden tree *n.m.* til·ler
line *n.f.* línia
lineage *n.m.* llinatge

linear *adj.* lineal
lined *adj.* folrat
linen *n.m.* lli
lingerie *n.f.* llenceria
linguist *n.* lingüista
linguistics *n.f.* lingüística
link *v.* enllaçar | *n.m.* enllaç
lion *n.m.* lleó
lip *n.m.* llavi
lipstick *n.m.* llapis de llavis
liquefy *v.* liquar
liqueur *n.m.* licor
liquid *n.m.* líquid
liquidate *v.* liquidar
liquidation *n.f.* liquidació
liquidity *n.f.* liquiditat
liquor *n.m.* licor
liquor store *n.f.* botiga de licors
list *n.f.* llista
listen *v.* escoltar
listener *n.* oient
liter *n.m.* litre
literal *adj.* literal
literary *adj.* literari
literature *n.f.* literatura
Lithuania *n.f.* Lituània
litigate *v.* litigar
litigation *n.m.* litigi
litter *v.* llançar escombraries | *n.f.* escombraries
little *adj.* petit | *n.f.* **a ~** una mica
live *v.* viure
livelihood *n.m.* mitjans de vida
lively *adj.* animat
liver *n.m.* fetge
living *adj.* viu
living room *n.f.* sala d'estar
lizard *n.m.* llangardaix
load *v.* carregar
loaf (of bread) *n.f.* barra de pa

loan v. prestar | n.m. préstec
loathe v. odiar
loathsome adj. odiós
lobby n.m. vestíbul
lobster n.f. llagosta
local adj. local
local train n.m. tren local
locally adv. localment
locate v. localitzar
located adj. situat
location n.m. lloc
lock v. tancar
lock out v. tancar a fora
locker n.m. armari
locker for baggage n.m. caseller
locomotive n.f. locomotora
locust n.f. llagosta
lodestar n.m. estel polar
log in/on v. iniciar una sessió
log out/off v. finalitzar una sessió
logic n.f. lògica
logical adj. lògic
lollipop n.f. piruleta
London n.m. Londres
lonely adj. sol
lonesome adj. sol
long adj. llarg
long-distance adj. llarga distància
long-distance call n.f. trucada de llarga distància
long-grain rice n.m. arròs llarg
long-term adj. llarg termini
long-term parking n.m. aparcament de llarg termini
longer adj. més llarg
longevity n.f. longevitat
longitude n.f. longitud
look v. mirar
look after v. cuidar
look around v. mirar al voltant

look for v. cercar
look forward to v. esperar
look like v. assemblar-se
loose adj. solt
loose-fitting adj. ample
loosely adv. balderament
lord n.m. senyor
lorry n.m. camió
lose v. perdre
lose blood v. perdre sang
lose one's way v. perdre el camí
loser n. perdedor
loss n.f. pèrdua
lost adj. perdut
lost and found office n.f. oficina d'objectes perduts
lot: a ~ of phr. molt(s)
lotion n.f. loció
lottery n.f. loteria
loud adj. sorollós
louder adv. més sorollós
loudly adv. sorollosament
loudness n.m. soroll
Louisiana n. Louisiana
lounge n.f. sala d'estar
love n.m. amor
lovely adj. preciós
lover n. amant
low adj. baix
low-calorie adj. baix en calories
low-fat adj. baix en greixos
lower adj. més baix | v. abaixar
lowland n.f. terres baixes
loyal adj. lleial
loyalty n.f. lleialtat
lozenge n.f. pastilla
lubricant n.m. lubricant
lubricate v. lubricar
lubrication n.f. lubricació
luck n.f. sort; **good ~!** phr. bona sort!

lucky *adj.* afortunat
lucrative *adj.* lucratiu
luggage *n.m.* equipatge
lukewarm *adj.* tebi
lullaby *n.f.* cançó de bressol
luminous *adj.* lluminós
lump *n.m.* bony
lunatic *n.* llunàtic
lunch *n.m.* dinar
lunch box *n.f.* carmanyola
lunchmeat *n.f.* carn freda

lunchtime *n.f.* hora de dinar
lung *n.m.* pulmó
lush *adj.* fresc
lust *n.f.* luxúria
Luxembourg *n.m.* Luxemburg
luxury *n.m.* luxe
luxury goods *n.m.* articles de luxe
lyrical *adj.* líric

M

macaroni *n.m.* macarrons
Macedonia *n.f.* Macedònia
macerate *v.* macerar
machine *n.f.* màquina
machine washable *adj.* rentable
a la rentadora
machinery *n.f.* maquinària
mackerel *n.m.* verat
mad *adj.* boig
madam *n.f.* senyora
made *adj.* fet
Madrid *n.m.* Madrid
magazine *n.f.* revista
magic *n.f.* màgia
magician *n.* mag
magnesium *n.m.* magnesi
magnet *n.m.* imant
magnetic *adj.* magnètic
magnetism *n.m.* magnetisme
magnificent *adj.* magnífic
magnitude *n.f.* magnitud
magpie *n.f.* garsa
maid *n.f.* cambrera
maiden name *n.m.* cognòm de
soltera
mail *n.m.* correu
mailbox *n.f.* bústia
main *adj.* principal
main course *n.m.* plat principal
main road *n.f.* carretera principal
main square *n.f.* plaça principal
main street *n.m.* carrer principal
Maine *n.* Maine
mainly *adv.* principalment
mainstream *n.m.* corrent dominant

maintain *v.* mantenir
maintenance *n.m.* manteniment
maize *n.m.* blat de moro
major *adj.* major
majority *n.f.* majoria
make *v.* fer
make fun of *v.* burlar-se de
make sure *v.* confirmar
make up *v.* constituir; **make
(something) up** inventar
maker *n.* fabricant
makeup *n.m.* maquillatge
malady *n.m.* mal
malaria *n.f.* malària
male *adj.* masculí | *n.m.* mascle
malice *n.f.* malícia
malicious *adj.* maliciós
malign *v.* difamar
malignant *adj.* maligne
mall *n.m.* centre comercial
mallet *n.f.* maça
malnutrition *n.f.* malnutrició
malpractice *n.f.* negligència
Malta *n.f.* Malta
malted *adj.* maltejat
mammal *n.m.* mamífer
mammoth *n.m.* mamut
man *n.m.* home
manage *v.* dirigir
management *n.f.* administració
manager *n.* gerent
managerial *adj.* directiu
mandarin orange *n.f.* mandarina
mandate *n.m.* mandat
mandatory *adj.* obligatori

mango *n.m.* mango
mania *n.f.* mania
manicure *n.f.* manicura
manifesto *n.m.* manifest
mannequin *n.f.* maniquí
manner *n.f.* manera
mansion *n.f.* casa gran
manslaughter *n.m.* homicidi
manual *adj./n.m.* manual
manual transmission *n.f.*
transmissió manual
manufacture *v.* fabricar
manufacturer *n.* fabricant
manufacturing *n.f.* fabricació
manure *n.m.* fems
manuscript *n.m.* manuscrit
many *pron.* molts
map *n.m.* mapa
maple syrup *n.m.* xarop d'auró
maraschino cherry *n.f.* cirera
marrasquino
marathon *n.f.* marató
marble *n.m.* marbre
March *n.m.* març
march *v.* marxar
margarine *n.f.* margarina
margin *n.m.* marge
marijuana *n.f.* marihuana
marinade *n.f.* marinada
marinated *adj.* marinat
marine *adj.* marí
marjoram *n.m.* marduix
mark *v.* marcar | *n.m.* marc
marked *adj.* marcat
marker *n.m.* retolador
market *n.m.* mercat
market price *n.m.* preu de mercat
marketing *n.m.* màrqueting
marketplace *n.m.* mercat
marmalade *n.f.* melmelada

marriage *n.m.* matrimoni
married *adj.* casat
marrow *n.f.* medul·la
marry *v.* casar-se
Mars *n.m.* Mart
marsh *n.m.* maresme
marshal *n.m.* mariscal
marshmallow *n.m.* núvol
martyr *n.* màrtir
marvelous *adj.* meravellós
Maryland *n.* Maryland
marzipan *n.m.* massapà
mascara *n.m.* rímel
mascot *n.f.* mascota
masculine *adj.* masculí
mashed potatoes *n.m.* puré de
patates
mask *n.f.* màscara
mass *n.f.* missa
Massachusetts *n.* Massachusetts
massacre *n.f.* matança, massacre
massage *n.m.* massatge
masseur *n.m.* massatgista
massive *adj.* massiu
master *n.m.* amo
masterpiece *n.f.* obra mestra
masturbate *v.* masturbar-se
mat *n.f.* estora
match *v.* igualar | *n.m.* igual
matches *n.m.* mistos
matching *adj.* igual
mate *n.* company
material *n.f.* material
mathematics *n.f.* matemàtiques
matinée *n.m.* matinal
matriculate *v.* matricular
matriculation *n.f.* matriculació
matrix *n.f.* matriu
matron *n.f.* matrona
matter *n.f.* matèria

mattress *n.m.* matalàs
mature *adj.* madur
maturity *n.f.* maduresa
mausoleum *n.m.* mausoleu
maxim *n.f.* màxima
maximize *v.* maximitzar
maximum *adj.* màxim
May *n.m.* maig
maybe *adv.* potser
mayonnaise *n.f.* maionesa
mayor *n.m.* alcalde
maze *n.m.* laberint
me *pron.* em, m', -em, 'm *(see page 8)*
mead *n.f.* aiguamel
meadow *n.m.* prat
meager *adj.* magre
meal *n.m.* àpat
mean *v.* significar
meaning *n.m.* significat
means *n.m.* mitjà
meanwhile *adv.* mentrestant
measles *n.m.* xarampió
measure *v.* mesurar
measurement *n.f.* mesura
meat *n.f.* carn
meatball *n.f.* mandonguilla
mechanic *n.* mecànic
mechanical *adj.* mecànic
mechanics *n.f.* mecànica
mechanism *n.m.* mecanisme
medal *n.f.* medalla
media *n.m.* mitjans de comunicació
mediate *v.* intercedir
mediation *n.f.* mediació
mediator *n.* mediador
medic *n.* metge
medical *adj.* mèdic
medication *n.m.* medicament

medicine *n.f.* medicina
medieval *adj.* medieval
mediocre *adj.* mediocre
mediocrity *n.f.* mediocritat
meditation *n.f.* meditació
Mediterranean *adj.* Mediterrani | *n.f.* Mediterrània
medium *adj.* mitjà
meet *v.* trobar
meeting *n.f.* trobada
meeting place *n.m.* lloc de trobada
megabyte *n.m.* megabyte
melancholy *n.f.* malenconia
meld *v.* fusionar
melody *n.f.* melodia
melon *n.m.* meló
melt *v.* fondre
member *n.m.* membre
membership *n.f.* afiliació
membrane *n.f.* membrana
memo *n.m.* memoràndum
memoir *n.f.* memòries
memorandum *n.m.* memoràndum
memorial *n.m.* memorial
memory *n.f.* memòria
menace *n.f.* amenaça
meningitis *n.f.* meningitis
menopause *n.f.* menopausa
menstruation *n.f.* menstruació
mental *adj.* mental
mentally *adv.* mentalment
menthol *n.m.* mentol
mention *v.* esmentar
menu *n.m.* menú
merchandise *n.f.* mercaderies
merchant *n.* comerciant
mercury *n.m.* mercuri
mere *adj.* mer
merge *v.* fusionar
meridian *n.m.* meridià

meringue *n.f.* merenga
Merry Christmas *phr.* Bon Nadal
mess *n.f.* brutícia
message *n.m.* missatge
message board *n.m.* fòrum
messenger *n.* missatger
metabolic *adj.* metabòlic
metabolism *n.m.* metabolisme
metal *n.m.* metall
metaphor *n.f.* metàfora
meteor *n.m.* meteor
meteorologist *n.* meteoròleg
meteorology *n.f.* meteorologia
meter *n.m.* metre
meter box *n.m.* comptador
method *n.m.* mètode
metro *adj./n.m.* metro
metro station *n.f.* estació de metro
metropolis *n.f.* metròpoli
metropolitan *adj.* metropolità
Mexican *adj./n.* mexicà
Mexico *n.m.* Mèxic
Michigan *n.* Michigan
microphone *n.m.* micròfon
microscope *n.m.* microscopi
microscopic *adj.* microscòpic
microwave *n.m.* microones
microwave oven *n.m.* microones
midday *n.m.* migdia
Middle East *n.m.* Pròxim Orient
middle *n.m.* mig
midnight *n.f.* mitjanit
midwife *n.f.* llevadora
might *n.f.* força
migraine *n.f.* migranya
mild *adj.* tranquil
mile *n.f.* milla
mileage *n.m.* quilometratge
milestone *n.f.* fita
military *adj.* militar

military service *n.m.* servei militar
milk *n.f.* llet
milkshake *n.m.* batut
milligram *n.m.* mil·ligram
millimeter *n.m.* mil·límetre
million *num.* milió
millionaire *n.* milionari
mime *n.m.* mim
minaret *n.m.* minaret
mince *v.* picar
minced meat *n.f.* carn picada
mind *n.f.* ment
mine *pos. pron.* el meu, la meva, els meus, les meves
mineral *n.m.* mineral
mineral water *n.f.* aigua mineral
miniature *n.f.* miniatura
minibar *n.m.* minibar
minimart *n.f.* botiga
minimize *v.* minimitzar
minimum *adj.* mínim
minister *n.* ministre
ministry *n.m.* ministeri
Minnesota *n.* Minnesota
minor *adj./n.* menor
minority *n.f.* minoria
mint *n.f.* menta
minuscule *adj.* minúscul
minute *n.m.* minut
mirror *n.m.* mirall
miscalculate *v.* calcular malament
miscarriage *n.m.* avortament espontani
mischief *n.f.* entremaliadura
mischievous *adj.* entremaliat
misconception *n.f.* equivocació
misconduct *n.f.* mala conducta
misdemeanor *n.m.* delicte
misgiving *n.m.* recel
mishap *n.m.* contratemps

miss *v. (emotion)* enyorar; *(be late for)* perdre
Miss *n.f.* senyoreta
missile *n.m.* míssil
missing *adj.* perdut
missionary *n.* missioner
Mississippi *n.* Mississipí
Missouri *n.* Missouri
mistake *n.m.* error
mistaken *adj.* equivocat
mistress *n.f.* mestressa
mistrial *n.m.* judici nul
misunderstanding *n.m.* malentès
mix *v.* barrejar
mixed *adj.* barrejat
mixture *n.f.* barreja
moat *n.m.* fossat
mobile *adj.* mòbil
mobile phone *n.m.* telèfon mòbil
mobility *n.f.* mobilitat
mockery *n.f.* burla
modal *adj.* modal
mode *n.f.* moda; *n.m.* mode
model *n.m.* model
modem *n.m.* mòdem
modern *adj.* modern
modest *adj.* modest
modification *n.f.* modificació
modify *v.* modificar
moisten *v.* humitejar
moisturizing cream *n.f.* crema hidratant
molar *n.m.* queixal
molasses *n.f.* melassa
mold *n.m. (for shaping)* motlle; *(fungus)* florit
Moldova *n.f.* Moldàvia
moldy *adj.* florit
mole *n.m.* talp
molecular *adj.* molecular

molecule *n.f.* molècula
molest *v.* assetjar
molestation *n.m.* assetjament
molten *adj.* fos
mom *n.f.* mama
moment *n.m.* moment
momentary *adj.* momentani
momentous *adj.* transcendental
momentum *n.m.* moment, impuls
Monaco *n.m.* Mònaco
monarch *n.* monarca
monarchy *n.f.* monarquia
monastery *n.m.* monestir
Monday *n.m.* dilluns
monetary *adj.* monetari
money *n.m.* diners
money order *n.m.* gir postal
monitor *n.m.* monitor
monkey *n.f.* mona
monogamy *n.f.* monogàmia
monologue *n.m.* monòleg
monopoly *n.m.* monopoli
monsoon *n.m.* monsó
Montana *n.* Montana
Montenegro *n.m.* Montenegro
month *n.m.* mes | *adv.* **next ~** mes que ve
monthly *adj.* mensual
monument *n.m.* monument
monumental *adj.* monumental
mood *n.m.* humor
moody *adj.* malhumorat
moon *n.f.* lluna
moor *n.m.* erm
moose *n.m.* ant
moot *adj.* inútil
mop *v.* pal de fregar
mope *v.* estar abatut
moped *n.m.* ciclomotor
moral *adj./n.m.* moral

moralist *n.* moralista
morally *adv.* moralment
morbid *adj.* mòrbid
morbidity *n.f.* morbositat
more *adj.* més
moreover *adv.* a més
morning *n.m.* matí; *n.f. (early ~)* matinada
morning-after pill *n.f.* píndola del dia després
morphine *n.f.* morfina
morsel *n.m.* mos
mortal *adj./n.* mortal
mortality *n.f.* mortalitat
mortar *n.m.* morter
mortgage *n.f.* hipoteca
mortify *v.* mortificar
mosaic *n.m.* mosaic
Moscow *n.m.* Moscou
mosque *n.f.* mesquita
mosquito *n.m.* mosquit
mosquito bite *n.f.* picada de mosquit
mosquito net *n.f.* mosquitera
moss *n.f.* molsa
most *adv.* molt
mostly *adv.* principalment
motel *n.m.* motel
moth *n.f.* arna
mother *n.f.* mare
mother-in-law *n.f.* sogra
motherhood *n.f.* maternitat
motif *n.m.* motiu
motion *n.m.* moviment
motion sickness *n.f.* cinetosi
motivate *v.* motivar
motivated *adj.* motivat
motivation *n.f.* motivació
motive *n.m.* motiu
motor *n.m.* motor

motorbike *n.f.* motocicleta
motorboat *n.f.* llanxa
motorcycle *n.f.* motocicleta
motorway *n.f.* autopista
mottle *adj.* clapejat
motto *n.m.* lema
mound *n.m.* pujol
mount *v.* pujar
mountain *n.f.* muntanya
mountain bike *n.f.* BTT (Bicicleta Tot Terreny)
mountain chain *n.f.* serra
mountain climbing *n.m.* muntanyisme
mountain pass *n.f.* collada
mountain path *n.m.* camí de muntanya
mountain range *n.f.* serra
mountaineer *n.* muntanyenc
mountainous *adj.* muntanyós
mourn *v.* lamentar
mournful *adj.* trist
mourning *n.m.* dol
mouse *(zool./tech.) n.m.* ratolí
mousse *n.f.* mousse
moustache *n.m.* bigoti
mouth *n.f.* boca
mouthful *n.f.* glopada
movable *adj.* movible
move *v.* moure
movement *n.m.* moviment
movie *n.f.* pel·lícula
movie theater *n.m.* cinema
moving *adj.* commovedor
Mr. *abbr.* Sr.
Mrs. *abbr.* Sra.
Ms. *abbr.* Senyoreta
much *adj.* molt
mucus *n.m.* moc
mud *n.m.* fang

muddle v. confondre
muddy adj. fangós
muesli n.m. musli
muffin n.m. muffin
muffle v. esmorteir
muffler n.m. silenciador
mug n.f. tassa
mule n.m. mul
mull v. considerar
mulled wine n.m. vi calent
mullet n.f. llissa
mullion n.m. mainell
multilateral adj. multilateral
multimedia adj. multimèdia
multinational adj. multinacional
multiped n.f. cotxinilla
multiple adj. múltiple
multiplex cinema n.m. multicinemes
multiplication n.f. multiplicació
multiplicity n.f. multiplicitat
multiply v. multiplicar
multitude n.f. multitud
mumble v. mussitar
mummy n.f. mòmia
mumps n.f. galteres
munch v. mastegar
mundane adj. mundà
municipal adj. municipal
municipality n.m. municipi
munificent adj. munífic
munitions n.f. municions
mural n.m. mural
murder v. assassinar | n.m.
  assassinat
murderer n. assassí
murderous adj. assassí
murmur v. murmurar | n.m.
  murmuri
muscle n.m. múscul

muscular adj. muscular
muse n.f. musa
museum n.m. museu
mush n.f. farinetes
mushroom n.m. bolet
music n.f. música
music store n.f. botiga de discos
musical adj. musical
musical instrument n.m.
  instrument musical
musician n. músic
musk n.m. mesc
musket n.m. mosquet
musketeer n.m. mosqueter
Muslim adj./n. musulmà
muslin n.f. mussolina
mussel n.m. musclo
must v. haver de
mustache n.m. bigoti
mustard n.f. mostassa
mustard greens n.f. mostassa
  bruna
muster n.f. assemblea
musty adj. ranci
mutant adj. mutant
mutation n.f. mutació
mute adj. mut
mutilate v. mutilar
mutilation n.f. mutilació
mutinous adj. amotinat
mutiny n.m. motí
mutter v. murmurar
mutton n.f. carn de be
mutual adj. mutu
muzzle n.m. morro
my pos. adj. el meu, la meva, els
  meus, les meves
myalgia n.f. miàlgia
myopia n.f. miopia
myself pron. jo mateix

mysterious *adj.* misteriós
mystery *n.m.* misteri
mystic *adj./n.* místic
mystical *adj.* místic
mysticism *n.m.* misticisme

mystify *v.* desconcertar
myth *n.m.* mite
mythical *adj.* mític
mythology *n.f.* mitologia

N

nail *v.* clavar | *n.m. (tool)* clau;
 n.f. (hand or foot) ungla
naive *adj.* ingenu
naked *adj.* nu
name *n.m.* nom
napkin *n.m.* tovalló
narcissism *n.m.* narcisisme
narcissist *n.* narcisista
narcosis *n.f.* narcosi
narcotic *n.m.* narcòtic
narrative *n.f.* narrativa
narrator *n.* narrador
narrow *adj.* estret
nascent *adj.* naixent
nasty *adj.* repugnant
nation *n.f.* nació
national *adj.* nacional
national anthem *n.m.* himne
 nacional
nationalism *n.m.* nacionalisme
nationality *n.f.* nacionalitat
nationalization *n.f.* nacionalització
nationalize *v.* nacionalitzar
native *adj./n.* nadiu
natural *adj.* natural
natural sciences *n.f.* ciències
 naturals
naturally *adv.* naturalment
nature *n.f.* natura
nature reserve *n.f.* reserva
 natural
nature trail *n.m.* sender
naughty *adj.* entremaliat
nausea *n.f.* nàusea
nauseous *adj.* nauseabund

naval *adj.* naval
nave *n.f.* nau
navel *n.m.* melic
navigate *v.* navegar
navigation *n.f.* navegació
navigator *n.* navegant
navy *n.f.* marina
near *adj.* proper
near-sightedness *n.f.* miopia
nearby *adj.* proper
nearest *adj.* més proper
nearly *adv.* gairebé
neat *adj.* pulcre
neatly *adv.* pulcrament
Nebraska *n.* Nebraska
nebula *n.f.* nebulosa
necessarily *adv.* necessàriament
necessary *adj.* necessari
neck *n.m.* coll
necklace *n.m.* collaret
nectar *n.m.* nèctar
nectarine *n.f.* nectarina
need *v.* necessitar
needle *n.f.* agulla
negative *adj.* negatiu
neglect *v.* negligir
negligence *n.f.* negligència
negotiate *v.* negociar
negotiation *n.f.* negociació
neighbor *n.* veí
neighborhood *n.m.* barri
neighboring *adj.* veí
neither *adv.* ni
neolithic *adj.* neolític
nephew *n.m.* nebot

nepotism *n.m.* nepotisme
Neptune *n.m.* Neptú
nerve *n.m.* nervi
nervous *adj.* nerviós
nervous system *n.m.* sistema nerviós
nervously *adv.* nerviosament
nest *n.m.* niu
net *n.f.* xarxa
net weight *n.m.* pes net
Netherlands *n.m.* Països Baixos
nettle *n.f.* ortiga
network *n.f.* xarxa
neurologist *n.* neuròleg
neurology *n.f.* neurologia
neurosis *n.f.* neurosi
neuter *adj.* neutre
neutral *adj.* neutral
neutralize *v.* neutralitzar
neutron *n.m.* neutró
Nevada *n.* Nevada
never *adv.* mai
never mind *phr.* no importa
nevertheless *adv.* no obstant
new *adj.* nou
New Hampshire *n.* Nou Hampshire
New Jersey *n.* Nova Jersey
New Mexico *n.* Nou Mèxic
New Year *n.m.* any nou
New Year's Day *n.m.* any nou
New Year's Eve *n.m.* nit de cap d'any
New York *n.* Nova York
New Zealand *n.f.* Nova Zelanda
newly *adv.* recentment
news *n.f.* notícies
newspaper *n.m.* diari
newsstand *n.m.* lloc de diaris
next *adj.* pròxim

next month *adv.* mes que ve
next to *prep.* al costat de
next week *adv.* setmana que ve
next year *adv.* any que ve
nib *n.m.* plomí
nibble *v.* mossegar | *n.f.* mossegada; *(of a fish)* picada
Nicaragua *n.f.* Nicaragua
nice *adj.* agradable
nicely *adv.* agradablement
nickname *n.m.* sobrenom
nicotine *n.f.* nicotina
niece *n.f.* neboda
night *n.f.* nit
night club *n.f.* discoteca
nightlife *n.f.* vida nocturna
nightmare *n.m.* malson
nihilism *n.m.* nihilisme
nimble *adj.* àgil
nimbus *n.m.* nimbe
nine *num.* nou
nineteen *num.* dinou
nineteenth *adj.* dinovè
ninetieth *adj.* norantè
ninety *num.* noranta
ninth *adj.* novè
nitrogen *n.m.* nitrogen
no *adv.* no
no one *pron.* ningú
nobility *n.f.* noblesa
noble *adj.* noble
nobleman *n.m.* noble
nobody *pron.* ningú
node *n.m.* node
noise *n.m.* soroll
nominal *adj.* nominal
nomination *n.f.* nominació
nominee *n.* candidat
non-alcoholic *adj.* sense alcohol
nonchalance *n.f.* indiferència

nonchalant *adj.* indiferent
none *pron.* cap
non-fiction *n.f.* no-ficció
nonlinear *adj.* no lineal
nonreturnable *adj.* no retornable
nonsense *n.m.* disbarat
non-smoker *n.* no fumador
non-smoking *adj.* de no fumador
non-stick *adj.* antiadherent
nonstop *adj.* sense parar
noodle *n.m.* fideu
noon *n.m.* migdia
nor *conj.* ni
norm *n.f.* norma
normal *adj.* normal
normalize *v.* normalitzar
normally *adv.* normalment
north *n.m.* nord
North America *n.f.* Amèrica del Nord
North American *adj.* nord-americà
North Carolina *n.* Carolina del Nord
North Dakota *n.* Dakota del Nord
northeast *adj./n.m.* nord-est
northern *adj.* del nord
northwest *adj./n.m.* nord-oest
Norway *n.f.* Noruega
nose *n.m.* nas
nostalgia *n.f.* nostàlgia
nosy *adj.* tafaner
not *adv.* no
notable *adj.* notable
notably *adv.* notablement
notary *n.* notari
notation *n.f.* notació
note *n.f.* nota
notebook *n.m.* quadern

noteworthy *adj.* notable
nothing *pron.* res
notice *v.* notar
noticeable *adj.* evident
notification *n.f.* notificació
notify *v.* notificar
notion *n.f.* noció
notoriety *n.f.* notorietat
notorious *adj.* notori
nougat *n.m.* torró
noun *n.m.* substantiu
nourish *v.* nodrir
nourishment *n.m.* aliment
novel *n.f.* novel·la
novelist *n.* novel·lista
novelty *n.f.* novetat
November *n.m.* novembre
now *adv.* ara
nowhere *adv.* enlloc
nuclear *adj.* nuclear
nuclear bomb *n.f.* arma nuclear
nuclear energy *n.f.* energia nuclear
nuclear physics *n.f.* física nuclear
nuclear power station *n.f.* central nuclear
nuclear testing *n.m.* assaigs nuclears
nuclear tests *n.m.* assaigs nuclears
nuclear weapons *n.f.* armes nuclears
nucleus *n.m.* nucli
nude *adj.* nu
nudist beach *n.f.* platja nudista
nuisance *n.f.* molèstia
number *n.m.* número
number plate *n.f.* matrícula
numerator *n.m.* numerador
numerous *adj.* nombrós
nun *n.f.* monja

nunnery *n.m.* convent
nurse *n.* infermer
nursery *n.m.* jardí d'infants
nut *n.f.* nou
nutmeg *n.f.* nou moscada
nutrient *n.m.* nutrient

nutrition *n.f.* nutrició
nutritious *adj.* nutritiu
nutty *adj.* de nou
nylon *n.m.* niló

O

oak *n.m.* roure
oasis *n.m.* oasi
oath *n.m.* jurament
oatmeal *n.f.* civades
oats *n.f.* civades
obese *adj.* obès
obesity *n.f.* obesitat
obey *v.* obeir
obituary *n.m.* obituari
object *v.* objectar | *n.m.* objecte
objection *n.f.* objecció
objectionable *adj.* objectable
objective *n.m.* objectiu
oblation *n.f.* oblació
obligation *n.f.* obligació
obligatory *adj.* obligatori
oblige *v.* obligar
oblique *adj.* oblic
obliterate *v.* obliterar
obliteration *n.f.* obliteració
oblivion *n.m.* oblit
oblivious *adj.* inconscient
obnoxious *adj.* desagradable
obscene *adj.* obscè
obscenity *n.f.* obscenitat
obscure *adj.* obscur
obscurity *n.f.* obscuritat
observance *n.f.* observança
observation *n.f.* observació
observatory *n.m.* observatori
observe *v.* observar
observer *n.* observador
obsess *v.* obsessionar
obsession *n.f.* obsessió
obsolete *adj.* obsolet

obstacle *n.m.* obstacle
obstinacy *n.f.* obstinació
obstinate *adj.* obstinat
obstruct *v.* obstruir
obstruction *n.f.* obstrucció
obstructive *adj.* obstructiu
obtain *v.* obtenir
obtainable *adj.* assequible
obtuse *adj.* obtús
obvious *adj.* obvi
obviously *adv.* òbviament
occasion *n.f.* ocasió
occult *adj.* ocult
occupancy *n.f.* ocupació
occupant *n.* ocupant
occupation *n.f.* ocupació
occupied *adj.* ocupada
occupy *v.* ocupar
occur *v.* ocórrer
occurrence *n.f.* ocurrència
ocean *n.m.* oceà
Oceania *n.f.* Oceania
o'clock *adv.* at two ~ a les dues
octagon *n.m.* octàgon
October *n.m.* octubre
octopus *n.m.* pop
ocular *adj./n.m.* ocular
oculist *n.* oculista
odd *adj.* estrany
oddly *adv.* estranyament
odds *n.f.* probabilitat
ode *n.f.* oda
odious *adj.* odiós
odium *n.m.* odi
odometer *n.m.* comptaquilòmetres

odor *n.f.* olor
odorous *adj.* olorós
odyssey *n.f.* odissea
of *prep.* de
of course *phr.* és clar
off *adv.* lluny; *(switch, etc.)* apagat
offal *n.m.* menuts
offence *n.m.* delicte
offend *v.* ofendre
offense *n.m.* delicte
offensive *adj.* ofensiu
offer *v.* oferir | *n.f.* oferta
offering *n.f.* ofrena
office *n.f.* oficina
office building *n.m.* edifici
 d'oficines
officer *n.* oficial
official *adj.* oficial
officially *adv.* oficialment
officiate *v.* oficiar
officious *adj.* oficiós
offline *adj.* desconnectat
offset *v.* compensar
offshoot *n.f.* derivació
offside *adj.* fora de joc
offspring *n.f.* descendència
often *adv.* sovint
oftentimes *adv.* sovint
ogle *v.* mirar amb insinuació
Ohio *n.* Ohio
oil *n.m.* oli; *(fuel)* petroli
oil filter *n.m.* filtre d'oli
oil painting *n.f.* pintura a l'oli
oily *adj.* oliós
ointment *n.m.* ungüent
OK / okay *interj.* d'acord
Oklahoma *n.* Oklahoma
okra *n.f.* ocra
old *adj.* vell
old age *n.f.* vellesa

old-fashioned *adj.* passat de moda
oligarchy *n.f.* oligarquia
olive *n.f.* oliva
olive oil *n.m.* oli d'oliva
Olympic Games *n.m.* Jocs
 Olímpics
omelet *n.f.* truita
omen *n.m.* presagi
ominous *adj.* ominós
omission *n.f.* omissió
omit *v.* ometre
omnipotence *n.f.* omnipotència
omnipotent *adj.* omnipotent
omnipresence *n.f.* omnipresència
omnipresent *adj.* omnipresent
omniscience *n.f.* omnisciència
omniscient *adj.* omniscient
omnivorous *adj.* omnívor
on *prep.* a, en; sobre
on board *phr.* a bord
on duty *phr.* de servei
on foot *phr.* a peu
once *adv.* una vegada
oncologist *n.* oncòleg
oncology *n.f.* oncologia
one *num.* un
one another *phr.* l'un a l'altre
one time *adv.* una vegada
onerous *adj.* onerós
onion *n.f.* ceba
online *adj.* en línia
onlooker *n.* espectador
only *adv.* només
onto *prep.* sobre
onyx *n.m.* ònix
opacity *n.f.* opacitat
opal *n.m.* òpal
opaque *adj.* opac
open *v.* obrir | *adj.* obert
open up *v.* obrir-se

opening *n.f.* obertura
opening night *n.f.* estrena
openly *adv.* obertament
opera *n.f.* òpera
opera house *n.m.* teatre d'òpera
operate *v.* operar
operating system *n.m.* sistema
operatiu
operation *n.f.* operació
operational *adj.* operatiu
operative *n.* operari
operator *n.* operador
opiate *n.m.* opiaci
opinion *n.f.* opinió
opium *n.m.* opi
opponent *n.* oponent
opportunism *n.m.* oportunisme
opportunity *n.f.* oportunitat
oppose *v.* oposar
opposite *adj.* oposat
opposition *n.f.* oposició
oppress *v.* oprimir
oppression *n.f.* opressió
oppressor *n.* opressor
opthalmologist *n.* oftalmòleg
optical *adj.* òptic
optician *n.* òptic
optimism *n.m.* optimisme
optimist *n.* optimista
optimistic *adj.* optimista
optimum *adj.* òptim
option *n.f.* opció
optional *adj.* opcional
optometrist *n.* optometrista
opulence *n.f.* opulència
opulent *adj.* opulent
or *conj.* o
oracle *n.m.* oracle
oracular *adj.* profètic
oral *adj.* oral

orally *adv.* oralment
orange *n.f.* taronja
orange blossom *n.f.* tarongina
orange juice *n.m.* suc de taronja
orange peel *n.f.* pell de taronja
oration *n.m.* discurs
orator *n.* orador
oratory *n.f.* oratòria
orbit *v.* orbitar | *n.f.* òrbita
orchard *n.m.* hort
orchestra *n.f.* orquestra
orchestral *adj.* orquestral
ordeal *n.f.* ordalia
order *v.* demanar | *n.m.* ordre
orderly *adj.* ordenat
ordinal *n.* ordinal
ordinance *n.f.* ordenança
ordinary *adj.* ordinari
ore *n.f.* mena
oregano *n.f.* orenga
Oregon *n.* Oregon
organ *n.m.* òrgan
organic *adj.* orgànic
organism *n.m.* organisme
organization *n.f.* organització
organizational *adj.* organitzatiu
organize *v.* organitzar
orgasm *n.m.* orgasme
oriental *adj.* oriental
orientate *v.* orientar
origin *n.m.* origen
original *adj.* original
original version *n.f.* versió
original
originally *adv.* originalment
originator *n.* autor
ornament *n.m.* ornament
orphan *n.* orfe
orphanage *n.m.* orfenat
orthodox *adj.* ortodox

oscillate *v.* oscil·lar
oscillation *n.f.* oscil·lació
ostracism *n.m.* ostracisme
ostrich *n.m.* estruç
other *adj.* altre
otherwise *adv.* altrament
otter *n.f.* llúdriga
ought to *v.* haver de
ounce *n.f.* unça
our *pos. adj.* el nostre, la nostra, els nostres, les nostres
ours *pron.* el nostre, la nostra, els nostres, les nostres
ourselves *pron.* nosaltres mateixos
oust *v.* expulsar
out *adv.* fora
out-of-print *adj.* exhaurit
out-patient *adj.* ambulatori
outbox *n.f.* safata de sortida
outbreak *n.m.* brot
outburst *n.m.* rampell
outcast *n.* marginat
outcome *n.m.* resultat
outcry *n.m.* clamor
outdated *adj.* antiquat
outdo *v.* excedir
outdoor(s) *adj.* a l'aire lliure
outer *adj.* exterior
outfit *n.m.* equip
outgoing *adj. (person)* extrovertit; *(clerical)* de sortida
outing *n.f.* excursió
outlandish *adj.* extravagant
outlast *v.* sobreviure
outlaw *n.* bandit
outlet *n.f.* sortida
outline *v.* esquematitzar | *n.m.* esquema; *(shape)* contorn
outlive *v.* sobreviure
outlook *n.f.* perspectiva

outpost *n.m.* lloc d'avançada
output *n.f.* sortida
outrage *n.f.* indignació
outrageous *adj.* escandalós
outrun *v.* córrer més ràpid que
outset *n.m.* principi
outshine *v.* eclipsar
outside *adv.* fora
outsider *n.* foraster
outskirts *n.m.* afores
outspoken *adj.* franc
outstanding *adj.* excepcional
oval *adj.* oval
ovary *n.m.* ovari
ovation *n.f.* ovació
oven *n.m.* forn
oven mitt *n.m.* guant de cuina
over *adj.* sobre
overall *adv.* en general
overcast *adj.* ennuvolat
overcharge *v.* cobrar massa
overcoat *n.m.* abric
overcome *v.* superar
overdone *adj.* exagerat
overdose *n.f.* sobredosi
overdraft *n.m. (banking)* descobert
overdraw *v. (banking)* girar al descobert
overdue *adj.* endarrerit
overhanging *adj.* voladís
overhear *v.* sentir per casualitat
overheat *v.* sobreescalfar
overlap *v.* superposar
overload *v.* sobrecarregar
overlook *v.* mirar des de dalt
overnight *adv.* durant la nit
overrule *v.* desautoritzar
overrun *v.* cobrir totalment
overseas *adv.* a ultramar

oversight *n.m.* descuit
overtake *v.* atrapar
overtime *n.f.* hores extraordinàries
overweight *adj.* sobrepès
owe *v.* deure
owl *n.m.* mussol
own *adj.* propi | *v.* posseir
owner *n.* propietari

ownership *n.f.* propietat
oxidation *n.f.* oxidació
oxtail *n.f.* cua de bou
oxygen *n.m.* oxigen
oyster *n.f.* ostra
ozone layer *n.f.* capa d'ozó
ozone *n.m.* ozó

P

p.m. *adv. (early)* a la tarda, *(later)* al vespre
pace *n.m.* pas
pacemaker *n.m.* marcapassos
pacific *adj.* pacífic
Pacific Ocean *n.m.* Oceà Pacífic
pacifier *n.m.* xumet
pacify *v.* pacificar
pack *v.* empaquetar
package *n.m.* paquet
packet *n.m.* paquet
pad *n.m.* farcit; *(paper)* bloc
paddle *v.* remar | *n.m.* rem
paddling pool *n.f.* piscina infantil
paddy *n.m.* camp d'arròs
padlock *n.m.* cadenat
page *n.f.* pàgina
pageant *n.f.* desfilada
pageantry *n.f.* pompa
pageview *n.f.* visita de pàgina
pagoda *n.f.* pagoda
paid *adj.* pagat
pail *n.f.* galleda
pain *n.m.* dolor
painful *adj.* dolorós
painfully *adv.* dolorosament
painkiller *n.m.* analgèsic
painstaking *adj.* meticulós
paint *v.* pintar | *n.f.* pintura
painter *n.* pintor
painting *n.m. (fine art)* quadre; *n.f. (activity)* pintura
pair *n.m.* parell
pajamas *n.f.* pijama
palace *n.m.* palau

palanquin *n.m.* palanquí
palatable *adj.* saborós
pale *adj.* pàl·lid
palette *n.f.* paleta
palm *n.m. (hand)* palmell; *n.f. (tree)* palma
palm oil *n.m.* oli de palma
Palm Sunday *n.m.* diumenge de rams
palmist *n.* quiromàntic
palmistry *n.f.* quiromància
palpable *adj.* palpable
palpitate *v.* palpitar
palpitation *n.f.* palpitació
palsy *n.f.* paràlisi
pamper *v.* consentir
pamphlet *n.m.* fullet
pan *n.f.* cassola
panacea *n.f.* panacea
Panama *n.m.* Panamà
pancake *n.m.* blini; *n.f.* crep
pancreas *n.m.* pàncrees
pane *n.m.* vidre
panegyric *n.m.* panegíric
panel *n.m.* plafó
panic *v.* espantar-se | *n.m.* pànic
panorama *n.m.* panorama
pant *v.* esbufegar | *n.m. (breath)* esbufec; *(clothing)* pantaló
panther *n.f.* pantera
pantomime *n.f.* pantomima
pantry *n.m.* rebost
pants *n.m.* pantalons, calçotets
pantyhose *n.m.* panti
pap smear *n.m.* frotis de Papa-nicolau

papaya *n.f.* papaia
paper *n.m.* paper; **pad of** ~ bloc
paprika *n.m.* pebre vermell
parable *n.f.* paràbola
parachute *n.m.* paracaigudes
parade *n.f.* desfilada
paradise *n.m.* paradís
paradox *n.f.* paradoxa
paraffin *n.f.* parafina
paragon *n.m.* model
paragraph *n.m.* paràgraf
Paraguay *n.m.* Paraguai
parallel *adj.* paral·lel
paralyse *v.* paralitzar
paralysis *n.f.* paràlisi
parameter *n.m.* paràmetre
paramount *adj.* suprem
paranoid *adj.* paranoic
paraphrase *v.* parafrasejar
paraplegic *adj./n.* paraplègic
parasite *n.m.* paràsit
parasol *n.m.* para-sol
parcel *n.m.* paquet
parchment *n.m.* pergamí
parchment paper *n.m.* paper
  pergamí
pardon *v.* perdonar | *n.m.* perdó
parent *n.m.* pare; *n.f.* mare
parenthesis *n.m.* parèntesi
Paris *n.m.* París
parish *n.f.* parròquia
parity *n.f.* paritat
park *v.* aparcar | *n.m.* parc
parking *n.m.* aparcament
parking garage *n.m.* edifici
  d'aparcament
parking meter *n.m.* parquímetre
parlance *n.m.* llenguatge
parliament *n.m.* parlament
parlor *n.f.* sala

parmesan cheese *n.m.* parmesà
parody *n.f.* paròdia
parole *n.f.* llibertat condicional
parrot *n.m.* lloro
parsley *n.m.* julivert
parsnip *n.f.* xirivia
parson *n.m.* rector
part *n.f.* part
part of speech *n.f.* categoria
  gramatical
part-time *adj.* temps parcial
partial *adj.* parcial
partially *adv.* parcialment
participant *n.* participant
participate *v.* participar
participle *n.m.* participi
particle *n.f.* partícula
particular *adj.* particular
particularly *adv.* particularment
partisan *adj./n.* partidista
partition *n.f.* partició
partly *adv.* en part
partner *n. (business)* soci; *n.f.*
  (personal) parella
partnership *n.m.* partenariat
partridge *n.f.* perdiu
party *n.f.* festa
pass *v.* passar | *n.m.* pas
passage *n.m.* passatge
passenger *n.* passatger
passion *n.f.* passió
passion fruit *n.m.* maracujà
passionate *adj.* apassionat
passionately *adv.* apassionadament
passive *adj.* passiu
passport *n.m.* passaport
passport photo *n.f.* foto de
  passaport
password *n.f.* contrasenya
past *n.m.* passat

pasta *n.f.* pasta
paste *v.* enganxar | *n.f.* pasta
pastel *adj./n.m.* pastel
pasteurized *adj.* pasteuritzat
pastime *n.m.* passatemps
pastry *n.f.* pasta
pastry shop *n.f.* rebosteria
pasture *n.f.* pastura
pat *n.m.* copet
patch *v.* apedaçar | *n.m.* pedaç
paté *n.m.* paté
patent *adj./n.f.* patent
path *n.m.* camí; sender
pathetic *adj.* patètic
pathos *n.m.* patetisme
patience *n.f.* paciència
patient *adj./n.* pacient
patriot *n.* patriota
patriotic *adj.* patriòtic
patriotism *n.m.* patriotisme
patrol *v.* patrullar | *n.f.* patrulla
patron *adj./n.m.* patró
patronage *n.m.* patrocini
patronize *v.* patrocinar
pattern *n.m.* patró
patty (hamburger ~) *n.m.*
 hamburguesa
pauper *n.* pobre
pause *v.* fer una pausa
pavement *n.m.* paviment
pavilion *n.m.* pavelló
paving stone *n.m.* llambordí
paw *n.f.* pota
pay *v.* pagar
pay phone *n.m.* telèfon públic
payable *adj.* pagable
payment *n.m.* pagament
pea *n.m.* pèsol
peace *n.f.* pau
peaceful *adj.* pacífic

peach *n.m.* préssec
peacock *n.m.* paó
peak *n.m.* cim
peanut *n.m.* cacauet
peapod *n.f.* tavella de pèsol
pear *n.f.* pera
pearl *n.f.* perla
pebble *n.m.* còdol
pebbly *adj.* pedregós
pecan *n.f.* pacana
peculiar *adj.* peculiar
pedagogy *n.f.* pedagogia
pedal *n.m.* pedal
pedant *n.* pedant
pedantic *adj.* pedant
pedantry *n.f.* pedanteria
pedestal *n.m.* pedestal
pedestrian *n.* vianant
pediatrician *n.* pediatre
pedigree *n.m.* pedigrí
peel *v.* pelar | *n.f.* pela
peeled *adj.* pelat
peep *v.* piular
peer *v.* fitar | *n.* igual
peg *n.f.* clavilla
pen *n.m.* bolígraf
penalize *v.* penalitzar
penalty *n.f.* pena
pence *n.m.* penics
pencil *n.m.* llapis
pending *adj.* pendent
pendulum *n.m.* pèndol
penetrate *v.* penetrar
penetration *n.f.* penetració
peninsula *n.f.* península
penis *n.m.* penis
penknife *n.f.* navalla
Pennsylvania *n.* Pennsilvània
penny *n.m.* penic
pension *n.f.* pensió

pensioner n. pensionista
pentagon n.m. pentàgon
penthouse n.m. àtic
people n.f. gent
pepper n.m. (spice) pebre;
  (vegetable) pebrot
peppermint n.f. menta
per prep. per
perceive v. percebre
percent n.m. per cent
percentage n.m. percentatge
perceptible adj. perceptible
perception n.f. percepció
perceptive adj. perceptiu
perch v. posar-se | n.f. perca
perfect adj. perfecte
perfection n.f. perfecció
perfectly adv. perfectament
perfidy n.f. perfídia
perform v. realitzar
performance n.f. actuació
performer n. executant
perfume n.m. perfum
perhaps adv. potser
peril n.m. perill
perilous adj. perillós
period n.m. (menstrual) període;
  (gram.) punt
periodic adj. periòdica
periodical n.f. revista
perish v. perir
perishable adj. perible
perjury n.m. perjuri
perm n.f. permanent
permanent adj. permanent
permanent collection n.f.
  col·lecció permanent
permanently adv. permanentment
permission n.m. permís
permit v. permetre | n.m. permís

permitted adj. permès
permutation n.f. permutació
pernicious adj. perniciós
perpendicular adj. perpendicular
perpetual adj. perpetu
perpetuate v. perpetuar
perplex v. deixar perplex
perplexity n.f. perplexitat
persecute v. perseguir
persecution n.f. persecució
perseverance n.f. perseverança
persevere v. perseverar
persimmon n.m. caqui
persist v. persistir
persistence n.f. persistència
persistent adj. persistent
person n.f. persona
personage n.m. personatge
personal adj. personal
personal computer (PC) n.m.
  ordinador personal (PC)
personality n.f. personalitat
personally adv. personalment
personification n.f. personificació
personnel n.m. personal
perspective n.f. perspectiva
perspiration n.f. transpiració
perspire v. transpirar
persuade v. persuadir
persuasion n.f. persuasió
pertain v. pertànyer
pertinent adj. pertinent
Peru n.m. Perú
perusal n.f. lectura detallada
peruse v. llegir detalladament
pervade v. penetrar
perverse adj. pervers
perversion n.f. perversió
perversity n.f. perversitat
pervert v. pervertir | n. pervertit

pessimism *n.m.* pessimisme
pessimist *n.* pessimista
pessimistic *adj.* pessimista
pest *n.f.* pesta, plaga
pesticide *n.m.* pesticida
pestilence *n.f.* pestilència
pet *v.* acariciar
petal *n.m.* pètal
petition *n.f.* petició
petrol *n.f.* gasolina
petticoat *n.m.* enagos
petulance *n.f.* impaciència
pewter *n.m.* peltre
pH *n.m.* pH
phantom *n.f.* fantasma
pharmacist *n.* farmacèutic
pharmacy *n.f.* farmàcia
phase *n.f.* fase
pheasant *n.m.* faisà
phenomenal *adj.* fenomenal
phenomenon *n.m.* fenomen
philanthropic *adj.* filantròpic
philanthropist *n.* filantrop
philanthropy *n.f.* filantropia
philological *adj.* filològic
philologist *n.* filòleg
philology *n.f.* filologia
philosopher *n.* filòsof
philosophy *n.f.* filosofia
phone *n.m.* telèfon
phone book *n.f.* guia telefònica
phone booth *n.f.* cabina telefònica
phone call *n.f.* trucada telefònica
　| *v.* **make a ~** fer una trucada
phone card *n.f.* targeta telefònica
phone number *n.m.* número de
　telèfon
phonetics *n.f.* fonètica
phosphorous *n.m.* fòsfor
photo *n.f.* foto

photocopier *n.f.* fotocopiadora
photocopy *n.f.* fotocòpia
photograph *n.f.* fotografia
photographer *n.* fotògraf
photography *n.f.* fotografia
phrasal verb *n.m.* verb amb
　partícules
phrase *n.f.* frase
phrasebook *n.m.* llibre de frases
phraseology *n.f.* fraseologia
physical *adj.* físic
physical therapy *n.f.* teràpia física
physically *adv.* físicament
physician *n.* metge
physicist *n.* físic
physics *n.f.* física
physiognomy *n.f.* fisonomia
piano *n.m.* piano
picarel *n.m.* gerret
pick *v. (flowers, etc.)* collir;
　(choose) triar
pick up *v.* recollir
pickaxe *n.m.* pic
picket *n.m.* piquet
pickle *v.* confitar | *n.m.* cogombret
pickled *adj.* confitat
pickup (truck) *n.f.* camioneta
picky *adj.* exigent
picnic *n.m.* pícnic
picnic area *n.f.* àrea de pícnic
picture *n.f.* imatge
picturesque *adj.* pintoresc
pie *n.m.* pastís
piece *n.m.* tros
pier *n.m.* embarcador
pierce *v.* foradar
pig *n.m.* porc
pigeon *n.m.* colom
pigment *n.m.* pigment
pigmy *n.m.* pigmeu

pike *(fish) n.m.* lluç de riu
pilaf *n.* pilaf
pile *v.* apilar | *n.f. (battery)* pila
pilfer *v.* rampinyar
pilgrim *n.* pelegrí
pilgrimage *n.f.* peregrinació
pill *n.f.* pastilla, píndola
pillar *n.m.* pilar
pillow *n.m.* coixí
pillowcase *n.f.* coixinera
pilot *v.* pilotar | *n.* pilot
pilot light *n.m.* pilot
pimiento *n.m.* pebrot
pimple *n.m.* gra
pin *v.* clavar | *n.f.* agulla
pinball machine *n.m.* joc del milió
pinch *v.* pessigar | *n.m. (squeeze)* pessic; *(measure)* polsim
pine *n.m.* pi
pineapple *n.f.* pinya
ping pong *n.m.* ping-pong
pink *adj.* rosa
pinnacle *n.m.* pinacle
pint *n.f.* pinta
pioneer *n.* pioner
pious *adj.* pietós
pipe *n.m. (water, etc.)* tub; *n.f. (tobacco)* pipa
piquant *adj.* picant
piracy *n.f.* pirateria
piranha *n.f.* piranya
pirate *n.m.* pirata
Pisces *n.m.* Peixos
pistachio *n.m.* pistatxo
pistol *n.f.* pistola
piston *n.m.* pistó
pita bread *n.f.* pita
pitch *v.* llançar
pitcher *n. (person)* llançador; *n.m. (container)* gerro

piteous *adj.* llastimós
pitfall *n.f.* trampa
pitiable *adj.* llastimós
pitiful *adj.* llastimós
pitiless *adj.* despietat
pittance *n.f.* misèria
pity *v.* compadir | *n.f.* llàstima; compassió
pivot *v.* pivotar
pizza *n.f.* pizza
pizzeria *n.f.* pizzeria
placard *n.m.* cartell
place *n.m.* lloc
place of birth *n.m.* lloc de naixement
placebo *n.m.* placebo
placid *adj.* plàcid
plague *n.f.* plaga
plain *adj.* natural | *n.f.* plana
plaintiff *n.* demandant
plan *n.m.* pla
plane *n.f.* avió
planet *n.m.* planeta
plank *n.m.* tauló
planning *n.f.* planificació
plant *v.* plantar | *n.f.* planta
plantain *n.m.* plàtan
plantation *n.f.* plantació
planting *n.f.* plantació
plasma *n.m.* plasma
plaster *n.m.* guix
plastic *n.m.* plàstic
plastic bag *n.f.* bossa de plàstic
plate *n.f.* placa
plateau *n.m.* altiplà
platform *n.f.* plataforma
platinum *n.m.* platí
platonic *adj.* platònic
platoon *n.m.* escamot
platter *n.f.* placa

play *v.* jugar | *n.f. (theater)* representació
player *n.* jugador
playground *n.m.* parc infantil
playing cards *n.f.* baralla de cartes
playing field *n.m.* camp de joc
plea *n.f.* petició
plead *v.* al·legar
pleasant *adj.* agradable
pleasantly *adv.* agradablement
pleasantry *n.f.* broma
please *phr.* si us plau
pleasing *adj.* agradable
pleasure *n.m.* plaer
plebiscite *n.m.* plebiscit
pledge *v.* prometre | *n.f.* promesa
plenty *adv.* prou
plight *n.m.* destret
plot *n.f. (land)* parcel·la; *(story)* trama; *n.m. (plan)* complot
plow *v.* llaurar | *n.f.* arada
plowman *n.* arador
pluck *v.* plomar
plug *n.m.* endoll
plum *n.f.* pruna
plumber *n.* lampista
plump *adj.* grassonet
plunder *v.* espoliar
plunge *v.* submergir
plural *adj./n.m.* plural
plus *conj.* més
ply *v.* exercir
pneumonia *n.m.* pneumònia
poached *adj.* escalfat
pocket *n.f.* butxaca
pod *n.f.* beina
poem *n.m.* poema
poet *n.* poeta
poetic *adj.* poètic

poetics *n.f.* poètica
poetry *n.f.* poesia
poignancy *n.f.* mordacitat
poignant *adj.* commovedor
point *n.f. (sharp)* punta
point of view *n.m.* punt de vista
point to *v.* assenyalar
pointed *adj.* punxegut
poise *v.* equilibrar | *n.m.* equilibri
poison *n.m.* verí
poisonous *adj.* verinós
poke *v.* burxar
poker *n.m.* pòquer
Poland *n.f.* Polònia
polar *adj.* polar
pole *n.m.* pal
police *n.f.* policia
police officer *n.* policia
police station *n.f.* comissaria
policy *n.f.* política
polish *v.* polir | *n.m.* poliment
polite *adj.* cortès
politely *adv.* cortesament
political *adj.* polític
politically *adv.* políticament
politician *n.* polític
politics *n.f.* política
poll *n.f.* enquesta
pollen *n.m.* pol·len
pollute *v.* contaminar
pollution *n.f.* contaminació
polo *n.m.* polo
polyester *n.m.* polièster
polygamous *adj.* polígam
polygamy *n.f.* poligàmia
polyglot *n.* poliglot
pomegranate *n.f.* magrana
pomp *n.f.* pompa
pomposity *n.f.* pompositat
pompous *adj.* pompós

pond *n.m.* estany
ponder *v.* ponderar, rumiar
pony *n.m.* poni
pool *n.f.* piscina
poor *adj.* pobre
pop *v.* punxar
pop music *n.f.* música pop
popcorn *n.f.* crispetes
Pope *n.m.* Papa
poppy *n.f.* rosella
popular *adj.* popular
popularity *n.f.* popularitat
population *n.f.* població
populous *adj.* populós
porcelain *n.f.* porcellana
porch *n.m.* porxo
pore *n.m.* porus
pork *n.f.* carn de porc
pork loin *n.m.* llom de porc
pork roast *n.m.* rostit de porc
pork sausage *n.f.* salsitxa de porc
porridge *n.f.* farinetes de civada
port *n.m.* port
portable *adj.* portàtil
portable crib *n.m.* bressol portàtil
portal *n.m.* portal
portend *v.* presagiar
porter *n.* porter
portfolio *n.f.* cartera
portico *n.m.* pòrtic
portion *n.f.* porció
portrait *n.m.* retrat
portray *v.* representar
Portugal *n.m.* Portugal
pose *v.* posar
position *n.f.* posició
positive *adj.* positiu
possess *v.* posseir
possession *n.f.* possessió
possessive *adj.* possessiu

possibility *n.f.* possibilitat
possible *adj.* possible
possibly *adv.* possiblement
post *n.m. (mail)* correu; *(position)* post
post office *n.f.* oficina de correus
postage *n.m.* franqueig
postage paid *n.m.* franqueig pagat
postal code *n.m.* codi postal
postbox *n.f.* bústia
postcard *n.f.* targeta postal
poster *n.m.* cartell
posterity *n.f.* posteritat
postman *n.m.* carter
postmaster *n.* administrador de correu
postpone *v.* ajornar
postponement *n.m.* ajornament
postscript *n.f.* postdata
posture *n.f.* postura
pot *n.f.* olla
pot roast *n.m.* rostit
potable *adj.* potable
potato *n.f.* patata
potato chips *n.f.* patates xips
potency *n.f.* potència
potential *adj.* potencial
pothole *n.m.* sot
potter *n.* terrissaire
pottery *n.f.* terrissa
pouch *n.f.* bossa
poultry *n.m.* aviram
pounce *v.* atacar
pound *v.* batre
pour *v.* vessar
poverty *n.f.* pobresa
powder *n.f.* pols
powdered *adj.* en pols
powdery *adj.* polsegós

power *n.m.* poder
power line *n.f.* línia elèctrica
power of attorney *n.m.* mandat
power outage *n.m.* tall d'energia
powerful *adj.* poderós
practicability *n.f.* practicabilitat
practical *adj.* pràctic
practically *adv.* pràcticament
practice *v.* practicar | *n.f.* pràctica
practitioner *n.* professional
pragmatic *adj.* pragmàtic
pragmatism *n.m.* pragmatisme
praise *v.* lloar | *n.f.* lloança
praiseworthy *adj.* lloable
praline *n.m.* praliné
prank *v.* bromejar | *n.f.* broma
prattle *v.* xerrar
prawn *n.f.* gamba
pray *v.* resar
prayer *n.f.* oració
preach *v.* predicar
preacher *n.* predicador
preamble *n.m.* preàmbul
precaution *n.f.* precaució
precautionary *adj.* preventiu
precede *v.* precedir
precedence *n.f.* precedència
precedent *n.m.* precedent
precept *n.m.* precepte
precious *adj.* preciós
precise *adj.* precís
precisely *adv.* precisament
precision *n.f.* precisió
precursor *n.m.* precursor
predator *n.m.* depredador
predecessor *n.* predecessor
predestination *n.f.* predestinació
predetermine *v.* predeterminar
predicament *n.m.* destret
predict *v.* predir

prediction *n.f.* predicció
predominance *n.m.* predomini
predominant *adj.* predominant
predominate *v.* predominar
preeminence *n.f.* preeminència
preeminent *adj.* preeminent
preface *n.m.* prefaci
prefect *n.m.* prefecte
prefer *v.* preferir
preference *n.f.* preferència
prefix *n.m.* prefix
pregnancy *n.m.* embaràs
pregnant *adj.* embarassada
prehistoric *adj.* prehistòric
prehistoric art *n.m.* art prehistòric
prejudice *n.m.* prejudici
prelate *n.m.* prelat
preliminary *adj.* preliminar
prelude *n.m.* preludi
premature *adj.* prematur
premeditate *v.* premeditar
premeditated *adj.* premeditat
premenstrual syndrome (PMS)
 n.f. síndrome premenstrual (SPM)
premier *n.* primer ministre
premiere *v.* estrenar | *n.f.* estrena
premises *n.m.* local
premium *n.f.* prima
premonition *n.f.* premonició
preoccupation *n.f.* preocupació
preoccupy *v.* preocupar
preparation *n.f.* preparació
prepare *v.* preparar
prepared *adj.* preparat
preponderance *n.f.* preponderància
preponderate *v.* preponderar
preposition *n.f.* preposició
prerequisite *n.m.* requisit
prerogative *n.f.* prerrogativa

prescient *adj.* prescient
prescribe *v.* prescriure; *(medical)* receptar
prescription *n.f.* recepta
presence *n.f.* presència
present *n.m.* present
presentation *n.f.* presentació
preservative *n.m.* conservant
preserve *v.* conservar
preserved *adj.* en conserva
preserves *n.f.* confitura
president *n.m.* president
press *v.* prémer | *n.f. (printing)* premsa
pressure *n.f.* pressió
pressurize *v.* pressionar
prestige *n.m.* prestigi
prestigious *adj.* prestigiós
presumably *adv.* presumiblement
presume *v.* presumir
presumption *n.f.* presumpció
presuppose *v.* pressuposar
presupposition *n.f.* pressuposició
pretence *n.f.* pretensió
pretend *v.* fingir
pretension *n.f.* pretensió
pretentious *adj.* pretensiós
pretext *n.m.* pretext
pretty *adv.* bonic
pretzel *n.m.* brètzel
prevail *v.* predominar
prevalence *n.m.* predomini
prevalent *adj.* predominant
prevent *v.* prevenir
prevention *n.f.* prevenció
preventive *adj.* preventiu
previous *adj.* anterior
previously *adv.* anteriorment
prey *n.f.* presa
price *n.m.* preu

price per liter *n.m.* preu per litre
prick *v.* punxar
pride *n.m.* orgull
priest *n.* sacerdot
prima facie *adj.* prima facie
primarily *adv.* principalment
primary *adj.* primari
prime *adj.* principal
prime minister *n.* primer ministre
primeval *adj.* primigeni
primitive *adj.* primitiu
prince *n.m.* príncep
princess *n.f.* princesa
principal *adj.* principal
principally *adv.* principalment
principle *n.m.* principi
print *v.* imprimir
printer *n.f.* impressora
printing *n.f.* impressió
prior *adj.* anterior
prioritize *v.* prioritzar
priority *n.f.* prioritat
prison *n.m.* presó
prisoner *n.* pres
privacy *n.f.* privadesa
private *adj.* privat
private property *n.f.* propietat privada
private room *n.f.* habitació privada
privately *adv.* en privat
privation *n.f.* privació
privatization *n.f.* privatització
privilege *n.m.* privilegi
prize *n.m.* premi
probability *n.f.* probabilitat
probable *adj.* probable
probably *adv.* probablement
probation *n.f.* llibertat vigilada
probe *v.* investigar | *n.f.* sonda

problem *n.m.* problema
problematic *adj.* problemàtic
procedure *n.m.* procediment
proceed *v.* procedir
proceeding *n.m.* procediment
proceeds *n.m.* beneficis
process *v.* processar | *n.m.* procés
processed *adj.* processat
procession *n.f.* processó
processor *n.m.* processador
proclaim *v.* proclamar
proclamation *n.f.* proclamació
proclivity *n.f.* proclivitat
procrastinate *v.* ajornar
procure *v.* obtenir
procurement *n.f.* obtenció
prodigal *adj.* pròdig
prodigality *n.f.* prodigalitat
produce *v.* produir | *n.m.* producte
produce market *n.m.* mercat de
  productes
producer *n.* productor
product *n.m.* producte
production *n.f.* producció
productivity *n.f.* productivitat
profane *adj.* profà
profess *v.* professar
profession *n.f.* professió
professional *adj./n.* professional
professor *n.* professor
profile *n.m.* perfil
profit *v.* guanyar | *n.m.* guany
profitability *n.f.* rendibilitat
profitable *adj.* rendible
profiteer *n.* especulador
profligate *adj.* malgastador
profound *adj.* profund
profoundity *n.f.* profunditat
profuse *adj.* profús
profusion *n.f.* profusió

progeny *n.f.* prole
program *n.m.* programa
progress *n.m.* progrés
progressive *n.* progressiu
prohibit *v.* prohibir
prohibited *adj.* prohibit
prohibition *n.f.* prohibició
project *v.* projectar | *n.m.* projecte
projectile *n.m.* projectil
projection *n.f.* projecció
projector *n.m.* projector
proliferate *v.* proliferar
proliferation *n.f.* proliferació
prolific *adj.* prolífic
prologue *n.m.* pròleg
prolong *v.* prolongar
prolongation *n.f.* prolongació
prominence *n.f.* prominència
prominent *adj.* prominent
promise *v.* prometre | *n.f.* promesa
promising *adj.* prometedor
promissory note *n.m.* pagaré
promote *v.* promoure
promotion *n.f.* promoció
prompt *adj.* puntual
promptly *adv.* puntualment
prone *adj.* propens
pronoun *n.m.* pronom
pronounce *v.* pronunciar
pronunciation *n.f.* pronunciació
proof *n.f.* prova
prop *v.* apuntalar | *n.m.* puntal
propaganda *n.f.* propaganda
propagandist *n.* propagandista
propagate *v.* propagar
propagation *n.f.* propagació
propel *v.* propulsar
proper *adj.* apropiat
properly *adv.* correctament
property *n.f. (quality)* propietat;
  n.m. (ownership) immoble

prophecy *n.f.* profecia
prophesy *v.* profetitzar
prophet *n.m.* profeta
proportion *n.f.* proporció
proportional *adj.* proporcional
proposal *n.f.* proposta
propose *v.* proposar
proposition *n.f.* proposició
propound *v.* proposar
proprietary *adj.* patentat
proprietor *n.* propietari
propriety *n.f.* propietat
prosaic *adj.* prosaic
prose *n.f.* prosa
prosecute *v.* processar
prosecution *n.f.* acusació
prosecutor *n.* fiscal
prosody *n.f.* prosòdia
prospect *n.f.* perspectiva
prospective *adj.* possible
prospectus *n.m.* prospecte
prosper *v.* prosperar
prosperity *n.f.* prosperitat
prosperous *adj.* pròsper
prostitute *n.f.* prostituta
prostitution *n.f.* prostitució
prostrate *adj.* postrat
prostration *n.f.* prostració
protagonist *n.* protagonista
protect *v.* protegir
protected *adj.* protegit
protection *n.f.* protecció
protein *n.f.* proteïna
protest *v.* protestar | *n.f.* protesta
Protestant *adj./n.* protestant
protocol *n.m.* protocol
proton *n.m.* protó
prototype *n.m.* prototip
proud *adj.* orgullós
proudly *adv.* orgullosament

prove *v.* provar, demostrar
proverb *n.m.* proverbi
provide *v.* proporcionar
provided *conj.* sempre que
provident *adj.* provident
providential *adj.* providencial
provider *n.m.* proveïdor
province *n.f.* província
provincialism *n.m.* provincialisme
provision *n.f.* provisió
provisionality *n.f.* provisionalitat
provisionally *adv.* provisionalment
provocation *n.f.* provocació
provocative *adj.* provocatiu
provoke *v.* provocar
prowess *n.m.* coratge
proximate *adj.* pròxim
proximity *n.f.* proximitat
proxy *n.m.* apoderat
prudence *n.f.* prudència
prudent *adj.* prudent
prune *n.f.* pruna
pry *v.* espiar
psalm *n.m.* salm
pseudonym *n.m.* pseudònim
psyche *n.f.* psique
psychiatrist *n.* psiquiatre
psychiatry *n.f.* psiquiatria
psychic *n.* endevinador
psychological *adj.* psicòlogic
psychologist *n.* psicòleg
psychopath *n.* psicòpata
psychotherapy *n.f.* psicoteràpia
psychotic *adj.* psicòtic
pub *n.m.* pub
puberty *n.f.* pubertat
public *adj.* públic
Public Limited Company (PLC)
  n.f. societat anònima
public transportation *n.m.*
  transport públic

publication *n.f.* publicació
publicity *n.f.* publicitat
publicly *adv.* públicament
publish *v.* publicar
publisher *n.* editor
publishing *n.f.* edició
pudding *n.m.* púding
puddle *n.m.* bassal
puerile *adj.* pueril
Puerto Rico *n.m.* Puerto Rico
puff *v.* bufar | *n.f.* bufada
puff-pastry *n.f.* pasta fullada
pull *v.* estirar
pulley *n.f.* politja
pullover *n.m.* jersei
pulp *n.f.* polpa
pulpit *n.m.* púlpit
pulsate *v.* bategar
pulsation *n.f.* pulsació
pulse *v.* polsar | *n.m.* pols
pump *v.* bombar | *n.f.* bomba
pumpernickel *n.m.* pa de sègol
pumpkin *n.f.* carbassa de rabequet
pun *n.m.* joc de paraules
punch *v.* donar un cop de puny |
  n.m. cop de puny
punctual *adj.* puntual
punctuality *n.f.* puntualitat
punctuate *v.* puntuar
punctuation *n.f.* puntuació
puncture *v.* punxar | *n.f.* punxada
pungent *adj.* picant
punish *v.* castigar

punishment *n.m.* càstig
pupil *n.f.* pupil·la
puppet *n.m.* titella
puppy *n.m.* cadell
purchase *v.* comprar | *n.f.* compra
purchaser *n.* comprador
pure *adj.* pur
puree *n.m.* puré
purely *adv.* purament
purgation *n.f.* purgació
purgative *adj.* purgant
purgatory *n.m.* purgatori
purge *v.* purgar | *n.f.* purga
purification *n.f.* purificació
purify *v.* purificar
purist *n.* purista
puritan *adj./n.* purità
purity *n.f.* puresa
purple *adj./n.f.* púrpura
purportedly *adv.* suposadament
purpose *n.m.* propòsit
purse *n.m.* moneder
pursue *v.* perseguir
pursuit *n.f.* persecució
pus *n.m.* pus
push *v.* empènyer | *n.f.* empenta
put *v.* posar
puzzle *n.f.* puzle, endevinalla
pygmy *n.* pigmeu
pyramid *n.m.* piràmide
pyre *n.f.* pira
python *n.m.* pitó

Q

quack *(of a duck)* v. clacar | n.f.
claca
quadrangle n.m. quadrangle
quadruple adj. quàdruple
quail n.f. guatlla
quaint adj. curiós
quake v. tremolar | n.m. terratrèmol
qualification n.f. qualificació
qualified adj. qualificat
qualify v. qualificar
quality n.f. qualitat
quandary n.m. dilema
quantity n.f. quantitat
quarantine n.f. quarantena
quarrel n.f. baralla
quarry n.f. pedrera
quarter n.m. *(time)* trimestre;
  (quantity) quart
quartered adj. a quarts
queen n.f. reina
quell v. sufocar
quench v. apagar
query v. preguntar | n.f. pregunta
quest n.f. recerca
question v. preguntar | n.f.
  pregunta

questionable adj. qüestionable
questionnaire n.m. qüestionari
queue n.f. cua
quibble v. subtilitzar | n.f.
  subtilesa
quiche n.f. quiche
quick adj. ràpid
quickest adj. més ràpida
quickly adv. ràpidament
quicksand n.f. arenes movedisses
quicksilver n.m. mercuri
quiet adj. tranquil
quieter adj. més tranquil
quietly adv. silenciosament
quinoa n.f. quinoa
quit v. deixar
quite adv. bastant
quiver v. tremolar
quixotic adj. quixotesc
quiz v. interrogar | n.m. concurs
quorum n.m. quòrum
quota n.f. quota
quotation n.f. citació
quote v. citar | n.f. citació

R

rabbi *n.m.* rabí
rabbit *n.m.* conill
race *v.* córrer | *n.f. (competition)* cursa; *(genetic)* raça
racial *adj.* racial
racism *n.m.* racisme
rack *n.m.* prestatge
racket *n.f.* raqueta
radiance *n.f.* resplendor
radiant *adj.* radiant
radiate *v.* radiar
radiation *n.f.* radiació
radiator *n.m.* radiador
radical *adj.* radical
radicalism *n.m.* radicalisme
radio *n.f.* ràdio
radish *n.m.* rave
radius *n.m.* radi
rag *n.m.* parrac
rage *n.f.* ràbia
ragout *n.m.* estofat
raid *v.* fer una incursió | *n.f.* incursió
rail *(train) n.m.* rail
railing *n.f.* barana
railroad *n.m.* ferrocarril
rain *v.* ploure | *n.f.* pluja
rainbow *n.m.* arc de Sant Martí
raincoat *n.m.* impermeable
rainy *adj.* plujós
raise *v. (height)* elevar; *(children/ animals)* criar
raisin *n.f.* pansa
rally *n.f.* manifestació | *v.* ajuntar-se
RAM *n.f.* RAM

ram *v.* maçonar | *n.m. (tool)* maçó; *(animal)* marrà
ramble *v.* passejar
ramp *n.f.* rampa
rampage *n.m.* aldarull
rampant *adj.* desenfrenat
rampart *n.m.* terraplè
rancor *n.m.* rancor
random *adj.* aleatori
range *n.m.* interval
ranger *n.* guardabosc
rank *n.m.* grau
ransack *v.* saquejar
ransom *n.m.* rescat
rape *v.* violar | *n.f.* violació
raped *adj.* violat
rapid *adj.* ràpid
rapidly *adv.* ràpidament
rapids *n.m.* ràpids
rappeling *n.m.* ràpel
rapport *n.f.* compenetració
rapt *adj.* absort
rapture *n.m.* èxtasi
rare *adj.* rar
rarely *adv.* rarament
rascal *n.* bergant
rash *n.f.* erupció
raspberry *n.m.* gerd
rat *n.f.* rata
rate *n.f.* taxa
rather *adv.* més aviat
ratify *v.* ratificar
ratio *n.f.* ràtio
ration *v.* racionar | *n.f.* ració
rational *adj.* racional

rationale *n.m.* raonament
rationality *n.f.* racionalitat
rationalize *v.* racionalitzar
rattle *v.* fer vibrar | *n.m.* sotragueig
ravage *v.* destrossar
rave *v.* delirar
raven *n.m.* corb
ravine *n.m.* barranc
raw *adj.* cru
ray *n.m.* raig
razor *n.f.* màquina d'afaitar
reach *v.* arribar
react *v.* reaccionar
reaction *n.f.* reacció
reactionary *adj./n.* reaccionari
reactor *n.m.* reactor
read *v.* llegir
reader *n.* lector
readily *adv.* fàcilment
reading *n.f.* lectura
ready *adj.* llest
real *adj.* real
real estate *n.m.* béns immobles
realism *n.m.* realisme
realist *n.* realista
realistic *adj.* realista
reality *n.f.* realitat
realization *n.f.* realització
realize *v.* realitzar
really *adv.* realment
realm *n.m.* regne
ream *n.f.* raima
reap *v.* segar, recollir
reaper *n.* segador
rear *adj.* posterior
reason *n.f.* raó
reasonable *adj.* raonable
reasonably *adv.* raonablement
reassure *v.* tranquil·litzar
rebate *n.f.* rebaixa

rebel *v.* rebel·lar | *n.* rebel
rebellion *n.f.* rebel·lió
rebellious *adj.* rebel
rebirth *n.m.* renaixement
rebound *v.* rebotar | *n.m.* rebot
rebuff *n.m.* rebuf
rebuild *v.* reconstruir
rebuilt *adj.* reconstruït
rebuke *v.* reganyar | *n.m.* regany
recall *v.* retirar
recede *v.* retrocedir
receipt *n.m.* rebut
receive *v.* rebre
receiver *n.m.* receptor
recent *adj.* recent
recently *adv.* recentment
reception *n.f.* recepció
receptionist *n.* recepcionista
receptor *n.m.* receptor
recess *v.* fer un descans | *n.m.* descans
recession *n.f.* recessió
recipe *n.f.* recepta
recipient *n.* receptor
reciprocal *adj.* recíproc
reciprocate *v.* reciprocar
recital *n.m.* recital
recitation *n.f.* recitació
recite *v.* recitar
reckon *v.* comptar
reclaim *v.* reclamar
reclamation *n.f.* reclamació
recluse *n.* reclús
recognition *n.m.* reconeixement
recognize *v.* reconèixer
recoil *v.* retrocedir
recollect *v.* recordar
recommend *v.* recomanar
recommendation *n.f.* recomanació
recommended *adj.* recomanat

recompense *n.f.* recompensa
reconcile *v.* reconciliar
reconciliation *n.f.* reconciliació
record *v.* gravar | *n.m.* disc
recorder *n.m.* gravadora
recording *n.f.* gravació
recount *v.* recomptar
recoup *v.* recuperar
recourse *n.m.* recurs
recover *v.* recuperar
recovery *n.f.* recuperació
recreate *v.* recrear
recruit *v.* reclutar | *n.* recluta
recruitment *n.m.* reclutament
rectangle *n.m.* rectangle
rectification *n.f.* rectificació
rectify *v.* rectificar
rectum *n.m.* recte
recur *v.* repetir
recurrence *n.f.* recurrència
recurrent *adj.* recurrent
recyclable *adj.* reciclable
recycle *v.* reciclar
recycling *n.m.* reciclatge
red *adj.* vermell
redeem *v.* redimir
redemption *n.f.* redempció
redirect *v.* redirigir
redress *v.* compensar
reduce *v.* reduir
reduced *adj.* reduït
reduction *n.f.* reducció
redundance *n.f.* redundància
redundancy *n.f.* redundància
redundant *adj.* redundant
reed *n.f.* canya
reef *n.m.* escull
reel *v.* enrotllar | *n.m.* rodet
refer to *v.* referir-se a
referee *n.* àrbitre

reference *n.f.* referència
referendum *n.m.* referèndum
refine *v.* refinar
refined *adj.* refinat
refinery *n.f.* refineria
reflect *v.* reflectir
reflection *n.m.* reflex
reflector *n.m.* reflector
reflex *n.m.* reflex
reflexive *adj.* reflexiu
reform *v.* reformar | *n.f.* reforma
reformation *n.f.* reformació
reformatory *n.m.* reformatori
reformer *n.* reformador
refrain *v.* abstenir-se
refresh *v.* actualitzar, refrescar
refreshing *adj.* refrescant
refreshment *n.m.* refresc
refrigeration *n.f.* refrigeració
refrigerator *n.f.* nevera
refuge *n.m.* refugi
refugee *n.* refugiat
refund *v.* reemborsar | *n.m.* reemborsament
refusal *n.m.* refús
refuse *v.* rebutjar | *n.f.* deixalles
refutation *n.f.* refutació
refute *v.* refutar
regal *adj.* regi
regard *n.m.* respecte
regarding *prep.* pel que fa a
regenerate *v.* regenerar
regeneration *n.f.* regeneració
regicide *n.m.* regicidi
regime *n.m.* règim
regiment *n.m.* regiment
region *n.f.* regió
regional *adj.* regional
register *v.* registrar
registration *n.f.* matrícula

registry *n.m.* registre
regret *v.* lamentar
regular *adj.* regular
regularly *adv.* regularment
regulate *v.* regular
regulation *n.f.* regulació
regulator *n.* regulador
regulatory *adj.* regulador
rehabilitate *v.* rehabilitar
rehabilitation *n.f.* rehabilitació
rehearsal *n.m.* assaig
rehearse *v.* assajar
reheat *v.* reescalfar
reign *v.* regnar | *n.m.* regnat
reimburse *v.* reemborsar
reimbursement *n.m.* reemborsament
reindeer *n.m.* ren
reinforce *v.* reforçar
reinforcement *n.m.* reforçament
reinstate *v.* reintegrar
reinstatement *n.f.* reintegració
reiterate *v.* reiterar
reiteration *n.f.* reiteració
reject *v.* rebutjar
rejection *n.m.* rebuig
rejoice *v.* alegrar
rejoinder *n.f.* rèplica
rejuvenate *v.* rejovenir
rejuvenation *n.m.* rejoveniment
relapse *v.* recaure | *n.f.* recaiguda
relate *v.* relatar
related (to) *adj.* relacionat amb
relation *n.f.* relació
relations *n.f.* relacions
relationship *n.f.* relació
relative *adj.* relatiu | *n.* parent
relatively *adv.* relativament
relax *v.* relaxar
relaxation *n.f.* relaxació

relaxed *adj.* relaxat
relaxing *adj.* relaxant
relay *n.m.* relleu
release *v.* alliberar
relent *v.* cedir
relentless *adj.* implacable
relevance *n.f.* rellevància
relevant *adj.* pertinent
reliable *adj.* de confiança
reliance *n.f.* dependència
relic *n.f.* relíquia
relief *n.m.* alleujament
relieve *v.* alleujar
religion *n.f.* religió
religious *adj.* religiós
relinquish *v.* cedir
relish *v. (like)* gaudir de | *n.m. (food)* condiment
reluctance *n.f.* desgana
reluctant *adj.* poc disposat
rely on *v.* comptar amb
remain *v.* romandre
remainder *n.f.* resta
remaining *adj.* restant
remains *n.f.* restes
remark *n.m.* comentari
remarkable *adj.* notable
remedy *n.m.* remei
remember *v.* recordar
remembrance *n.f.* recordança
remind *v.* recordar
reminder *n.m.* recordatori
reminiscence *n.f.* reminiscència
reminiscent *adj.* reminiscent
remission *n.f.* remissió
remit *v.* remetre
remittance *n.f.* remesa
remorse *n.m.* remordiment
remote *adj.* remot
removal *n.f.* eliminació

remove *v.* eliminar
remunerate *v.* remunerar
remuneration *n.f.* remuneració
Renaissance *n.m.* Renaixement
render *v.* fer
rendezvous *n.f.* cita
renew *v.* renovar
renewal *n.f.* renovació
renounce *v.* renunciar
renovate *v.* renovar
renovation *n.f.* renovació
renown *n.m.* renom
renowned *adj.* anomenat
rent *v.* llogar | *n.m.* lloguer
rental *n.m.* lloguer
renunciation *n.f.* renúncia
repair *v.* reparar | *n.f.* reparació
repairman *n.* reparador
reparable *adj.* reparable
repartee *n.f.* rèplica ràpida
repatriate *v.* repatriar
repatriation *n.f.* repatriació
repay *v.* tornar
repayment *n.m.* reemborsament
repeal *v.* abrogar
repeat *v.* repetir | *n.f.* repetició
repeated *adj.* repetit
repeatedly *adv.* repetidament
repel *v.* repel·lir
repellent *adj./n.m.* repel·lent
repent *v.* penedir-se
repentance *n.m.* penediment
repercussion *n.f.* repercussió
repetition *n.f.* repetició
replace *v.* reemplaçar, substituir
replacement *n.m.* reemplaçament;
 n. (person) substitut
replenish *v.* reomplir
replete *adj.* replet
replica *n.f.* rèplica

reply *v.* respondre | *n.f.* resposta
report *v.* relatar | *n.m.* informe
reporter *n.* periodista
repose *n.m.* repòs
repository *n.m.* repositori
represent *v.* representar
representation *n.f.* representació
representative *n.* representant
repress *v.* reprimir
repression *n.f.* repressió
reprimand *v.* reprendre | *n.f.*
 reprimenda
reprint *n.f.* reimpressió
reproach *v.* reprotxar | *n.m.*
 reprotxe
reproduce *v.* reproduir
reproduction *n.f.* reproducció
reproductive *adj.* reproductiu
reproof *n.f.* reprensió
reptile *n.m.* rèptil
republic *n.f.* república
republican *adj./n.* republicà
repudiate *v.* repudiar
repudiation *n.m.* repudi
repugnance *n.f.* repugnància
repugnant *adj.* repugnant
repulse *v.* repel·lir
repulsion *n.f.* repulsió
repulsive *adj.* repulsiu
reputation *n.f.* reputació
repute *v.* reputar | *n.f.* reputació
request *v.* sol·licitar | *n.f.* sol·licitud
require *v.* requerir
required *adj.* necessari
requirement *n.m.* requisit
requisite *adj.* necessari
requisition *n.m.* requeriment
rescue *v.* rescatar | *n.m.* rescat
research *v.* investigar | *n.f.* recerca
researcher *n.* investigador

resemblance *n.f.* semblança
resemble *v.* assemblar-se
reservation *n.f.* reserva
reserve *v.* reservar
reserved *adj.* reservat
reservoir *n.m.* embassament
reside *v.* residir
resident *n.* resident
residue *n.m.* residu
resign *v.* dimitir
resignation *n.f.* dimissió
resist *v.* resistir
resistance *n.f.* resistència
resolute *adj.* resolut
resolution *n.f.* resolució
resolve *v.* resoldre
resort *n.m.* complex turístic
resound *v.* ressonar
resource *n.m.* recurs
respect *v.* respectar | *n.m.* respecte
respectful *adj.* respectuós
respective *adj.* respectiu
respectively *adv.* respectivament
respiration *n.f.* respiració
respiratory system *n.f.* sistema respiratori
respite *n.f.* pausa
respond *v.* respondre
response *n.f.* resposta
responsibility *n.f.* responsabilitat
responsible *adj.* responsable
rest *v.* descansar | *n.m.* descans
restaurant *n.m.* restaurant
restoration *n.f.* restauració
restore *v.* restaurar
restored *adj.* restaurat
restrain *v.* refrenar
restraint *n.m.* control
restrict *v.* restringir
restricted *adj.* restringit

restriction *n.f.* restricció
restroom *n.m.* lavabo
restructure *v.* reestructurar
restructuring *n.f.* reestructuració
result *n.m.* resultat
resumé *n.m.* resum
resume *v.* reprendre
resumption *n.f.* represa
resurgence *n.m.* ressorgiment
retail *n.f.* venda al detall
retailer *n.* detallista
retailing *n.f.* venda al detall
retain *v.* retenir
retaliate *v.* represaliar
retaliation *n.f.* represàlia
retard *v.* retardar
retardation *n.m.* retard mental
retention *n.f.* retenció
retentive *adj.* retentiu
reticence *n.f.* reticència
reticent *adj.* reticent
retina *n.f.* retina
retinue *n.m.* seguici
retire *v.* jubilar-se
retired *adj.* jubilat
retirement *n.f.* jubilació
retort *v.* replicar | *n.f.* rèplica
retouch *v.* retocar
retrace *v.* retrocedir
retreat *v.* retir
retrieve *v.* recuperar
retrospect *n.f.* retrospecció
retrospection *n.f.* retrospecció
return *v.* tornar | *n.f.* tornada
returnable *adj.* retornable
reveal *v.* revelar
revel *v.* fer gresca
revelation *n.f.* revelació
revelry *n.f.* gresca
revenge *n.f.* venjança

revenue *n.m.* ingressos
revere *v.* reverenciar
reverence *n.f.* reverència
reverential *adj.* reverencial
reverie *n.m.* somni
reversal *n.f.* inversió
reverse *v.* invertir
revert *v.* revertir
review *v.* revisar | *n.f.* revista
revise *v.* revisar
revision *n.f.* revisió
revival *n.f.* revifalla
revive *v.* revifar
revocable *adj.* revocable
revocation *n.f.* revocació
revoke *v.* revocar
revolting *adj.* repugnant
revolution *n.f.* revolució
revolutionary *adj.* revolucionari
reward *n.f.* recompensa
rhetoric *n.f.* retòrica
rhetorical *adj.* retòric
rheumatic *adj.* reumàtic
rheumatism *n.m.* reumatisme
rhinoceros *n.m.* rinoceront
Rhode Island *n.* Rhode Island
rhubarb *n.m.* ruibarbre
rhyme *v.* rimar | *n.f.* rima
rhythm *n.m.* ritme
rhythmic *adj.* rítmic
rib *n.f.* costella
rib-eye steak *n.m.* ribeye
ribbon *n.f.* cinta
rice *n.m.* arròs
ricepaper *n.* paper d'arròs
rich *adj.* ric
rickets *n.m.* raquitisme
rickshaw *n.m.* rickshaw
rid *v.* eliminar
riddle *n.f.* endevinalla

ride *v.* *(horse)* anar a cavall;
(car) anar amb cotxe; *(bicycle)*
anar amb bicicleta | *n.m.* passeig,
viatge
rider *n.* genet
ridge *n.f.* cresta
ridicule *v.* ridiculitzar
ridiculous *adj.* ridícul
riding *n.f.* equitació
rifle *n.m.* rifle
right *adj.* dret, correcte
righteous *adj.* just
rightly *adv.* correctament
rigid *adj.* rígid
rigor *n.m.* rigor
rigorous *adj.* rigorós
rim *n.f.* vora
rind *n.f.* pell
ring *n.m.* anell
ringlet *n.m.* rínxol
ringworm *n.f.* tinya
rinse *v.* esbandir
riot *v.* provocar aldarulls | *n.m.*
aldarull
rip *v.* estripar
ripe *adj.* madur
ripple *v.* arrissar | *n.m.* ris
rippled *adj.* arrissat
rise *v.* pujar, ascendir
risk *n.m.* risc
ritual *n.m.* ritual
rival *n.* rival
rivalry *n.f.* rivalitat
river *n.m.* riu
rivulet *n.m.* rierol
roach *n.f.* panerola
road *n.f.* carretera
road map *n.m.* mapa de carreteres
roam *v.* vagar
roar *v.* rugir

roast *v.* rostir
roasted *adj.* rostit
rob *v.* robar
robbed *adj.* robat
robber *n.* lladre
robbery *n.m.* robatori
robe *n.m.* barnús; *n.f.* túnica
robot *n.m.* robot
rock *n.f.* roca
rocket *n.m.* coet
rod *n.f.* vara
roe *n.f.* fresa
rogue *n.m.* bergant
role *n.m.* paper
roll *v.* rodar | *n.m. (spiral of)* rotlle
rolling pin *n.m.* corró
romaine lettuce *n.m.* enciam romà
romance *n.m.* amor
Romania *n.f.* Romania
romantic *adj.* romàntic
Romanticism *n.m.* romanticisme
Rome *n.f.* Roma
romp *v.* jugar
rood *n.f.* creu
roof *n.f.* teulada
room *n.f.* habitació, sala
room service *n.m.* servei d'habitacions
room temperature *n.f.* temperatura ambient
roommate *n.* company d'habitació
rooster *n.m.* gall
root *n.f.* arrel
rope *n.f.* corda
rose *n.f.* rosa
rosemary *n.m.* romaní
rot *v.* podrir
rotary *adj.* rotatori
rotation *n.f.* rotació

rotisserie *n.m.* rostidoria
rotted *adj.* podrit
rotten *adj.* podrit
rough *adj.* aspre
roughly *adv.* aproximadament
round *adj.* circular
roundabout *n.f.* rotonda
rouse *v.* despertar
rout *n.m.* derrota
route *n.f.* ruta
routine *n.f.* rutina
rove *v.* recórrer
rover *n.* vagabund
row *n.f.* fila
rowing *n.m.* rem
royal *adj.* reial
royalty *n.f.* reialesa
rub *v.* fregar
rubber *n.m.* cautxú
rubbish *n.f.* escombraries
rubble *n.f.* runes
ruby *n.m.* robí
rucksack *n.f.* motxilla
rude *adj.* mal educat
rudely *adv.* grollerament
rudiment *n.m.* rudiment
rudimentary *adj.* rudimentari
rue *v.* lamentar
rueful *adj.* trist
ruffian *n.* rufià
ruffle *v.* crespar | *n.m.* volant
ruffled *adj.* volants
rug *n.f.* catifa
rugby *n.m.* rugbi
ruin *v.* arruïnar
ruined *adj.* arruïnat
ruins *n.f.* ruïnes
rule *v.* governar | *n.f.* regla
ruler *n.m. (for measure)* regle; *n. (governmental)* governant

rules *n.f.* normes
rum *n.m.* rom
rumor *n.m.* rumor
rump *n.f.* gropa
run *v.* córrer
runner *n.* corredor
running *n.f.* carrera a peu; *n.m.*
funcionament
rural *adj.* rural
ruse *n.m.* ardit
rush *v.* anar amb pressa | *n.f.*
pressa

Russia *n.f.* Rússia
Russian *adj./n.* rus
Russian Federation *n.f.*
Federació Russa
rust *n.m.* rovell
rustic *adj.* rústic
rusticity *n.f.* rusticitat
rusty *adj.* rovellat
rut *n.f.* rodera
rye *n.m.* sègol

S

Sabbath *n.m.* dissabte
sabotage *v.* sabotejar | *n.m.* sabotatge
saccharin *n.f.* sacarina
sack *n.m.* sac
sacrament *n.m.* sagrament
sacred *adj.* sagrat
sacrilege *n.m.* sacrilegi
sad *adj.* trist
saddle *n.f.* sella
sadism *n.m.* sadisme
sadly *adv.* amb tristesa
sadness *n.f.* tristesa
safe *adj.* segur
safely *adv.* sense perill
safety *n.f.* seguretat
safflower oil *n.m.* oli de càrtam
saffron *n.m.* safrà
sagacious *adj.* sagaç
sagacity *n.f.* sagacitat
sage *n.f.* sàlvia
Sagittarius *n.m.* Sagitari
sail *v.* navegar | *n.f.* vela
sailing *n.f.* navegació
sailor *n.* mariner
saint *n.* sant
salad *n.f.* amanida
salad dressing *n.m.* amaniment
salary *n.m.* sou
sale *n.f.* venda
sales *n.f.* vendes
sales receipt *n.m.* rebut
sales tax *n.m.* impost
saliva *n.f.* saliva
salmon *n.m.* salmó

salon *n.m.* saló
salt *n.f.* sal
salted *adj.* salat
salty *adj.* salat
salutation *n.f.* salutació
salute *v.* saludar | *n.f.* salutació
salvage *v.* recuperar | *n.f.* recuperació
salvation *n.f.* salvació
same *adj.* mateix
sample *n.f.* mostra
San Marino *n.m.* San Marino
sanatorium *n.m.* sanatori
sanctification *n.f.* santificació
sanctify *v.* santificar
sanction *n.f.* sanció
sanctuary *n.m.* santuari
sand *n.f.* sorra
sandal *n.f.* sandàlia
sandwich *n.m.* entrepà
sandy *adj.* sorrenc
sanitary *adj.* sanitari
sanitary napkin *n.f.* compresa
sanitation *n.m.* sanejament
sanitize *v.* desinfectar
sapling *n.m.* arbre jove
sapphire *n.m.* safir
sarcasm *n.m.* sarcasme
sarcastic *adj.* sarcàstic
sardine *n.f.* sardina
Satan *n.* Satanàs
satellite *n.m.* satèl·lit
satin *n.m.* setí
satire *n.f.* sàtira
satisfaction *n.f.* satisfacció

satisfied *adj.* satisfet
satisfy *v.* satisfer
satisfying *adj.* satisfactori
saturate *v.* saturar
saturated *adj.* saturat
saturation *n.f.* saturació
Saturday *n.m.* dissabte
sauce *n.f.* salsa
saucepan *n.f.* cassola
saucer *n.m.* platet
sauna *n.f.* sauna
sausage *n.f.* salsitxa
sautéed *adj.* saltat
savage *adj.* salvatge
save *v.* guardar
savings *n.m.* estalvis
savior *n.* salvador
savor *v.* assaborir
savory *adj.* salat
saw *n.f.* serra
say *v.* dir
saying *n.f.* dita
scab *n.f.* crosta
scaffold *n.f.* bastida
scald *v.* escaldar
scalding *adj.* escaldat
scale *v. (climb)* escalar; *(fish)* es-
  catar | *n.f. (for weighing)* escala;
  (of fish) escama
scallops *n.f.* vieira
scalp *n.m.* cuir cabellut
scalpel *n.m.* bisturí
scan *v.* escanejar
scandal *n.m.* escàndol
scanner *n.m.* escàner
scapegoat *n.m.* cap de turc
scar *n.f.* cicatriu
scare *v.* espantar
scared: to be ~ *v.* tenir por
scarf *n.f.* bufanda

scary *adj.* de por
scatter *v.* dispersar
scattered *adj.* dispers
scene *n.f.* escena
scenery *n.m.* paisatge
schedule *n.m.* horari
scheme *n.m.* pla
scholar *n.* erudit
school *n.f.* escola
science *n.f.* ciència
scientific *adj.* científic
scientist *n.* científic
scissors *n.f.* tisores
scope *n.m.* abast
score *v.* marcar | *n.m.* resultat
Scorpio *n.m.* Escorpí
scorpion *n.m.* escorpí
scotch *n.m.* whisky
Scotland *n.f.* Escòcia
scramble *v.* remenar
scrambled *adj.* remenat
scrape *v.* raspar
scratch *v.* ratllar
scream *v.* cridar
screen *n.f.* pantalla
screw *v.* cargolar | *n.m.* cargol
screwdriver *n.m.* tornavís
script *n.f.* guió
sculptor *n.* escultor
sculpture *n.f.* escultura
sea *n.* mar
sea bass *n.m.* llobarro
sea bream *n.m.* besuc
sea urchin *n.m.* eriçó de mar
seafood *n.m.* marisc
seal *v.* segellar | *n.m.* segell; *n.f.*
  (zool.) foca
sear *v.* marcir
search *v.* cercar | *n.f.* cerca
search engine *n.m.* motor de cerca

search warrant *n.m.* ordre de registre

seashore *n.f.* ribera

seasick *adj.* marejat

season *v.* assaonar | *n.f. (of the year)* estació

seasonal *adj.* estacional

seat *n.m.* seient

seat belt *n.m.* cinturó de seguretat

seaweed *n.f.* alga

second *adj./n.m. (numerical / in time)* segon

second opinion *n.f.* segona opinió

secondary *adj.* secundari

secondhand *adj.* de segona mà

secrecy *n.m.* secretisme

secret *adj./n.m.* secret

secretary *n.* secretari

secretly *adv.* secretament

section *n.f.* secció

sector *n.m.* sector

secular *adj.* secular

secure *v.* assegurar | *adj.* segur

security *n.f.* seguretat

sedative *n.m.* sedant

sediment *n.m.* sediment

see *v.* veure

seed *n.f.* llavor

seek *v.* buscar

seem *v.* semblar

segment *n.m.* segment

seize *v.* confiscar

seizure *n.f. (taking of)* confiscació; *(med.)* convulsió

select *v.* seleccionar

selection *n.f.* selecció

self *adj.* mateix

self-defense *n.f.* defensa personal

self-service *adj.* d'autoservei

selfish *adj.* egoista

sell *v.* vendre

seller *n.* venedor

semicolon *n.m.* punt i coma

seminar *n.m.* seminari

senate *n.m.* senat

senator *n.* senador

send *v.* enviar

sender *n.* remitent

senior *adj.* més gran

sense *v.* sentir | *n.m.* sentit

sensible *adj.* sensat

sensitive *adj.* sensible

sensitivity *n.f.* sensibilitat

sentence *n.f. (gram.)* frase; *(legal)* sentència

sentimental *adj.* sentimental

separate *v.* separar | *adj.* separat

separated *adj.* separat

separately *adv.* per separat

separation *n.f.* separació

September *n.m.* setembre

sequence *n.f.* seqüència

sequential *adj.* seqüencial

sequester *v.* segrestar

Serbia *n.f.* Sèrbia

series *n.f.* sèrie

serious *adj.* seriós

seriously *adv.* seriosament

serum *n.m.* sèrum

servant *n.* criat

serve *v.* servir

server *n.* servidor

service *n.m.* servei

serving *n.f.* ració

sesame *n.m.* sèsam

session *n.f.* sessió

set *v.* posar | *n.m.* set

setting *n.m.* ambient

settle *v.* resoldre

settlement *n.m.* establiment

seven *num.* set
seventeen *num.* disset
seventeenth *adj.* dissetè
seventh *adj.* setè
seventieth *adj.* setantè
seventy *num.* setanta
several *adj.* diversos
severe *adj.* sever
severely *adv.* severament
sew *v.* cosir
sewing *n.f.* costura
sewing machine *n.f.* màquina de cosir
sex *n.m.* sexe
sexism *n.m.* sexisme
sexual *adj.* sexual
sexuality *n.f.* sexualitat
sexually *adv.* sexualment
sexy *adj.* atractiu
shade *n.f. (for window)* ombra; *n.m. (of color)* matís
shadow *n.f.* ombra
shady *adj.* ombrejat
shake *v.* sacsejar
shallot *n.f.* escalunya
shallow *adj.* poc profund | *n.f. (~ water)* aigües baixes
shame *v.* avergonyir | *n.f.* vergonya
shampoo *n.m.* xampú
shank *n.m.* jarret
shape *v.* formar | *n.f.* forma
shaped *adj.* format
share *v.* compartir
shareholder *n.* accionista
shark *n.m.* tauró
sharp *adj.* agut
sharply *adv.* bruscament
shave *v.* afaitar-se
shaver *n.f.* maquineta d'afaitar
shaving brush *n.f.* brotxa d'afaitar

shaving cream *n.f.* crema d'afaitar
she *pron.* ella
sheep *n.f.* ovella
sheer *v.* desviar
sheet *n.m.* full
shelf *n.m.* prestatge
shell *n.f.* closca
shellfish *n.m.* marisc
shelter *n.m.* abric
sherbet *n.m.* sorbet
sheriff *n.m.* xèrif
sherry *n.m.* xerès
shield *n.m.* escut
shift *v.* canviar
shine *v.* brillar
shiny *adj.* brillant
ship *v.* enviar | *n.m.* vaixell
shipment *n.m.* carregament
shirt *n.f.* camisa
shiver *v.* tremolar | *n.m.* tremolor
shock *v.* xocar | *n.m.* xoc
shoe *n.f.* sabata
shoot *v.* disparar
shop *v.* comprar | *n.f.* botiga
shopkeeper *n.* botiguer
shoplifting *n.m.* furt
shopping *n.f.* compra
shore *n.f.* costa; riba
short *adj.* curt
shortage *n.f.* escassetat
shortcut *n.f.* drecera
shortly *adv.* aviat
shorts *n.m.* pantalons curts
shot *n.m.* tret
shoulder *n.f.* espatlla
shout *v.* cridar | *n.m.* crit
shovel *n.f.* pala
show *v.* mostrar | *n.m.* espectacle
shower *v.* dutxar-se | *n.f.* dutxa

shred *v.* estripar
shrimp *n.f.* gambeta
shrine *n.m.* santuari
shut *v.* tancar | *adj.* tancat
shutter *n.m. (window)* porticó;
 (camera) obturador
shuttle *n.m.* transbordador
shy *adj.* tímid
sibling *n.* germà
sick *adj.* malalt
sickness *n.f.* malaltia
side *n.m.* costat
sidebar *n.f.* barra lateral
sidewalk *n.f.* vorera
sideways *adj.* de costat
sieve *n.m.* tamís
sift *v.* garbellar
sight *n.f.* vista
sightseeing *n.m.* turisme
sightseeing tour *n.f.* visita turística
sign *v.* signar, firmar | *n.m.* senyal
signal *n.m.* senyal
signature *n.f.* signatura
significance *n.f.* significació
significant *adj.* significatiu
significantly *adv.* significativament
signpost *n.m.* pal indicador
silence *n.m.* silenci
silent *adj.* silenciós
silk *n.f.* seda
silly *adj.* ximple
silver *n.f.* plata | *adj.* de plata
similar *adj.* similar
similarity *n.f.* similaritat
simmer *v.* bullir a foc lent
simple *adj.* senzill
simply *adv.* senzillament
sin *v.* pecar | *n.m.* pecat
since *prep.* des de
sincere *adj.* sincer

sincerely *adv.* sincerament
sing *v.* cantar
singe *v.* socarrar
singer *n.* cantant
singing *n.m.* cant
single *adj.* sol, solter
singular *adj.* singular
sink *v.* enfonsar | *n.m.* lavabo
sir *n.m.* senyor
siren *n.f.* sirena
sirloin *n.m.* filet
sister *n.f.* germana
sit *v.* seure
site *n.m.* lloc
situation *n.f.* situació
six *num.* sis
sixteen *num.* setze
sixteenth *adj.* setzè
sixth *adj.* sisè
sixtieth *adj.* seixantè
sixty *num.* seixanta
size *n.f.* mida
skate *v.* patinar | *n.m.* patí
skeleton *n.m.* esquelet
sketch *v.* esbossar | *n.m.* esbós
skewer *v.* enfilar | *n.f.* broqueta
skewered *adj.* enfilat
ski *v.* esquiar | *n.m.* esquí
skill *n.f.* habilitat
skilled *adj.* expert
skillet *n.f.* paella
skim milk *n.f.* llet desnatada
skin *n.f.* pell
skirt *n.f.* faldilla
skull *n.m.* crani
sky *n.m.* cel
slang *n.m.* argot
slash *v.* apunyalar
slaw *n.f.* coleslaw
sleep *v.* dormir | *n.f.* dormida

sleeper *n.* dorment
sleeping bag *n.m.* sac de dormir
sleeping car *n.m.* vagó llit
sleeping pill *n.f.* pastilla per dormir
sleepy *adj.* endormiscat
sleeve *n.f.* màniga
slice *v.* llescar | *n.f.* llesca
slide *v.* lliscar | *n.f. (photography)* diapositiva
slight *adj.* lleuger
slightly *adv.* lleugerament
slim *adj.* prim
sling *n.m.* cabestrell
slip *v.* relliscar
slipper *n.f.* sabatilla
slope *n.m.* pendent
Slovakia *n.f.* Eslovàquia
Slovenia *n.f.* Eslovènia
slow *adj.* lent
slowly *adv.* lentament
SLR camera *n.f.* càmera rèflex
small *adj.* petit
smaller *adj.* menor
smart *adj.* intel·ligent
smash *v.* trencar
smell *v.* olorar | *n.m.* olor
smile *v./n.m.* somriure
smoke *v.* fumar | *n.m.* fum
smoked *adj.* fumat
smoker *n.* fumador
smoking *n.m.* fumar
smooth *adj.* llis
smoothie *n.m.* smoothie
smoothly *adv.* suaument
snack *n.m.* snack
snail *n.m.* cargol
snake *n.f.* serp
sneaker *n.f.* sabatilla
snore *v.* roncar

snow *v.* nevar | *n.f.* neu
so *adv.* tan
soap *n.m.* sabó
soccer *n.m.* futbol
sociable *adj.* sociable
social *adj.* social
socialist *adj./n.* socialista
socially *adv.* socialment
society *n.f.* societat
sock *n.m.* mitjó
socket *(electrical) n.m.* endoll
soda *n.f.* soda
sodium *n.m.* sodi
soft *adj.* suau
soft drink *n.f.* soda
softly *adv.* suaument
software *n.m.* programari
soil *n.m.* sòl
sojourn *n.m.* sojorn
solar *adj.* solar
sold *adj.* venut
soldier *n.* soldat
sole *n.f.* sola
solid *adj.* sòlid
solo *n.m.* solo
soloist *n.* solista
solution *n.f.* solució
solve *v.* resoldre
solvent *n.m.* dissolvent
some *pron.* alguns
somebody *pron.* algú
somehow *adv.* d'alguna manera
someone *pron.* algú
something *pron.* alguna cosa
sometimes *adv.* de vegades
somewhat *adv.* una mica
somewhere *adv.* en algun lloc
son *n.m.* fill
son-in-law *n.m.* gendre
song *n.f.* cançó

songwriter *n.* compositor
soon *adv.* aviat
soothe *v.* calmar
sophisticated *adj.* sofisticat
sorbet *n.m.* sorbet
sore *adj.* adolorit | *n.f.* nafra
sorghum *n.m.* sorgo
sorrel *n.f.* agrella
sorry *adj.* llastimós; **I'm ~** *phr.* ho sento
sort *v.* ordenar | *n.f.* mena
soufflé *n.m.* suflé
soul *n.f.* ànima
sound *n.m.* sonar
soup *n.f.* sopa
sour *adj.* agre
source *n.f.* font
south *n.m.* sud
South Africa *n.f.* Sud-Àfrica
South America *n.f.* Amèrica del Sud
South Carolina *n.* Carolina del Sud
South Dakota *n.* Dakota del Sud
southern *adj.* del sud
souvenir *n.m.* record
sow *v.* sembrar
sowing *n.f.* sembra
soy *n.f.* soja
soy milk *n.f.* llet de soja
soy sauce *n.f.* salsa de soja
soya *n.f.* soja
soybean *n.f.* soja
space *n.m.* espai
spacebar *n.f.* barra d'espai
spade *n.f.* pala
spaghetti *n.m.* espaguetis
Spain *n.f.* Espanya
Spanish *adj.* espanyol | *n.m.* espanyol, castellà

spare *adj.* de recanvi
spare part *n.f.* peça de recanvi
sparkling *adj.* escumós
spatula *n.f.* espàtula
speak *v.* parlar
speaker *n. (person)* parlant; *n.m. (audio equipment)* altaveu
special *adj.* especial
specialist *n.* especialista
specialize *v.* especialitzar-se
specialized *adj.* especialitzat
specially *adv.* especialment
specialty *n.f.* especialitat
species *n.f.* espècie
specific *adj.* específic
specifically *adv.* específicament
specification *n.f.* especificació
specify *v.* especificar
specimen *n.m.* espècimen
spectacles *n.f.* ulleres
spectator *n.* espectador
spectrum *n.m.* espectre
speech *n.m.* discurs
speed *n.f.* velocitat
speed limit *n.m.* límit de velocitat
speedometer *n.m.* velocímetre
spell *v.* lletrejar | *n.m. (magic)* conjur
spelling *n.f.* ortografia
spend *v.* gastar
sperm *n.m.* espermatozoide
spherical *adj.* esfèric
spice *v.* especiar | *n.f.* espècia
spicy *adj.* picant
spider *n.f.* aranya
spill *v.* vessar | *n.m.* vessament
spin *v.* fer girar
spinach *n.m.* espinacs
spinal column *n.f.* columna vertebral

spine *n.f.* espinada
spire *n.f.* agulla
spirit *n.m.* esperit
spirits *(alcohol)* *n.f.* begudes espirituoses
spiritual *adj.* espiritual
spit *v.* escopir | *n.f.* saliva
spite *n.m.* despit
spleen *n.f.* melsa
splinter *n.f.* estella
split *v.* dividir | *n.f.* divisió
spoil *v.* malmetre
spoke *n.m.* raig
spoken *adj.* parlat
sponge *n.f.* esponja
sponge cake *n.m.* pa de pessic
sponsor *v.* patrocinar | *n.* patrocinador
spoon *n.f.* cullera
spoonful *n.f.* cullerada
spork *n.m.* spork
sport *n.m.* esport
sports *n.m.* esports
spot *v.* localitzar | *n.f. (mark)* taca; *n.m. (place)* lloc
spouse *n.* cònjuge
sprain *v.* torçar | *n.f.* torçada
sprained *adj.* torçat
spray *v.* ruixar | *n.m.* esprai
spread *v.* estendre
spreadsheet *n.m.* full de càlcul
spring *n.f. (season)* primavera; *(coil)* molla; *n.m. (water)* font
sprinkle *v.* esquitxar
sprout *v.* brotar | *n.m.* brot
squab *n.m.* colomí
square *n.m.* quadrat; *n.f. (city)* plaça
squash *v.* aixafar | *n.m. (fruit)* carabassó

squeeze *v.* esprémer
squid *n.m.* calamar
squirrel *n.m.* esquirol
stable *adj.* estable | *n.f.* quadra
stables *n.m.* estables
stadium *n.m.* estadi
staff *n.m.* personal
stage *n.f. (level)* etapa; *n.m. (theater)* escenari
stain *v.* tacar | *n.f.* taca
stained glass *n.m.* vitrall
stainless steel *n.m.* acer inoxidable
stair *n.f.* escala
staircase *n.f.* escala
stairway *n.f.* escala
stairwell *n.f.* escala
stake *n.f.* estaca
stale *adj.* ranci
stamp *v.* segellar | *n.m.* segell
stand *v.* estar dempeus
standard *adj./n.m.* estàndard
standing *adj.* dempeus
stanza *n.f.* estrofa
star *n.f.* estrella
starch *n.m.* midó
stare *v.* mirar fixament
starfish *n.f.* estrella de mar
start *v.* començar | *n.m.* començament
state *n.m.* estat
state of emergency *n.m.* estat d'emergència
statement *n.f.* declaració
station *n.f.* estació
statistic *n.f.* estadística
statistical *adj.* estadístic
statue *n.f.* estàtua
status *n.m.* estat
statute *n.m.* estatut
statutory *adj.* estatutari

stay *v.* quedar-se
steadily *adv.* establement
steady *adj.* estable
steak *n.m.* bistec
steal *v.* robar
stealing *n.m.* robatori
steam *n.m.* vapor
steamer *n.m. (ship)* vaixell de vapor; *n.f. (for food)* olla de vapor
steel *n.m.* acer
steep *adj.* costerut
steeply *adv.* abruptament
steer *v.* conduir
steering wheel *n.m.* volant
stem *n.f.* tija
step *v.* caminar | *n.m. (stairs)* esglaó; *(phase)* pas
sterile *adj.* estèril
sterilize *v.* esterilitzar
sterilized *adj.* esterilitzat
sterling *n.f.* lliura esterlina
stew *n.m.* estofat
stewed *adj.* estofat
stick *v.* enganxar | *n.m.* pal
sticky *adj.* enganxós
stiff *adj.* rígid
stiffly *adv.* rígidament
still *adj.* quiet | *adv.* encara
stimulate *v.* estimular
stimulus *n.m.* estímul
sting *v.* picar | *n.f.* picada
stir *v.* remenar
stir-fry *n.* saltar
stitch *v.* cosir | *n.m.* punt
stock *(monetary) n.m.* estoc
stock exchange *n.f.* borsa
stockings *n.f.* mitges
stolen *adj.* robat
stomach *n.m.* estómac
stomachache *n.m.* mal d'estómac

stone *n.f.* pedra
stool *n.m.* tamboret
stop *v.* aturar
stopper *n.m.* tap
stopwatch *n.m.* cronòmetre
store *v.* emmagatzemar | *n.m.* magatzem
stork *n.f.* cigonya
storm *n.f.* tempesta
stormy *adj.* tempestuós
story *n.f.* història
storyboard *n.m.* guió il·lustrat
stove *n.f.* estufa
straight *adj.* dret
strain *v.* estirar | *n.f.* tensió
strange *adj.* estrany
strangely *adv.* estranyament
stranger *n.* desconegut
strategic *adj.* estratègic
strategically *adv.* estratègicament
strategy *n.f.* estratègia
straw *n.f.* palla
strawberry *n.f.* maduixa
stream *n.m.* corrent
street *n.m.* carrer
streetcar *n.m.* tramvia
strength *n.f.* força
stress *n.m.* estrès
stressed *adj.* estressat
stressful *adj.* estressant
stretch *v.* estirar | *n.f.* estirada
stretcher *n.f.* llitera
strict *adj.* estricte
strictly *adv.* estrictament
strike *v. (hit)* colpejar; *(protest)* fer vaga | *n.f. (protest)* vaga
striking *adj.* magnífic
string *n.m.* cordill
stringy *adj.* fibrós
strip *v.* despullar | *n.f.* tira

stripe *n.f.* ratlla
striped *adj.* ratllat
stroke *n.m. (med.)* accident vascular cerebral (AVC)
stroll *v.* passejar | *n.f.* passejada
strong *adj.* fort
strongly *adv.* fortament
structural *adj.* estructural
structurally *adv.* estructuralment
structure *n.f.* estructura
strudel *n.m.* strudel
struggle *v.* lluitar | *n.f.* lluita
stubborn *adj.* tossut
stuck *adj.* enganxat
student *n.* estudiant
studio *n.m.* estudi
study *v.* estudiar | *n.m.* estudi
stuff *v.* farcir
stuffed *adj.* farcit
stuffing *n.m.* farcit
stun *v.* atordir
stunning *adj.* extraordinari
stupid *adj.* estúpid
sturgeon *n.m.* esturió
style *n.m.* estil
stylistic *adj.* estilístic
subject *n.m.* tema
submit *v.* presentar
subpoena *n.f.* citació
subscribe *v.* subscriure
subscriber *n.* abonat
subscription *n.f.* subscripció
subsequent *adj.* subsegüent
subsequently *adv.* subsegüentment
subsidiary *n.m.* filial
substance *n.f.* substància
substantial *adj.* substancial
substantially *adv.* substancialment
substitute *v.* substituir | *adj./n.* suplent

subtitles *n.m.* subtítols
subtle *adj.* subtil
suburb *n.m.* suburbi
subway *n.m.* metro
subway station *n.f.* estació de metro
succeed *v.* tenir èxit
success *n.m.* èxit
successful *adj.* reeixit
successfully *adv.* amb èxit
such *pron.* tal
suck *v.* xuclar
sudden *adj.* sobtat
suddenly *adv.* de cop i volta
suffer *v.* patir
suffering *n.m.* patiment
sufficient *adj.* suficient
sufficiently *adv.* suficientment
suffix *n.m.* sufix
sugar *n.m.* sucre
sugar-free *adj.* sense sucre
suggest *v.* suggerir
suggestion *n.m.* suggeriment
suit *n.m.* vestit
suitable *adj.* apropriat
suitcase *n.f.* maleta
suite *n.f.* suite
suited *adj.* adequat
sum *n.f.* suma
summary *n.m.* resum
summer *n.m.* estiu
summon *v.* convocar
summons *n.f.* citació
sun *n.m.* sol
sunblock *n.f.* protector solar
sunburn *n.f.* cremada
sundae *n.m.* sundae
Sunday *n.m.* diumenge
sunflower *n.m.* gira-sol
sunflower oil *n.m.* oli de gira-sol

sunglasses *n.f.* ulleres de sol
sunlight *n.f.* llum del sol
sunny *adj.* assolellat
sunrise *n.f.* sortida del sol
sunset *n.f.* posta del sol
sunshade *n.* para-sol
sunshine *n.f.* llum del sol
sunstroke *n.f.* insolació
suntan lotion *n.f.* crema solar
suntan *n.m.* bronzejat
super *n.* súper
superb *adj.* magnífic
superior *adj.* superior
superlative *adj./n.m.* superlatiu
supermarket *n.m.* supermercat
supervise *v.* supervisar
supervision *n.f.* supervisió
supper *n.m.* sopar
supplement *n.m.* suplement
supplier *n.* proveïdor
supplies *n.m.* subministraments
supply *v.* subministrar | *n.m.*
  subministrament
support *v.* suportar | *n.m.* suport
supporter *n.* partidari
suppose *v.* suposar
suppository *n.m.* supositori
suppress *v.* suprimir
supreme *adj.* suprem
sure *adj.* segur
surely *adv.* segurament
surf *v.* fer surf | *n.f.* onades
surface *v.* emergir | *n.f.* superfície
surfboard *n.f.* taula de surf
surfer *n.* surfista
surfing *n.m.* surf
surgeon *n.* cirurgià
surgery *n.f.* cirurgia
Suriname *n.m.* Surinam
surname *n.m.* cognom

surplus *adj./n.m.* excedent
surprise *v.* sorprendre | *n.f.*
  sorpresa
surprised *adj.* sorprès
surprising *adj.* sorprenent
surprisingly *adv.* sorprenentment
surrender *v.* rendir
surround *v.* envoltar
surrounding *adj.* al voltant
surroundings *n.m.* voltants
surveillance *n.f.* vigilància
survey *v.* inspeccionar | *n.f.*
  inspecció
survival *n.f.* supervivència
survive *v.* sobreviure
sushi *n.m.* sushi
suspect *v.* sospitar | *n.* sospitós
suspicion *n.f.* sospita
suspicious *adj.* sospitós
sustain *v.* sostenir
sustainable *adj.* sostenible
swallow *v.* empassar | *n.f.* empas-
  sada; *(bird)* oreneta
swamp *n.m.* pantà
swear *v.* jurar
sweat *v.* suar | *n.f.* suor
sweater *n.m.* suèter
sweatshirt *n.f.* dessuadora
Sweden *n.f.* Suècia
sweep *v.* escombrar
sweet *adj.* dolç
sweet potato *n.m.* moniato
sweetener *n.m.* edulcorant
swell *v.* inflar
swelling *n.f.* inflor
swim *v.* nedar
swimming *n.f.* natació
swimming pool *n.f.* piscina
swimsuit *n.m.* banyador
swindle *v.* estafar

swing *v.* gronxar | *n.f.* oscil·lació
Swiss *adj.* suís
Swiss chard *n.f.* bleda
switch *v.* canviar; *(~ on)* engegar; *(~ off)* apagar | *n.m.* canvi; *(electric)* interruptor
Switzerland *n.f.* Suïssa
swollen *adj.* inflat
sword *n.f.* espasa
swordfish *n.m.* peix espasa
syllable *n.f.* síl·laba
symbol *n.m.* símbol
symmetry *n.f.* simetria

sympathetic *adj.* comprensiu
sympathy *n.f.* compassió
symphony *n.f.* simfonia
symptom *n.f.* símptoma
synagogue *n.f.* sinagoga
syndrome *n.f.* síndrome
synthesis *n.f.* síntesi
synthetic *adj.* sintètic
syringe *n.f.* xeringa
syrup *n.m.* xarop
system *n.f.* sistema

table   246   Tennessee

T

table *n.f.* taula
tablecloth *n.f.* estovalles
tablespoon *n.f.* cullerada
tablet *n.f.* tauleta
tableware *n.f.* vaixella
taboo *adj.* tabú
tackle *v.* placar
tag *n.* etiqueta
tail *n.f.* cua
tailor *n.m.* sastre
take *v.* prendre
take-out food *n.m.* menjar per emportar
tale *n.m.* conte
talent *n.m.* talent
talented *adj.* talentós
talk *v.* parlar
tall *adj.* alt
tampon *n.m.* tampó
tan *adj./n.m.* broncejat
tangerine *n.f.* mandarina
tangy *adj.* picant
tank *(gas ~) n.m.* dipòsit
tap *v.* copejar | *n.m.* copet
tape *n.f.* cinta
tapestry *n.m.* tapís
tapioca *n.f.* tapioca
target *n.m.* objectiu
tarragon *n.m.* estragó
tart *adj.* acre | *n.m.* pastís
tartar sauce *n.f.* salsa tàrtara
task *n.f.* tasca
taste *v.* degustar | *n.m.* gust
Taurus *n.m.* Taure
tax *v.* gravar | *n.m.* impost

taxation *n.m.* impostos
taxi *n.m.* taxi
taxpayer *n.* contribuent
tea *n.m.* te
teach *v.* ensenyar
teacher *n.* mestre
teaching *n.m.* ensenyament
team *n.m.* equip
tear *v.* esquinçar | *n.m. (rip)* esquinç; *n.f. (of the eye)* llàgrima
teaspoon *n.f.* cullereta
technical *adj.* tècnic
technique *n.f.* tècnica
technology *n.f.* tecnologia
teddy bear *n.m.* osset de peluix
telecommunications *n.f.* telecomunicacions
telegram *n.m.* telegrama
telephone *n.m.* telèfon
telescope *n.m.* telescopi
television *n.f.* televisió
tell *v.* dir
temperature *n.f.* temperatura
temple *n.m. (religious)* temple; *n.f. (head)* templa
temporarily *adv.* temporalment
temporary *adj.* temporal
ten *num.* deu
tenant *n.* inquilí
tend *v.* tendir
tendency *n.f.* tendència
tender *adj.* tendre
tenderloin *n.m.* llom
tendon *n.m.* tendó
Tennessee *n.* Tennessee

tennis *n.m.* tennis
tense *n.m.* temps
tension *n.f.* tensió
tent *n.f.* tenda
tenth *adj.* desè
term *n.m.* termini
terminal *n.f.* terminal
terminus *n.f.* estació terminal
terra-cotta *n.f.* terracota
terrace *n.f.* terrassa
terrible *adj.* terrible
terribly *adv.* terriblement
terrific *adj.* excel·lent
territory *n.m.* territori
terrorism *n.m.* terrorisme
terrorist *n.* terrorista
test *n.f.* prova
testicle *n.m.* testicle
testimony *n.m.* testimoni
tetanus *n.m.* tètanus
Texas *n.* Texas
text *n.m.* text
textile *n.m.* tèxtil
texture *n.f.* textura
than *conj.* que, de
thank *v.* agrair
thankful *adj.* agraït
thanks *n.m.* agraïment | *phr.* gràcies
Thanksgiving *n.m.* Dia d'Acció de Gràcies
that *dem. adj. (near)* aquest(a), *(far)* aquell(a) | *dem. pron.* allò | *rel. pron.* que
the *def. art.* el, els *(pl.)*, la, les *(pl.)*
theater *n.m.* teatre
theft *n.m.* furt
their *pos. adj. pl.* el seu, la seva, els seus, les seves
theirs *pron. pl.* el seu, la seva, els seus, les seves

them *pron.* els, les
theme *n.m.* tema
themselves *pron. pl.* ells mateixos, elles mateixes
then *adv.* llavors
theoretical *adj.* teòric
theory *n.f.* teoria
therapeutic *adj.* terapèutic
therapy *n.f.* teràpia
there *adv.* allí, allà
therefore *adv.* per tant
thermometer *n.m.* termòmetre
thermos *n.m.* termos
these *pron.* aquests, aquestes
they *pron.* ells, elles
thick *adj.* espès
thickly *adv.* densament
thickness *n.m.* gruix
thief *n.* lladre
thigh *n.f.* cuixa
thin *adj.* prim
thing *n.f.* cosa
think *v.* pensar
thinking *n.m.* pensament
third *adj.* tercer
thirst *n.f.* set
thirsty *adj.* assedegat
thirteen *num.* tretze
thirteenth *adj.* tretzè
thirtieth *adj.* trentè
thirty *num.* trenta
this *pron.* aquest(a)
thorough *adj.* exhaustiu
thoroughly *adv.* exhaustivament
those *adj.* aquells, aquelles
though *conj.* encara que
thought *n.m.* pensament
thousand *num.* mil
thousandth *adj.* mil·lèsim
thread *v.* enfilar | *n.m.* fil

threat *n.f.* amenaça
threaten *v.* amenaçar
threatening *adj.* amenaçador
three *num.* tres
thrill *v.* emocionar | *n.f.* emoció
thrilled *adj.* emocionat
thrilling *adj.* emocionant
throat *n.f.* gola
thrombosis *n.f.* trombosi
through *prep.* a través de
throughout *prep.* al llarg de
throw *v.* tirar
thumb *n.m.* polze
thunder *n.m.* tro
Thursday *n.m.* dijous
thus *adv.* així
thyme *n.f.* farigola
ticket *n.m.* bitllet
tide *n.f.* marea
tidy *adj.* ordenat
tie *v.* lligar | *n.f. (necktie)* corbata
tier *n.m.* nivell
tight *adj.* estret
tightly *adv.* estretament
tights *n.m.* pantis
tilapia *n.f.* tilàpia
tile *n.f.* rajola, teula
till *prep.* fins a
time *n.m.* temps
timer *n.m.* temporitzador
timetable *n.m.* horari
tin *n.m. (metal)* estany; *n.f. (container)* llauna
tiny *adj.* minúscul
tip *n.f. (point)* punta; *(gratuity)* propina
tire *v. (get sleepy)* cansar | *n.m. (wheel)* pneumàtic
tired *adj.* cansat
tiring *adj.* fatigós

tissue *n.m. (biology)* teixit; *(paper)* mocador
title *n.m.* títol
to *prep.* a
toad *n.m.* gripau
toast *v.* torrar | *n.f.* torrada
toaster *n.f.* torradora
toaster oven *n.m.* forn torradora
tobacco *n.m.* tabac
today *adv.* avui
toe *n.m.* dit del peu
toenail *n.f.* ungla del peu
toffee *n.m.* caramel
tofu *n.m.* tofu
together *adv.* juntament
toilet *n.m.* lavabo
toilet paper *n.m.* paper higiènic
token *n.f.* fitxa
toll *n.m.* peatge
tomato *n.m.* tomàquet
tomorrow *adv.* demà
ton *n.f.* tona
tone *n.m.* to
tongue *n.f.* llengua
tonic water *n.f.* aigua tònica
tonight *adv.* aquesta nit
tonsil *n.f.* amígdala
tonsilitis *n.f.* amigdalitis
too *adv. (amount)* massa; *(also)* també
tool *n.f.* eina
toolbar *n.f.* barra d'eines
toolbox *n.f.* caixa d'eines
tooth *n.f.* dent
toothache *n.m.* mal de queixal
toothbrush *n.m.* raspall de dents
toothpaste *n.f.* pasta de dents
toothpick *n.m.* escuradents
top *n.m.* part superior
topic *n.m.* tema

topping *n.f.* guarnició
torn *adj.* estripat
torrent *n.m.* torrent
torte *n.m.* pastís
tortoise *n.f.* tortuga
torture *v.* torturar | *n.f.* tortura
toss *v.* llançar | *n.m.* llançament
total *adj.* total
totally *adv.* totalment
touch *v.* tocar | *n.m.* toc
tough *adj.* dur
tour *v.* anar de viatge | *n.m.* viatge
tourist *n.* turista
tow *v.* remolcar
toward(s) *prep.* cap a
towel *n.f.* tovallola
tower *n.f.* torre
town *n.f.* ciutat
toxic *adj.* tòxic
toxin *n.f.* toxina
toy *n.f.* joguina
trace *v.* traçar | *n.f.* rastre
track *n.f.* pista
trade *v.* comerciar | *n.m.* comerç
trader *n.* comerciant
trading *n.m.* comerç
tradition *n.f.* tradició
traditional *adj.* tradicional
traditionally *adv.* tradicionalment
traffic *n.m.* trànsit
tragedy *n.f.* tragèdia
trail *n.m.* camí
trailer *n.m.* tràiler
train *v. (practice)* entrenar | *n.m.* *(railroad)* tren; **local** ~ tren local
train station *n.f.* estació de tren
trained *adj.* entrenat
trainer *n.* entrenador
training *n.m.* entrenament
tramway *n.m.* tramvia

transaction *n.f.* transacció
transcript *n.f.* transcripció
transfer *v.* transferir | *n.f.* transferència
transform *v.* transformar
transformation *n.f.* transformació
transfusion *n.f.* transfusió
transit *n.m.* trànsit
transition *n.f.* transició
translate *v.* traduir
translation *n.f.* traducció
translator *n.* traductor
transmission *n.f.* transmissió
transmit *v.* transmetre
transparent *adj.* transparent
transplant *v.* trasplantar | *n.m.* trasplantament
transport *v.* transportar | *n.m.* transport
transportation *n.m.* transport
trap *v.* atrapar | *n.f.* trampa
trash *n.f.* escombraries
travel *v.* viatjar | *n.m.* viatge
traveler *n.* viatger
tray *n.f.* safata
treasure *n.m.* tresor
treasury *n.f.* tresoreria
treat *v.* tractar
treatment *n.m.* tractament
treaty *n.m.* tractat
tree *n.m.* arbre
trek *n.f.* excursió
tremendous *adj.* tremend
trend *n.f.* tendència
trespass *v.* violar la propietat
trespassing *n.f.* violació
trial *n.m.* judici
triangle *n.m.* triangle
tribe *n.m.* tribu
tribute *n.m.* tribut

trick *v.* enganyar | *n.m.* truc
trim *v.* retallar
trimming *n.f.* guarnició
trip *n.m.* viatge
tripod *n.m.* trípode
triumph *n.m.* triomf
trolley *n.m.* carretó
tropical *adj.* tropical
trouble *n.f.* problema
trousers *n.m.* pantalons
trout *n.f.* truita
truck *n.m.* camió
true *adj.* veritable
truffle *n.f.* tòfona
truly *adv.* veritablement
trunk *n.m. (tree)* tronc; *(car)* maleter
trust *v.* tenir confiança en | *n.f.* confiança
truth *n.f.* veritat
try *v.* provar
T-shirt *n.f.* samarreta
tube *n.m.* tub
Tuesday *n.m.* dimarts
tumor *n.m.* tumor
tuna *n.f.* tonyina
tune *v.* afinar | *n.f.* melodia

tunnel *n.m.* túnel
turbot *n.f.* turbot
Turkey *n.f.* Turquia
turkey *n.m.* gall dindi
turmeric *n.f.* cúrcuma
turn *v.* girar | *n.m.* gir
turnip *n.m.* nap
turnover *n.f.* facturació
turret *n.f.* torreta
turtle *n.f.* tortuga
tutor *n.* tutor
tutorial *n.m.* tutorial
TV *n.f.* TV
tweezers *n.f.* pinces
twelfth *adj.* dotzè
twelve *num.* dotze
twentieth *adj.* vintè
twenty *num.* vint
twice *adv.* dues vegades
twin *n.* bessó
twist *v.* torçar-se | *n.f.* torçada
two *num.* dos, dues
type *v.* teclejar | *n.m. (printing)* tipus
typical *adj.* típic
typically *adv.* típicament

U

ugly *adj.* lleig
Ukraine *n.f.* Ucraïna
ulcer *n.f.* úlcera
ultimate *adj.* últim
ultimately *adv.* finalment
ultrasound *n.m.* ultrasò
umbrella *n.f.* paraigua
unable *adj.* incapaç
unacceptable *adj.* inacceptable
unbearable *adj.* inaguantable
uncertain *adj.* incert
uncertainty *n.f.* incertesa
uncle *n.m.* oncle
uncomfortable *adj.* incòmode
unconscious *adj.* inconscient
under *prep.* sota
underground *adj.* subterrani
underline *v.* subratllar
underlying *adj.* subjacent
underneath *prep.* sota
underpants *n.m.* calçotets
understand *v.* entendre, comprendre
understanding *n.f.* comprensió
undertake *v.* emprendre
undertaking *n.f.* empresa
underwater *adj.* submarí
underwear *n.f.* roba interior
undo *v.* desfer
undoubtedly *adv.* indubtablement
undress *v.* despullar
unemployed *adj.* aturat
unemployment *n.f.* desocupació
uneven *adj.* desigual
unexpected *adj.* inesperat

unexpectedly *adv.* inesperadament
unfair *adj.* injust
unfairly *adv.* injustament
unfamiliar *adj.* desconegut
unfortunate *adj.* desafortunat
unfortunately *adv.* desafortunadament
unfriendly *adj.* antipàtic
unfurnished *adj.* sense mobles
unhappiness *n.f.* infelicitat
unhappy *adj.* infeliç
unhealthy *adj.* malsà
uniform *n.m.* uniforme
unimportant *adj.* insignificant
uninterrupted *adj.* ininterromput
union *n.f.* unió
unique *adj.* únic
unit *n.f.* unitat
unite *v.* unir
united *adj.* unit
United Kingdom (UK) *n.m.* Regne Unit
United States of America (USA) *n.m.* Estats Units d'Amèrica (EUA)
universe *n.m.* univers
university *n.f.* universitat
unkind *adj.* poc amable
unknown *adj.* desconegut
unless *conj.* llevat que
unlike *prep.* diferent
unlikely *adj.* improbable
unlimited *adj.* il·limitat
unload *v.* descarregar
unlock *v.* obrir

unlucky *adj.* desafortunat
unmarried *adj.* solter
unnecessary *adj.* innecessari
unpleasant *adj.* desagradable
unplug *v.* desconnectar
unreasonable *adj.* irraonable
unripe *adj.* immadur
unsafe *adj.* insegur
unsanitary *adj.* antihigiènic
unsatisfied *adj.* insatisfet
unscrew *v.* afluixar
unstable *adj.* inestable
unsteady *adj.* inestable
unsuccessful *adj.* infructuós
untidy *adj.* desordenat
until *prep.* fins
unusual *adj.* rar
unusually *adv.* extraordinàriament
unwilling *adj.* reticent
unwillingly *adv.* a contracor
unzip *v.* obrir la cremallera
up *adv.* amunt
updated *adj.* actualitzat
uphill *adj.* costa amunt
upon *prep.* a, en
upper *adj.* superior
upset *v.* trasbalsar
upsetting *adj.* pertorbador

upside down *adv.* al revés
upstairs *adv.* a dalt
upward *adj.* ascendent
upwards *adv.* cap amunt
urban *adj.* urbà
urge *v.* instar | *n.m.* impuls
urgent *adj.* urgent
urinate *v.* orinar
urine *n.f.* orina
URL *n.m. (tech.)* URL
Uruguay *n.m.* Uruguai
us *pron.* nosaltres
usage *n.m.* ús
use *v.* usar | *n.m.* ús
used *adj.* usat
useful *adj.* útil
useless *adj.* inútil
user *n.* usuari
username *n.m.* nom d'usuari
usual *adj.* habitual
usually *adv.* habitualment
usury *n.f.* usura
Utah *n.* Utah
utensil *n.m.* estri
utility *n.f.* utilitat
utterance *n.f.* pronúncia

V

vacancy *n.m.* vacant
vacant *adj.* vacant
vacate *v.* desocupar
vacation *n.f.* vacances
vaccinate *v.* vacunar
vaccination *n.f.* vacunació
vaccine *n.f.* vacuna
vagina *n.f.* vagina
valet *n.m.* ajudant de cambra
valid *adj.* vàlid
validate *v.* validar
validation *n.f.* validació
valley *n.f.* vall
valuable *adj.* valuós
valuables *n.m.* objectes de valor
valuation *n.f.* valoració
value *n.m.* valor
van *n.f.* furgoneta
vanilla *n.f.* vainilla
vapor *n.m.* vapor
variable *adj.* variable
variation *n.f.* variació
varied *adj.* variat
variety *n.f.* varietat
various *adj.* diversos
vary *v.* variar
vase *n.m.* gerro
vast *adj.* vast
Vatican City *n.f.* Ciutat del Vaticà
vault *n.f.* volta
veal *n.f.* vedella
vector *n.m.* vector
vegan *adj./n.* vegà
vegetable *n.f.* verdura
vegetarian *adj./n.* vegetarià

vegetation *n.f.* vegetació
vehicle *n.m.* vehicle
veil *n.m.* vel
vein *n.f.* vena
velocity *n.f.* velocitat
velvet *n.m.* vellut
vendor *n.* venedor
venereal *adj.* veneri
Venezuela *n.f.* Veneçuela
venison *n.f.* cérvol
venom *n.m.* verí
ventilator *n.m.* ventilador
venture *v.* aventurar | *n.f.* aventura
venue *n.m.* lloc
verb *n.m.* verb
verdict *n.m.* veredicte
Vermont *n.* Vermont
verse *n.m.* vers
version *n.f.* versió
vertical *adj.* vertical
very *adv.* molt
via *prep.* via
vibrate *v.* vibrar
vibration *n.f.* vibració
victim *n.* víctima
victorious *adj.* victoriós
victory *n.f.* victòria
video *n.m.* vídeo
view *n.f.* vista
viewer *n.* espectador
viewpoint *n.m.* punt de vista
village *n.m.* poble
vinaigrette *n.f.* vinagreta
vine *n.f.* vinya
vinegar *n.m.* vinagre

vineyard *n.f.* vinya
vintage *n.f.* verema
viola *n.f.* viola
violate *v.* violar
violation *n.f.* violació
violence *n.f.* violència
violent *adj.* violent
violently *adv.* violentament
violin *n.m.* violí
violinist *n.* violinista
virgin *n.f.* verge
Virginia *n.* Virgínia
Virgo *n.f.* Verge
virtual *adj.* virtual
virtual reality *n.f.* realitat virtual
virtually *adv.* virtualment
virtue *n.f.* virtut
virus *n.m.* virus
visa *n.m.* visat
visible *adj.* visible
vision *n.f.* visió
visit *v.* visitar | *n.f.* visita
visitor *n.* visitant
visor *n.f.* visera

visual *adj.* visual
vital *adj.* vital
vitamin *n.f.* vitamina
vocabulary *n.m.* vocabulari
vocal *adj.* vocal
vodka *n.m.* vodka
voice *n.f.* veu
voicemail *n.m.* correu de veu
void *v.* invalidar | *n.m.* buit
volcano *n.m.* volcà
volleyball *n.m.* voleibol
voltage *n.m.* voltatge
volume *n.m.* volum
voluntarily *adv.* voluntàriament
voluntary *adj.* voluntari
volunteer *n.* voluntari
vomit *v.* vomitar | *n.m.* vòmit
vote *v.* votar | *n.m.* vot
voter *n.* votant
vow *v.* jurar | *n.m.* vot
vowel *n.f.* vocal
voyage *n.m.* viatge

W

wafer *n.f.* oblia
waffle *n.f.* gofra
wage *n.m.* salari
waist *n.f.* cintura
wait *v.* esperar
waiter *n.m.* cambrer
waitress *n.f.* cambrera
waiver *n.f.* renúncia
wake *v.* despertar
Wales *n.m.* Gal·les
walk *v.* caminar | *n.f.* passejada
walkway *n.f.* passarel·la
wall *n.f.* paret
wallet *n.f.* cartera
walnut *n.f.* nou
wander *v.* vagar
want *v.* voler
war *n.f.* guerra
wardrobe *n.m.* armari
warehouse *n.m.* magatzem
warm *v.* escalfar | *adj.* calent
warmer *adj.* més calent
warmth *n.f.* calor
warn *v.* advertir
warning *n.m.* advertiment
warrant *n.f.* ordre
warranty *n.f.* garantia
wart *n.f.* berruga
wash *v.* rentar
washbasin *n.m.* rentamans
washing machine *n.f.* rentadora
Washington *n.* Washington
Washington, DC *n.m.* Washington DC
washroom *n.m.* lavabo

wasp *n.f.* vespa
waste *v.* malgastar
watch *v.* mirar | *n.m. (clock)* rellotge
watchmaker *n.* rellotger
water *n.f.* aigua; **drinkable** ~ aigua potable; **fresh** ~ aigua dolça
water-skiing *n.m.* esquí aquàtic
watercolor *n.f.* aquarel·la
watercress *n.m.* créixens
waterfall *n.f.* cascada
watermelon *n.f.* síndria
waterproof *adj.* impermeable
wave *n.f.* onada
wax *n.f.* cera
waxwork *n.f.* figura de cera
way *n.f. (method)* manera; *n.m. (path)* camí
we *pron.* nosaltres
weak *adj.* feble
weakness *n.f.* debilitat
wealth *n.f.* riquesa
wealthy *adj.* ric
weapon *n.f.* arma
wear *v.* portar
weather *n.m.* temps
web *n.m.* web; *n.f. (spider ~)* teranyina
webpage *n.f.* pàgina web
website *n.m.* lloc web
wedding *n.m.* casament
Wednesday *n.m.* dimecres
week *n.f.* setmana | *adv.* **next** ~ setmana que ve
weekday *n.m.* dia laborable

weekend *n.m.* cap de setmana
weekly *adj.* setmanal
weigh *v.* pesar
weight *n.m.* pes
weird *adj.* estrany
welcome *v.* acollir | *n.m.* acolliment | *phr.* benvingut!
well *adv.* bé
west *n.m.* oest
West Virginia *n.* Virgínia de l'Oest
western *adj.* occidental
wet *adj.* mullat
wetsuit *n.m.* vestit humit
whale *n.f.* balena
what *adj.* quin(a) | *pron.* què
whatever *pron.* el que
wheat *n.m.* blat; **whole ~** blat integral
wheat germ *n.m.* germen de blat
wheel *n.f.* roda
wheelchair *n.f.* cadira de rodes
wheezing *n.f.* sibilació
when *adv.* quan
whenever *adv.* quan, sempre que
where *adv.* on
whereas *conj.* mentre que
wherever *adv.* a qualsevol lloc
whether *conj.* si
whey *n.m.* sèrum de llet
which *pron.* quin(a)
while *conj.* mentre
whip *v.* fuetejar | *n.m.* fuet
whisker *n.m.* bigotis
whiskey *n.m.* whisky
whisper *v.* murmurejar | *n.m.* murmuri
whistle *v.* xiular | *n.m.* xiulet
white *adj.* blanc
who *pron.* qui

whoever *pron.* qualsevol
whole *adj.* tot
whole wheat *n.m.* blat integral
whom *pron.* qui
whose *adj.* de qui
why *adv.* per què
wide *adj.* ample
widely *adv.* àmpliament
widespread *adj.* estès
widow *n.f.* vídua
widower *n.m.* vidu
width *n.f.* amplada
wife *n.f.* dona
wild *adj.* salvatge
wildcat *n.m.* gat salvatge
wildlife *n.f.* fauna
wildly *adv.* salvatgement
will *n.f.* voluntat
willing *adj.* disposat
willingly *adv.* de bona gana
willingness *n.f.* bona disposició
win *v.* guanyar
wind *n.m.* vent
windbreaker *n.f.* jaqueta
windmill *n.m.* molí de vent
window *n.f.* finestra
windshield *n.f.* parabrisa
windsurfing *n.m.* windsurf
windy *adj.* ventós
wine *n.m.* vi
wineglass *n.f.* copa
winery *n.m.* vinateria
wing *n.f.* ala
winner *n.* guanyador
winning *adj.* guanyador
winter *n.m.* hivern
wipe *v.* eixugar
wire *n.m.* fil
wireless *adj.* sense fil
Wisconsin *n.* Wisconsin

wisdom *n.f.* saviesa
wise *adj.* prudent
wish *v.* desitjar | *n.m.* desig
wit *n.m.* enginy
witch *n.f.* bruixa
witchcraft *n.f.* bruixeria
with *prep.* amb
withdraw *v.* retirar
withdrawal *n.f.* retirada
wither *v.* marcir
within *adv.* dins
without *prep.* sense
witness *v.* presenciar | *n.* testimoni
wolf *n.m.* llop
woman *n.f.* dona
women *n.f. pl.* dones
wonder *v.* preguntar-se
wonderful *adj.* meravellós
wood *n.f.* fusta
wooden *adj.* de fusta
woods *n.m.* bosc
wool *n.f.* llana
word *n.f.* paraula
word processing *n.m.* processament de textos
work *v.* treballar | *n.m.* treball
worker *n.* treballador
working *adj.* que treballa
workout *v.* fer exercici | *n.m.* exercici

workshop *n.m.* taller
world *n.m.* món
worldwide *adj.* mundial
worm *n.m.* cuc
wormwood *n.m.* donzell
worried *adj.* preocupat
worry *v.* preocupar
worrying *adj.* preocupant
worse *adj.* pitjor
worship *v.* adorar | *n.f.* adoració
worst *adj.* pitjor
worth *adj./n.m.* valor
worthy *adj.* digne
wound *v.* ferir | *n.f.* ferida
wounded *adj.* ferit
wrap *v.* embolicar
wrapped *adj.* embolicat
wrapping *n.m.* embolcall
wrist *n.m.* canell
writ *n.m.* ordre
write *v.* escriure
writer *n.* escriptor
writing *n.f.* escriptura
written *adj.* escrit
wrong *adj.* incorrecte
wrongly *adv.* incorrectament
Wyoming *n.* Wyoming

X-Y-Z

x-ray *n.m.* raig X

yacht *n.m.* iot
yam *n.m.* nyam
yard *n.m.* *(of a house)* pati; *n.f.* *(measurement)* iarda
yarrow *n.f.* milfulles
yawn *v.* badallar | *n.m.* badall
yeah *interj* sí
year *n.m.* any | *adv.* **next** ~ any que ve
yeast *n.m.* llevat
yell *v.* cridar | *n.m.* crit
yellow *adj.* groc
yes *adv.* sí
yesterday *adv.* ahir
yet *adv.* encara
yield *v.* rendir
yoga *n.m.* ioga
yogurt *n.m.* iogurt
yolk *n.m.* rovell
you *pron.* tu (*sing.*, *fam.*), vostè (*sing.*, *form.*), vosaltres (*pl.*, *fam.*), vostès (*pl.*, *form.*)
young *adj.* jove

your *pos. adj. sing.* el teu, la teva, els teus, les teves; *pl.* el vostre, la vostra, els vostres, les vostres
yours *pron. sing.* el teu, la teva, els teus, les teves; *pl.* el vostre, la vostra, els vostres, les vostres
yourself *pron. fam.* tu mateix; *form.* vostè mateix
youth *n.f.* joventut
yo-yo *n.m.* io-io

zebra *n.f.* zebra
zero *num.* zero
zest *n.f.* pell de llimona
zinc *n.m.* zinc
zip *v.* tancar la cremallera
zip code *n.m.* codi postal
zipper *n.f.* cremallera
Zodiac *n.m.* zodíac
zombie *n.* zombi
zone *n.f.* zona
zoning *n.f.* zonificació
zoo *n.m.* zoo
zucchini *n.m.* carbassó